PROF. DR. THEODOR BERGMANN

Division of Comparative International Farm Policies,
University of Stuttgart-Hohenheim, Federal Republic Germany

The Development Models of India, the Soviet Union and China

A COMPARATIVE ANALYSIS

1977
Van Gorcum, Assen / Amsterdam, The Netherlands

© 1977 Van Gorcum & Comp. B.V., P.O.B. 43, Assen, The Netherlands

ISBN 90 232 1497 8

Printed in The Netherlands by Van Gorcum, Assen

CONTENTS

VIII

LIST OF TABLES

LIST OF CHARTS

LIST OF FIGURES

India

Soviet Union

China

Synopsis

1. INTRODUCTION

This book attempts a comparative analysis of the development models, objectives and achievements of the three most populous nations of the world – India, the Soviet Union and China, each of which has embarked on a path of planned and accelerated economic growth, technical modernisation and social change. Their way and standard of life, their achievements and failures are of prime concern to humanity as a whole for economic and political reasons. These three nations – no matter how many, if any, nuclear weapons they may have stockpiled – are today world powers of the first order on the strength of the sheer size of their population and their development problems. As shown in Table 1.1, they account for almost half the world's population.

Table 1.1.: Selected indicators of India, Soviet Union and China

Item	Unit	India	Soviet Union	China
Area	mill. sq. km	3,280	22,042	9,597
Population				
1961	millions	439	216	673 [1]
1971	millions	547	244	785 [2]
1974	millions	574	251	814
Population density 1974	inhabitants/sq. km	179	11	82
growth rate 1961-71	per cent	24.6	13.0	16.6
Agricultural land 1971	1,000 ha	178,680	608,731	327,000
Agricultural land/inhabitant	ha	0.32	2.48	0.41
Production				
Grain 1971	million tonnes	113	174	217
Steel 1974	million tonnes	7	135	26
Coal-lignite 1974	million tonnes	77	515 [3]	?
Oil 1974	million tonnes	7	457	?

[1] 1960; [2] 1970; [3] 1973

Sources: Statistical yearbooks

I

The three states started their take-off at different points in time, characterised by different world levels of technology and science, and in a different phase of human knowledge and experience. The Soviet Union after 1917 set out to follow the entirely new and hitherto untried course of economic planning and a methodical, preconceived and controlled social transformation. It is viewed here as the model of the settled, completed revolution. The proclaimed aim was a socialist society, which finally should pass into a classless, communist society after certain transitions and further transformations.

China after 1949 followed a somewhat similar pattern. But, after some time, the model was subjected to modifications, which at first perhaps were no more than adaptations to the country's specific conditions, but at a later stage embodied new concepts differing basically from the Soviet model. These differences eventually came to a head in a political confrontation, and even a number of minor military incidents, with the Soviet Union. For the process and the modes of transformation the repeated revolutionary mobilisation of the masses was envisaged, thus introducing another model of social change.

India, finally, also aimed at a socialist commonwealth, though not in Marxist terms. In fact, she embarked after 1949 on a development model which tried to merge planning and private profit, to fuse a private with a public sector, to mediate between the urgent needs of social reform and the resistance of the privileged castes and classes. She has embraced the principle of gradualism and pursues a course of cautious reform.

The three nations coexist in a special three-cornered relationship, to be discussed in chapter 5.8.5. Their models are offered to developing countries of the "third world"[1] for imitation, allowing for adjustments to meet specific cases. China and India, in particular, seem to be competing with each other in economic achievements, and the outside world, in the first place countries with development problems of their own, eagerly observes the progress and the relative position of each.

The present book seeks to collect, present and discuss a number of data relevant to the main problem of transition from an agrarian to an industrial society. The author has endeavoured to provide data on long-term developments rather than pictures of the momentary situation at a certain point in time, though the inevitable cutting off of statistical graphs at the date of finalising the book introduces a certain arbitrariness, maybe even bias. The thorough description of the three countries follows a sequence dictated by technical expediency. India, not embarking on a Marxist idea of development, stands apart. China followed the Soviet model for a certain period, as outlined above, and will thus be discussed after the USSR.

The last part deals with the basic problems of applying quantitative indicators and evaluation to different socio-economic systems, and goes on to discuss the comparable quantitative aspects. This should offer students and research workers in this field some hints for an understanding of the problems and an assessment of the three models, their relative advantages and disadvantages, their successes, and failures.

The reader must be warned to guard against a number of pitfalls inherent in the subject and the presentation of the book. The first lies in the word "model". For some it might imply the invitation to follow it or copy it, if successful. This would be a complete misunderstanding. The task here is to understand recent history and to separate the specific features from those of more general validity. Nothing can or should be copied, since the prerequisites differ from country to country.

The second danger lies in the belief that the successful or ruling party or group is historically right or justified, just because it has been successful. This is a crude misinterpretation of history. Even the defeated contributes to history, if only by lucid criticism of the rulers.

The third pitfall is due to the fact that recent history is closer to politics than earlier history. If we lack an awareness of our own subjective bias, we are easily misled into believing that our view equals reality.

The technical difficulties, on the other hand, seem less burdensome, though they, too, imply barriers to research. There are discrepancies in the available data; China for a long time published no statistical information at all, while Soviet statistics have fundamentally improved with time. Most complete are those of India, though the wealth of empirical and statistical data veils some inevitable imprecisions. Thus, certain quantitative contradictions cannot be avoided.

The problem of comparability, however, seems more difficult to solve, since data and indices are system-bound and tied to certain phases of development. This issue will be dealt with in section 5.9.

Nevertheless, it seemed well worth while to try to overcome the difficulties, because the subject stimulates our critical thinking and helps us to rid ourselves of ethnocentrism. Capitalism was able to develop the productive forces to a high degree, though only in a small part of the world and for a small part of mankind. The vast majority does not yet share the goods of culture and technology, it suffers from hunger, poverty, epidemics, illiteracy. It continues to live in agrarian societies, partly in archaic conditions. The transition to a new industrial society is one of the major problems of our time. How can this transition be guided? Where does it lead? Our model, successful in Western Europe and Northern America, is not acceptable for the most populous nations of the world for three main reasons:

a. it was financed through exploitation of what are now the developing nations;
b. the developed capitalist nations are much smaller in terms of population;
c. the process took about 150 years, but the developing nations cannot be expected to wait so long.

The three models analysed here are today beset by problems, but they represent three great powers of tomorrow, interlinked in a particular triangular relationship. We must seek to understand their problems of transition.

The author's field of research is concerned mainly with farm policies and their international comparison. For this work he had to integrate several concepts and methods of other disciplines, which are often called upon to contribute to studies in agricultural policies. Forming part of the social sciences, this particular academic discipline is more prone to political bias than are natural sciences. To counterbalance this higher degree of subjectivity and the influence of personal political preferences, it is necessary for any worker in this field to be always aware of his own political bias and to inform the public of this position.

In the present study, the problems are considered and evaluated from the point of view of critical, independent Marxism. This implies that the critical tools of Marxian sociology are being used to understand the development, the problems, achievements and failures of socialist societies, too, and to discover the factors influencing the degree of achievement. In the pre-Stalin era the term "critical Marxism" would have been a pleonasm. Since Stalin and the regimented uniformity of pseudo-Marxist thinking it has come to have a meaning.

The book owes its origin to an invitation extended to the author by some professors of modern history at the University of Göttingen, in particular Professor Dr. Helga Grebing, to give a course on historical transitions from agrarian to industrial society. Following discussions, some basic reading material was offered to the students. Later this was enlarged and revised and new data were added.

My thanks are due to Prof. Grebing for the initial inspiration, to Mrs. B. Neef for patient typing of a difficult text, to Dr. L. Furtmuller for vetting and correcting the English text and to Mrs. J. Watts for typing the revised text. The responsibility for errors and for the political position taken is the author's alone. Nevertheless he expresses the hope that the book may stimulate other research workers to discuss the issue, express criticism and offer comments.

Stuttgart-Hohenheim, December 1976

2. INDIA – MODEL OF GRADUALIST REFORM

2.1. *The facts*

2.1.1. *Recent history – time chart*

1498	Discovery of the sea route to India; European interest is aroused.
1526-1658	Mogul Empire (Islamic) in India.
1612-1613	British colonial policy begins.
About 1700	Decay of Mogul Empire; Marathis form their own state against the last Mogul Emperor Aurangzeb.
1600-1858	East-India Company (British) is the exponent and agent of British colonial policy and economic exploitation.
1664	East-India Company (French) founded – Dutch, Portuguese and French colonialists are expelled by the British.
1750-1858	Official British rule is established.
1773	East-India Company is slowly transformed into British administration; border wars against Afghanistan, incorporation of Burma.
1835	British secondary education system is introduced.
1857-1858	Great Sepoy rebellion.
1858	East-India Company is finally dissolved and entirely transferred into the Anglo-Indian administrative service.
1858-1914	India is British Crown Colony.
1875	Peasant riots in the Deccan (Poona area).
1876-1887	Conquest of Baluchistan.
1885	Foundation of Indian National Congress.
1903-1904	Conquest of Tibet, further British expansion. The infrastructure is developed and the country opened up: railways, harbours, roads, irrigation.
1919	Amritsar massacre.
1919-1935	Limited Indian self-administration, first steps of reform.
1920	First civil disobedience movements are organised.
1937	First regional elections of State assemblies.
1947	Independence, partition into India and (East and West) Pakistan.

Writing in 1853, Karl Marx evaluated British rule as follows:
"England has to fulfil a double mission in India: one destructive, and
the other regenerating – the annihilation of old Asiatic society, and
the laying the material foundations of Western society in Asia...
The British were the first conquerors superior, and therefore in-
accessible to Hindu civilisation. They destroyed it by breaking up
the native communities, by uprooting the native industry, and by
levelling all that was great and elevated in the native society. The
historic pages of their rule in India report hardly anything beyond
that destruction. The work of regeneration hardly transpires
through a heap of ruins. Nevertheless it has begun...
The ruling classes of Great Britain have had till now but an acciden-
tal, transitory and exceptional interest in the progress of India. The
aristocracy wanted to conquer it, the moneyocracy [plutocracy] to
plunder it and the millocracy [barons of industry] to undersell it.
But now the tables are turned. The millocracy have discovered that
the transformation of India into a reproductive country has become
of vital importance to them, and that, to that end, it is necessary
above all to gift her with means of irrigation and of internal communication. They intend now drawing a net of railroads over India.
And they will do it. The results must be inappreciable [i.e. – in-
calculable]." (Karl Marx, 'Future results of British rule in India'
(original in English), *New York Daily Tribune*, 8th August 1853,
see *Selected works* vol. 2, Moscow-London 1942, pp. 658f.)

1947-1964	Jawaharlal Nehru is Prime Minister – with brief inter-ruptions.
1948	Mahatma Gandhi, by then retired from active politics, is assassinated.
1951	Vinoba Bhave starts his land gift movement. The Planning Commission inaugurates the first five year plan, to be followed by four further plans. Main objectives are: Industrialisation, land reform. India as a neutral big power mediates in several conflicts of world politics.
1954	Chou En-lai, then China's Minister of Foreign Affairs, visits India and jointly with Nehru announces the five principles of coexistence.
1957-1959	Border conflicts with China begin.
1962-1963	Border war with China destroys Nehru's long-term efforts for peaceful collaboration.
1964-1965	Lal Bahadur Shastri Prime Minister after Nehru's death.
1965	Short border war with Pakistan. The Soviet Union mediates at a conference in Tashkent.

1965	Indira Gandhi succeeds to premiership after Shastri's death. Unrest and riots due to hunger, linguistic tensions, religious tensions, oppression of separatist tribes in the border regions.
1969-1970	Split of Congress Party, Indira Gandhi retains rank-and-file support, while the dominant sections of the party machine oppose her.
1971, March	In the All-India elections, Indira Gandhi's new Congress wins a two-thirds majority in the House of the People.
August	Friendship treaty with the Soviet Union.
December	War of secession brings independence to East Pakistan, now forming the State of Bangladesh.
1972, April	Elections in most Federal States lead to overwhelming victories of the new Congress (except in Tamil Nadu).
1975	Sikkim is integrated into India as the 23rd state.[2]
1975, June	After internal political difficulties and an adverse court sentence, Indira Gandhi proclaims a state of emergency, jails opposition leaders and announces radical economic measures.
1976, March	Indira Gandhi's Congress is defeated in general elections by a united opposition front. Morarji Desai as leader of the Janata Party succeeds as Prime Minister.

2.1.2. *Natural conditions*
The country covers more than three million sq km and stretches from
latitude 8.4°–37.2° north,   3,200 km north to south,
longitude 68.7°–97.2° east,   3,400 east to west.
The Indian sub-continent's natural frontiers coincide largely with the coastline of the Indian Ocean and the Bay of Bengal; they are almost wholly identical with the State's political frontiers. The northern frontier is formed by the Himalayan mountains. Only the Western frontier against (West) Pakistan and the Eastern frontier with Bangladesh are not natural; they were drawn according to religious rather than geographical considerations.

The Indian mainland can be divided into three main geographical regions:
1. Himalayan mountain zone;
2. Indo-Gangetic plain, formed by the three river systems of Indus, Ganges and Brahmaputra. To this zone belong several river systems, fed by Himalayan waters and thus carrying water all the year round owing to heavy rainfalls and snow. It is one of the largest alluvial regions of the world, very densely populated, with very small varia-

tions of altitude. The alluvium has considerable depth; it is formed in the west largely through wind deposition, in the east through fluvial sedimentation transported by mountain rivers;

3. Southern peninsula. This is separated from the Indo-Gangetic plain by mountain ranges. The coastline is bordered by the western and eastern Ghats, rising to an altitude of 2,500 m. Interposed between the Ghats and the sea is a strip of lowland plain, narrow in the west, broader in the east. The river systems, short and with small catchment areas, are entirely dependent on rainfall and thus carry water only seasonally or with very heavy seasonal fluctuations. Some are losing themselves in the Rajasthan desert without ever reaching the sea. The important river systems are Mahanadi, Godavari, Krishna, Cauvery, all running into the bay of Bengal, and Mahi and Narmada, flowing into the Arabian Sea or Indian Ocean.

In the greater part of the country a tropical-subtropical climate prevails. There are four seasons: December-March cold weather, April-May hot, June-September rainy season, October-November season of south-westerly monsoons. Temperatures in the north and the interior show strong seasonal variations, with very high maxima in summer. In the south, east and in the coastal regions the climate is hot without marked fluctuations.

New Delhi: January minimum 6.3° – maximum 21.4°C
May   "   26.0° –   "   40.4°C
Trivandrum: March   "   25.3° –   "   31.5°C.

Rainfall is very low and insufficient for intensive cropping in Rajasthan (average annual rainfall in Bikaner 291 mm). In the mountains and the coastal plains bordering the Ghats heavy rains are registered (Cherrapunji in Assam 10,800 mm). Rainfall is mostly concentrated within a period of 2-3 months, with the rest of the year completely dry. Irrigation and economy in the use of water are, thus, indispensable requirements of agriculture and culture.

Water availability also determines natural vegetation. It varies from rich, tropical jungle in the humid zones to the xerophilous plants in dry and arid regions and to the complete absence of vegetation in the deserts of Rajasthan. Crops of all climates are cultivated in the several parts of the country. Plants of the moderate zones – potatoes, wheat, barley – are cultivated in the north and in the mountains up to an altitude of 2400 m. Maize, cotton and tobacco, demanding a warmer climate, are grown in vast regions of the country. Tropical crops – e.g. rice, mango, pineapple, coconuts, coffee, pepper, vanilla – are planted in the south and east. Tea-growing estates are concentrated in the blue hills of southern India, in the hills and plains of Assam and the foothills of the Himalayas.

2.1.3. Politico-administrative structure

India is a federative republic with a central government in New Delhi and currently 23 federal states. In 1956, a first restructuring of the state system, based in the main on the geographical distribution of languages, consolidated the many remnants of feudal and colonial rule into 15 states. Since then, some states have been divided, some Union territories and border regions were granted statehood and, finally, Sikkim was integrated as the 23rd state. The constitution is that of a parliamentary democracy with universal franchise. The Congress Party has formed the central government continuously since independence in 1947. Since its overwhelming victory in 1972, it has ruled also in most of the states. State governments are controlled by State legislative assemblies. The central government faces two houses, one constituted by direct elections, the second representing the states. The vote is universal, equal, secret and direct, but protection is provided for scheduled castes and tribes.[3]

The most important parties at national level are:
1. Swatantra: conservative, pro-capitalist, now merged with No. 4 and a few others into Indian People's Party (BLD = Bharatiya Lok Dal);
2. Jana Sangh Hindu Mahasabha: conservative, almost reactionary, orthodox Hindu, strove to maintain ban on the slaughter of cows and to perpetuate the caste system; now in the main merged with BLD;
3. Congress: "socialist" objectives, popular party with various factions and pressure groups;
4. Praja Socialist Party: right-wing socialist, strongly nationalist, anti-communist, anti-Chinese, in the main merged with BLD;
5. Samyukta Socialist Party: Left-wing socialist;
6. Communist Party of India: sympathises with Moscow, at present supports Indira Gandhi's government;
7. Communist Party of India (M): position quite close to 6, more critical of Congress Party, friendlier towards Peking;
8. Communist Party of India (ML) (Naxalites): promotes and organises armed struggle, sympathises strongly with the "Chinese path", now split into two factions;
9. Congress (O)[4]: very conservative, pro-Western, opposes the government in economic, internal and foreign policies;
10. Bharatiya Lok Dal: new alliance of several former parties and politicians aiming at a replacement of the ruling Congress.

The three communist parties' influence today is largely regional. In Kerala, however, CPI and CPI (M) are competing, though sometimes also coexisting and cooperating. – Furthermore, there are important

Table 2.1.: Demographic data by states 1971/74

State	Area (1000 sq. km) 1974	Population 1971 (million)	Population 1974 (million)	Population 1974 per sq. km	Population growth (1971-74) per cent	Literates 1971 per mille	Rural population 1971 in % of total population	Scheduled castes and tribes 1971 in % of total population
Andhra Pradesh	277	43.5	46.3	167	6.4	246	80.7	17.1
Assam	79	14.6	16.4	208	12.3	288	91.6	18.9
Bihar	174	56.4	59.7	343	5.9	198	90.0	22.9
Gujarat	196	26.7	28.9	147	8.2	357	71.9	20.8
Haryana	44	10.0	10.8	246	8.0	267	82.2	18.9
Himachal Pradesh	56	3.5	3.6	64	2.9	313	92.9	26.3
Jammu & Kashmir	222	4.6	4.9	22	6.5	183	81.7	8.3
Karnataka (Mysore)	192	29.3	31.3	163	6.8	315	75.7	13.9
Kerala	39	21.3	23.0	589	8.0	602	83.7	9.6
Madhya Pradesh	443	41.6	45.1	101	8.4	221	83.7	33.1
Maharashtra	308	50.4	54.1	175	7.3	391	68.8	11.9
Manipur	22	1.1	1.1	50	0	328	86.8	32.7
Meghalaya	22.5	1.0	1.1	49	10.0	284	87.0	80.9
Mizoram	21	0.3	.	.	.	(509)[1]	(88.4)[1]	.
Nagaland	17	0.5	0.5	29	0	273	90.1	88.6
Orissa	156	21.9	23.5	151	7.3	261	91.7	38.2
Punjab	50	13.6	14.4	288	5.9	334	76.2	24.7
Rajasthan	342	25.8	27.8	81	7.8	188	82.4	27.9
Sikkim	7	0.2	0.2	29	0	.	.	.
Tamil Nadu	130	41.2	43.9	338	6.6	394	69.7	18.6
Tripura	10.5	1.6	1.7	162	6.3	309	92.2	41.4
Uttar Pradesh	294	88.3	93.3	317	5.7	216	86.0	21.2
West Bengal	88	44.3	47.6	541	7.4	331	75.4	25.6
Union Territories	215	6.3	.	.	.	500	31.3[2]	.
All India	3,207	547.4	574	179	4.9	295	80.1	21.5

[1]) Mizoram was 1971 part of Assam   [2]) The most important part of the Union territories is New Delhi

Sources: Census (1971); Five-Year Plan (1973)

parties, active and influential in certain States only, like the DMK, which ruled in Tamil Nadu until 1976.

In the federative states, strong centrifugal forces are at work. Regional differences are considerable: the regions differ in terms of natural conditions, population density, education and literacy, percentage of scheduled castes and tribes, irrigation, intensity of land use etc. (see Table 2.1. and Fig. 2.1.). Five of the states are larger in area than the Federal Republic of Germany, one has more inhabitants (Uttar Pradesh), 7 have populations in excess of 40 million.

2.1.4. *Population explosion*

Since 1921, the population has been growing steadily, and at an increasing rate (see Table 2.2. and Fig. 2.2.). From 1921 to 1971, the population increased from 251 to 547 millions, i.e. by 118 per cent. While in the first decade after 1921 the growth rate was 11 per cent, it rose in the last decade to 24.7 per cent. Mortality showed a steep decline, while fertility hardly changed at all. Man adapts his sexual and reproduction behaviour too slowly to improved hygiene and decreasing infant mortality. Life expectancy has improved, in itself a desirable development. So far all population forecasts have been exceeded. A large-scale migration from the land has not been possible until now. Thus, the main determinants of population trends have changed adversely (see Table 2.3.).

Population growth as such is neither a stimulant nor a hindrance for development. In sparsely populated countries it stimulates and calls for more intensive farm production.[5] In the Federal Republic of Germany, the influx of refugees was a main factor of economic growth after 1945. The Netherlands are more densely populated than Germany and economically prosperous. In India, on the other hand, the population explosion is harmful under present conditions. The slow growth of production is balanced by more mouths to feed and thus has no positive psychological effect. The material and socio-psychological effect of economic progress as a spur to effort and performance is thus weakened.

2.1.5. *Socio-cultural framework*

Literacy. – In the country as a whole, 71 per cent of the total population were still illiterates in 1971, as compared with 82 per cent of those over 4 years of age in 1961. There are vast differences regarding literacy between rural and urban populations, between the States and between the castes (see Table 2.1.). Kerala and Gujarat rank highest, Jammu-and-Kashmir and Rajasthan lowest.

Language. – Fifteen main languages and about 200 minor languages are spoken. The main languages (e.g. Hindi, Bengali, Marathi, Gujarati,

Fig. 2.1. India: Population and area of the federal states 1974

Table 2.2.: Population trends

A. *1891-1975*

	Millions	Decadal growth rate %	Agricultural in percent of total population
1891	235		
1901	236	—	66.5
1911	252	+ 5.7	72.2
1921	251	− 0.3	73.0
1931	279	+ 11.0	67.0
1941	319	+ 14.2	75.0
1951	361	+ 13.3	70.0
1961	439	+ 21.5	72.0
1971	547	+ 24,7	68.6
1975	604	.	.

B. *Projections 1961-2001 (millions)*

		1961	1966	1971	1976	1981	1991	2001
1958	Coale u. Hoover [1])	424	473	532	601			
1958	UN	417	456	503	−			
1960	Central Statistical Office New Delhi	431	480	528	568			
1960	Agarwal	423	472	526	574			
1961	Planning Commission	−	492	555	625			
1964	Planning Commission	−	495	560	630			
1966	UN expert mission most favourable projection [2])			539	586	622	668	
	most unfavourable projection [3])			549	629	725	983	
1968	Pandit I [3])	439	497	568	655	762	1,047	1,460
	II [4])	439	497	563	635	701	804	916
	III [5])	439	497	565	625	670	757	858
	(IV [6])	372	388	409	433	459	511	562)

[1]) Unchanged growth rate
[2]) Rapid decrease of fertility ⎫
[3]) Unchanged fertility   ⎬ projection for years 1970, 1975, 1980, 1990
[4]) Accelerated decrease of fertility from five-year period 1966-71
[5]) Fertility decreased by half from mid-term of fourth Five-Year Plan
[6]) Decreased fertility according to the Japanese model – by 50 percent during the decade 1947-57

Sources: Census etc.

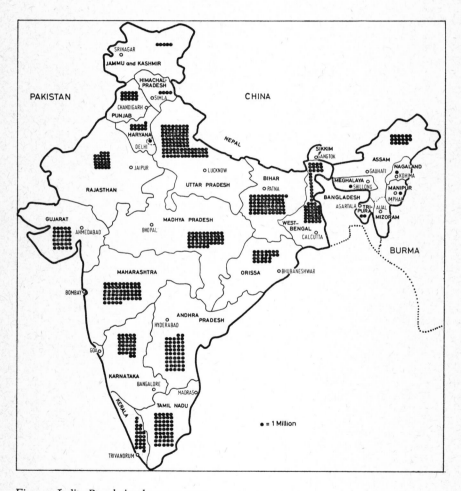

Fig. 2.2. India: Population by states 1975

Table 2.3.: Main determinants of population growth

Decade	Birth rate	Death rate per thousand + year	Birth ./. death	Life expectancy years males	females
1911-20	48.1	47.2	0.9	19.4	20.9
1921-30	46.4	36.3	10.1	26.9	26.6
1931-40	45.2	31.2	14.0	32.1	31.4
1941-50	39.9	27.4	12.5	32.5	31.7
1951-60	41.7	22.8	18.9	41.9	40.6
1961-70	39.9	18.1	21.8	47.0	45.6
Projections					
1971-76	35.6	15.2	20.4	51.3	49.6
1976-81	29.6	12.8	16.8	53.3	52.6
1981-86	24.8	11.1	13.7	56.0	55.3

Source: Statistical outline (1975)

Tamil, Malayalam) have a literature of their own. English is still the lingua franca and will probably remain so for a long time to come. Indians from north and south can communicate only in English and for ethnic and economic reasons the non-Hindi-speaking states will not accept Hindi as an official language.

Religion. – The people are overwhelmingly of Hindu religion (83 per cent). Furthermore, there are 11 per cent Moslems, 2.6 per cent Christians, 2 per cent Buddhists and Sikhs, and smaller percentages of Jains and Jews. – Hinduism has no organised church, let alone religious dogmas. The temples are built, maintained and used for worship by the castes. The clergy are mostly not employees, but "free-lancing" mendicant priests (saddhus).

The main idea of Hinduism is reincarnation. According to his behaviour in his present life or in earlier lives man is re-born as a higher or as a lower creature. Thus a human soul can live in an animal; accordingly, believing Hindus must not eat meat. – This doctrine gives solace to the faithful in enduring the misery of their lives, and teaches the oppressed to practise humility and submission in the face of their predetermined destiny.[6]

2.1.6. *Economic system and socio-economic conditions*

2.1.6.1. Economic structure

India has a developing agrarian economy and aims at rapidly overcoming the development lag. The Planning Commission of the Central

Government and the corresponding commissions attached to the state governments can only give advice and general guide-lines. In the economy, public and private sectors exist side by side. Public sector activities include the construction of dams for irrigation and hydroelectric power, as well as railways and steel plants; supplying of water and electricity; manufacture of heavy machinery and aircraft; takeovers and preservation of bankrupt private enterprises; furthermore an attempt has been made to nationalise the banking system. The rest of the economy – the major part – is left to the private sector, which, for instance, runs one large steel plant, as against four in the public sector. Administration and state enterprises, in the first place the railways, are the biggest employers. Workers and employees in the industrial sector form only a small part of the economically active population, about 11 per cent (see Table 2.4.). Exports have so far originated chiefly in the field of agricultural produce and textiles. Gradually, industrial goods are coming into the picture. The currency is not convertible; foreign trade, therefore, is largely directed or supervised by government and based on barter agreements.

Table 2.4.: Economically active population and gross national product by sectors 1971

Sectors	Economically active		Gross national product [1]	
	Thousand	p.c.	Milliard Rs.	p.c.
1. Agriculture, forestry, hunting, fishing	129,963	72.1	177.4	46.2
2.1. Power + water	532	0.3	4.5	1.2
2. Mining + quarrying	923	0.5	3.8	1.0
3. Industrial processing	17,068	9.5	54.2	14.1
4. Construction	2,215	1.2	20.9	5.5
2. Production	20,738	11.5	83.4	21.8
3.1. Commerce, banking, insurance	10,038 [2]	5.6	39.6	10.3
2. Transport + communications	4,401	2.4	20.6	5.4
3. Other services	14,018	7.8	62.3	16.3
3. Services	28,457	15.8	122.5	32.0
4. Activities not sufficiently identified	1,215	0.6	–	–
Total economically active	180,373	100.0	383.3	100.0

[1] At current prices
[2] Including catering

Source: Länderkurzberichte (1974)

The economic system, then, is a mixed one, in which public and private sector, planning and profit-directed production supplement, even while competing with, each other. Public investment is directed into those branches and subsectors where in the short term at best small profits are expected. Indeed, Indian entrepreneurs are not prepared to invest in long-term projects or to take risks. Myrdal (1957) defines the function of planning as follows:

"... The explanation why a region or a country has a stagnating economy is that it cannot compete successfully. And, from this point of view, the whole meaning of a national plan is to give investment such protection from the market forces as will permit it to be undertaken in spite of the fact that it would not be remunerative according to private business calculations. It is here that the national state comes in as representing the common and long-term interests of the community at large." (p. 87)

The two sectors compete for scarce resources (foreign currency for imports of machinery or semi-finished goods). The political influence of the private sector is strong, whereas the impact of the Planning Commission varies, but is generally weak.

In 1971, more than 80 per cent of the population lived in villages, 69 per cent engaged in farming. The distinctive functions of the castes have been blurred, yet the caste system has survived. The population increases rapidly, but rural migration to the towns or emigration to foreign countries has hardly been possible. Rather, there is forced re-migration or repatriation from the new nationalist states in Asia and Africa. Rural artisans, ruined by early industrialisation, also returned to the land. Fields are thus being continually fragmented, and the operational units are decreasing in size. Unemployment and underemployment are endemic in the villages.

2.1.6.2. Socio-economic conditions
In 1967/68 families of landless labourers – no less than about 60 million people in 13.5 million households – lived on a level still below that of the small and marginal cultivators (see Table 2.5.). Each of these households of between 4 and 5 persons had on average a spendable annual income of 1,052 Rs., i.e. 230 Rs. per head.

According to another survey, farmworkers were employed 255 days, women 168 days per year. Low wages and underemployment result in a low family income. Those 10 per cent of the population mostly belong to the lowest caste, the harijans or untouchables. They have experienced hardly any material improvement since independence.

The 5 million factory workers had annual earnings averaging 2,355 Rs.

Table 2.5.: Living standards of agricultural labour households

	Unit	1950/51	1956/57	1963/64	1967/68
1. Rural households	million	58.90	66.60	67.56	70.47
2. Agric. labour households	million	17.90	16.30	14.12	13.47
a. with land	million	8.94	6.99	5.48	–
b. without land	million	8.96	9.31	8.64	–
a. with land	%	49.9	42.9	38.8	–
b. without land	%	50.1	57.1	61.2	–
3a. Persons/AL household		4.30	4.40	4.47	4.50
3b. AL + dependents	million	76.97	71.72	63.12	60.62
4a. Earners/AL household		2.0	2.2	2.0	2.1
4b. AL	million	35.8	35.9	28.2	28.3
5. Daily wages: men	Rs.	1.09	0.96	?	?
women	Rs.	0.68	0.59	?	?
6a. Working days/year: men		283	255	?	?
women		?	168	?	?
6b. Unemployed days/year: men		82	110	?	?
women		?	197	?	?
7. Annual income					
a. AL household at current prices Rs.		447	437	660	1,052
b. AL household at constant prices 1950/51 Rs.		447	412.5	487	499
c. per capita at current prices Rs.		104	99	148	230
d. per capita at constant prices 1950/51 Rs.		104	94	109	111
8. All-India working class consumer price index 1949 = 100		101	107	137	213

Source: The anatomy... (1968)

Their living standards and consumption, therefore, must remain low, except for cereals and pulses. Meat consumption is confined to limited groups and is as yet of no importance for the vast majority. Protein intake is low and the diet is deficient in nutritive value (see also Table 2.6.).

On average, expenditure on consumption is low, with wide variations between the social strata. The poorest decile (10 per cent) of the rural consumers had a share of 3.6 per cent of total rural consumption, while the top decile consumed 25.3 per cent. The differential is 1 : 7. In 1963/64 average monthly expenditure was 24.3 Rs., with variations ranging from 8 to 67 Rs. Another survey (see Table 2.7.) showed that 22 per cent of the population lived in conditions of destitution.[7] The percentage varied between 4 per cent in Assam and 30 per cent in Kerala.

The few surveys of rural employment problems present a picture of general unemployment, combined with spells of employment during

Table 2.6.: Annual per capita consumption of selected commodities 1951-1971

Commodity	Unit	India			Fed. Rep. Germany 1970/71
		1951	1961	1971 [1])	
Cereals	kg	122	146	145	67.6
Pulses	kg	21.7	24.8	19.7	1.1
Sugar	kg	3.0	4.7	3.6	34.3
Peanut butter	kg	0.5	0.8	0.9	26.6 [3])
Tea	gr.	251	291	436	145
Coffee	gr.	53	105	80	4,010
Cloth	m				
mill		8.5	9.3	6.7	18.3
decentralized sector		2.5	5.5	6.1	–
Electricity (private consumption)	kWh				4,339 [4])
Coal	kg	4.5	6.0	5.3	1,400 [4])
Paper	gr	616	1,012	1,420	17,400
Cigarettes	pieces	57	76	111	1,948
	per million head				
Bicycles	head	1,100	2,030	3,960	?
Radio receivers	,,	228	792	3,299	168,000 [5])
Sewing machines	,,	200	730	770	?
Cars	,,	610	500	630 [2])	37,600

[1]) Estimates
[2]) Cars, jeeps and similar vehicles
[3]) Edible fat without water
[4]) Total consumption
[5]) Radio + TV sets

Sources: The crisis of the seventies (1971); Statistisches Jahrbuch (1973)

brief seasonal peaks. During those peak periods, however, the demand for labour cannot be fully met, owing to lack of technical equipment and nutritional deficiencies. The shortage of all types of energy – human, animal and mechanical – and the vast number of labourers cause economic waste and delay in the performance of field operations. The rhythms of nutrition and work are out of phase instead of being synchronised. When the demand for labour is at its highest in the ploughing and harvesting seasons, nutrition and work performance are at their lowest point. Conversely, when the storage rooms are full, there is no work.

In spite of all efforts to industrialise the country, registered unemployment has risen steadily. In 1965/66, it was estimated to reach 10 million.[8] To this the even larger numbers of unregistered unemployed and under-

Table 2.7.: Consumer expenditure and poverty by states 1963/64

State	Consumer expenditure per head + month Rs.	Persons below poverty line [1] – per cent
Andhra Pradesh	22.1	26.6
Assam	28.0	3.9
Bihar	22.0	23.4
Gujarat	25.4	17.5
Jammu + Kashmir	28.5	7.6
Kerala	21.4	30.4
Madhya Pradesh	24.3	25.3
Madras	25.6	20.8
Maharashtra	26.2	22.8
Mysore	21.7	29.4
Orissa	20.1	28.0
Punjab (+ Haryana)	29.8	14.5
Rajasthan	24.7	22.4
Uttar Pradesh	22.3	26.7
West Bengal	28.1	13.2
Union territories	32.3	9.0
India	24.3	22.4

[1] Poverty line: urban population with per capita expenditure below 18 Rs/month
rural population with per capita expenditure below 13 Rs/month

Source: The anatomy... (1968)

employed have to be added. For the last few years, official estimates of unemployment were altogether omitted as a useless exercise.

2.2. *Farm production, agrarian structure and agrarian reform*

2.2.1. *Farm production*
For field crops water is the decisive minimum factor, apart from fertilisers and other inputs, which can be increased more easily, i.e. with less investment. Production, of course, depends on natural conditions. In the deserts and desert-like regions, there are no or no secure harvests, in other regions only one crop. Where irrigation is assured, two crops per year can be grown.

There are 21 million ha of fallow, as against a cropped acreage of 139.4 million ha, of which 114,8 millions were cropped once, 24.6 millions twice (1971-72) (see Table 2.8). The irrigated acreage has been increased,[9] but can be expanded even more, while the fallow will have to be diminished. Reclamation of wasteland is still possible, though the

Table 2.8.: Land utilization 1950/51-1971/72 (million hectares)

	1950/51	1955/56	1968/69	1971/72
1. Forests	40.5	51.3	62.7	65.8
2. Not available for cultivation	47.5	48.4	48.1	45.8
3. Other uncultivated land excluding fallow	49.4	38.9	34.3	33.4
4. Fallow	28.1	24.1	23.1	21.3
5. Total cropped area	131.9	147.3	159.2	164.0
a. Net area sown	118.7	129.2	137.6	139.4
b. Area sown more than once	13.2	18.1	21.6	24.6
6. a. Gross irrigated area	22.6	25.6	33.8	38.6
b. Total net irrigated area	20.8	22.8	27.9	31.6
7. a. Area recorded	284.2	291.9	305.8	305.7
b. Area not recorded	42.0	36.1	22.2	22.4
8. Total geographical area	326.3	328.0	328.0	328.0

Source: Brief on Indian agriculture (annually)

extent is unknown; estimates vary widely. The potential depends partly upon available capital and technology.

The cropping pattern as a whole is varied; crops of all climatic zones can be grown, as mentioned above; but within each region cropping and nutrition are more uniform. Transport conditions are relatively poor, owing to vast distances and lack of rolling stock. Therefore the balancing of supply and demand between the regions and states is hampered, particularly at times of food deficiencies and harvest failures.

Table 2.9. gives a picture of long-term changes in cropping patterns and intensity over the past 23 years. – Rice is the most important food grain. The acreage was expanded during the past 23 years and the yield also increased, so that the total crop more than doubled. Various strains of millet and sorghum are also of great importance in terms of acreage, which however is not reflected in the size of the harvests. Mostly they are grown as a second crop and thus tend to suffer from lack of humidity. Moreover, efforts to improve seed quality were quite inadequate. Wheat, on the other hand, recorded increases both in acreage and yield; thus during the relevant period, crops have grown by 242 per cent. Even so, average yields are still as low as for rice. Pulses, very important for the proteins in the diet, are almost stationary in performance, with low yields. The acreage of oil-seeds has expanded by 41 per cent, the harvest by 69 per cent. Sugar-cane, one of the important cash-crops, also recorded a higher acreage and a substantial increase in yields. Other export cash-crops, too, have shown an upward trend, though the develop-

Table 2.9.: Acreage, harvest and yield of principal crops

	Acreage (1000 ha)		Harvest (1000 to)		Yield (dt per ha)	
	1950/51	1973/74	1950/51	1973/74	1950/51	1973/74
Rice, polished	30,810	38,010	20,576	43,742	6.7	11.5
Millets	31,402	37,534	11,270	20,073	3.6	5.3
Corn	3,159	6,021	1,729	5,643	5.5	9.4
Wheat	9,746	19,057	6,462	22,072	6.6	11.6
Barley	3,113	2,624	2,378	2,327	7.6	8.9
Total cereals	78,230	103,246	42,414	93,857	(5.4	9.1)
Pulses	19,091	22,882	8,411	9,754	(4.4	4.3)
Total foodgrains	97,321	126,128	50,825	103,611	(5.2	6.0)
Peanuts	4,494	6,900	3,481	5,798	7.7	8.4
Sesamum	2,204	2,358	445	486	2.0	2.1
Rape + mustard	2,071	3,428	762	1,692	3.7	4.9
Linseed	1,403	1,876	367	471	2.6	2.5
Castor beans	555	529	103	235	1.9	4.4
Total oilseeds	10,727	15,090	5,158	8,682	(4.8	5.8)
Potatoes	240	533	1,660	4,626	69	87
Sugarcane [1])	1,707	2,722	5,705	14,046	33.4	51.6
Tobacco	357	446	261	441	7.3	9.9
Cotton	5,882	7,601	590	1,152	0.9	1.5
Jute (dry)	571	792	596	1,112	10.4	14.0
Tea	314	360	275	468	8.8	13.0
Coffee [2])	83	146 [3])	25	92	2.7	6.3
Black pepper	80	122	26	36	2.6	3.0
Chillies (dry)	592	732	351	488	5.9	6.7
Ginger (dry)	17	24	15	38	8.8	15.8

[1]) Harvest and yield in terms of gur, brown, semi-refined sugar
[2]) Harvested acreage
[3]) 1972/73

Sources: Statistical abstract, Brief on Indian agriculture, Economic survey, FAO Production yearbook

ment was fitful and subject to heavy fluctuations from year to year, which do not appear in the table, where only the first and last year of the period of reference are shown.[10] Thus, the general picture is one of a slow, but steady growth of crop production.[11] Yields per hectare, however, remain very low, though even here a slow improvement can be seen.

The use of fertilisers increases slowly. In addition to growing home production, large quantities have been imported. The expansion of the fertiliser industry proceeds slowly and does not meet the plan targets. Thus, the physiological needs will not be covered for a long time to come. Furthermore, even if fertilisers are available, the problem remains as to whether the small and dwarf cultivators will be able to purchase them and thus to break the vicious circle of subsistence farming, low yields, poverty, hunger.

The country has the largest cattle population in the world (239 million head of bovines and buffaloes), with the lowest average performance (see Table 2.10.). If these figures are related to cropped acreage or to population, they show an excessive density, due to the fact that orthodox Hindus are strict vegetarians and do not consume any meat.

Table 2.10.: Livestock 1951-1974 (millions)

Category/age	1951	1961	1966	1972	1976 [1]
Cattle					
males over 3 years	61.8	72.5	73.4	74.6	
females over 3 years	49.9	54.2	54.7	56.8	
young stock	43.6	48.8	48.1	47.5	
total	155.3	175.5	176.2	178.9	130.6
Buffaloes					
males over 3 years	6.8	7.7	8.2	8.1	
females over 3 years	21.9	25.0	26.2	29.5	
young stock	14.7	18.5	18.6	20.3	
total	43.4	51.2	53.0	57.9	61.2
Sheep	39.1	40.2	42.0	40.4	40.0
Goats	47.2	60.9	64.6	68.0	70.0
Horses and ponies	1.5	1.3	1.2	1.0	1.0
Other livestock [2]	6.4	7.3	7.2	8.8	8.9
Poultry	73.6	114.3	115.4	136.8	154.0
Sex ratio (males : females = 1 : ...)					
Cattle over 3 years	0.8	0.7	0.7	0.8	
Buffaloes over 3 years	3.2	3.2	3.2	3.6	

[1]) Estimates
[2]) Mainly camels + donkeys

Source: Brief on Indian agriculture (1975)

Vegetarianism of the Hindu type implies prohibition of slaughter by caste Hindus. But cows and buffaloes are milked and used for draft purposes. There is practically no fodder production, nor are there any breeding activities, which, of course, would imply the elimination of unproductive animals. Animal husbandry is not integrated with arable farming, a combination that generally results in mutual benefits and increased production. Milk production, therefore, is in its infancy. Untapped production reserves are particularly large in animal husbandry. But all activities of technical improvement are barred or severely hampered by social and religious taboos.

Plantations are listed in Indian statistics under industries. In large-scale enterprises mainly tea, rubber, coffee and oranges are produced, in some farms also sugar-cane. These farms produce cash crops for marketing only and their structure is relatively capital-intensive. They do not communicate with, or influence, their peasant environment, since they have established an autonomous circulation of capital. Some agricultural economists speak of dualism, a dichotomous agrarian sector composed of two separate parts without interaction. Others call it the formation of economic enclaves. The products are mainly exported in their original form as raw materials, or they are partly processed for finishing in the countries of destination. Since production as well as marketing and export were, and partly still are, economically controlled by foreigners, the profits are rarely, if at all, available for re-investment in the country.

2.2.2. *Agrarian structure and rural social relations*
Ownership of land is acutely polarised and fragmented. According to the 1971 census, 23 million cultivators are virtually landless, with dwarf holdings of under half a hectare. They account for almost one third of all operational holdings but for only 3.4 per cent of the total acreage (see Table 2.11.).[12] Another 26 million have little land, between 0.5 and 2 ha. This second group – over one third of the total – holds 17 per cent of the cultivated land. Another 10.7 million cultivate 2-4 ha, which under average Indian condition might be sufficient to feed a family, with marginal and varying marketable surpluses. The 10 million cultivators holding 4-20 ha can be described as peasants or farmers; they represent 14 per cent of all holders and farm 37 per cent of the agricultural land. The remaining 635,000, under 1 per cent of the total, holding over 13 per cent of the land, are large-scale farmers, some of them possibly capitalist entrepreneurs.

Most of the tiny holdings are insufficient to feed, maintain and employ an average family, not to speak of capital formation for intensification or

Table 2.11.: Operational holdings by size – 1971

Size class (ha)	Holdings 1000	Percent actual	Percent cumu-lative	Area hectares 1000	Percent actual	Percent cumu-lative
- 0.5	23,178	32.9	32.9	5,446	3.3	3.3
0.5- 1	12,503	17.7	50.6	9,097	5.6	8.9
1- 2	13,432	19.1	69.7	19,285	11.9	20.8
2- 3	6,722	9.5	79.2	16,359	10.1	30.9
3- 4	3,959	5.6	84.8	13,646	8.4	39.3
4- 5	2,684	3.8	88.6	11,929	7.3	46.6
5-10	5,248	7.4	96.0	36,306	22.4	69.0
10-20	2,135	3.0	99.0	28,521	17.6	86.6
20-30	401	0.6	99.6	9,345	5.8	92.4
30-40	120	0.2	99.8	4,177	2.6	95.0
40-50	49	0.1	99.9	2,051	1.3	96.3
50-	65	0.1	100.0	5,971	3.7	100.0
Total	70,494	100.0		162,133	100.0	

		mln.	percent	mln. ha	percent
Marginal	- 1	35.7	50.6	14.5	8.9
Small	1- 2	13.4	19.0	19.3	11.9
Semi-medium	2- 4	10.7	15.2	30.0	18.5
Medium	4-10	7.9	11.3	48.2	29.8
Large	10-	2.8	3.9	50.1	30.9
Total		70.5	100.0	162.1	100.0

Source: All India report (1975)

of a factor contribution towards general economic development. They live at subsistence level. Even the most equal distribution of land among the cultivators by a radical and efficient agrarian reform would offer no economic solution, for all its positive social effects: each family would then hold 2.3 ha.

According to an earlier survey of 1959/60, 87.5 per cent of all cropped land was owned by the cultivators, only 12.5 per cent was held on lease. Official figures, however, seem to overrate the extent of peasant owner-ship and to underrate share-cropping and tenancy, which are very common. In this respect, statistics seem to indicate the official objectives of agrarian reform rather than its actual results.

The British administration introduced the tax-farming system.

Collection of land-tax was transferred to a tax-farmer (zamindar) against fixed fees; there was no limit or check on what he took from the cultivators. Many zamindars recruited sub-zamindars, who followed the same system. In some regions, several tiers of subletting are recorded. Thus, large uncontrolled groups of unproductive exploiters were established with the administration's blessings. In certain regions the amount of tax to be delivered to the state was permanently fixed (permanent settlement), in other regions the amounts due from the zamindars were checked after a certain time and re-assessed, to adapt them to changing conditions (temporary settlement). These methods made it possible in that agrarian country with no fiscal administration to tap the most important source of revenue, that is the farming sector. At the same time a new stratum of politically dependent, privileged supporters of colonial rule was created. The cultivators became more and more indebted; land was concentrated in fewer and fewer hands, as the earlier owners lost their titles. Gradually, the tax-farmers became proprietors and landlords.

In some regions – particularly Bombay and Madras[13] – taxes were collected according to the *ryotwari* system. The cultivators had to pay their tax either individually or as a village community directly to government administration. This system is seen by some as advantageous, since the ryot in that way comes close to the status of an economically independent peasant. Other economists and historians see it as a form of direct dependence on the state.

As for tenant farmers – more aptly described as share-croppers – they mostly had to pay 50 per cent of the gross yield by way of rent. If the landlord lends his tractor for works in the fields, he may extract as much as 75 per cent.

Tenancy based on fixed cash payment, as in modern capitalist economies, such as Great Britain or the Federal Republic of Germany, is completely different from the share-cropping practised in India. Leasing of entire farms with buildings, drainage etc. implies a certain division of economic functions with positive effects. The landlord owns the land and has to invest in farm buildings, drainage, soil conservation, hedges and other long-term productive ventures. The tenant, then, contributes all mobile or short-term capital: labour, animals, equipment, seeds, fertilisers etc. He pays the fixed rent in cash, but is not compelled to invest capital in land etc. Thus, two persons or two sources capitalise the farm enterprise, and utilisation by the tenant is settled for an extended period (9 or 12 years, subject to renewal). – In share-cropping, on the other hand, nobody invests; the landlord is uninterested or unwilling, the cultivator incapable. Two persons, or rather two families, try hard to draw on the same land with a minimum of inputs. – Share-cropping in itself is an obstacle to investment, since all expenses and risks are born by the investing cultivator, while the non-investing landlord receives half of all additional yields.

The cultivator borrows money from the village usurer and sells his surplus produce to the private merchant or dealer. Landlord, money-lender and middleman form an unholy trinity; frequently they are of the same caste or family, dominate the village economically, socially and politically. The "farm", insufficient even to feed the family, offers no chance of capital formation. The payments due to the absentee landlord from the small cultivator are not used for investment, but for urban, sometimes conspicuous consumption.

Frequently it is being claimed, and has been claimed for a long time, that the poor spend vast amounts on family feasts. This is a doubtful proposition. As long ago as 1875, British inquiry committees rejected this view as irrelevant.

2.2.3. *Agrarian reform and land gift movement*
The rural population contributed substantially to the independence movement led by the Congress Party, and to its final success. In 1947-1950, peasant revolutions occurred in Andhra Pradesh and Kashmir. In Telengana (Andhra Pradesh), peasant soviets were formed. In these circumstances, the Congress Party was compelled to initiate a legal agrarian reform. Only the general legislation was centrally prepared in New Delhi: jurisdiction lies largely with the states. General objectives of agrarian reform are:
1. Abolition of tax-farming, security of tenants;
2. abolition of share-cropping;
3. reduction of land-rent for tenants;
4. improved living conditions for landless labourers;
5. cooperative organisation of farming with the final goal of establishing self-governing cooperative villages;
6. fairer distribution of land-ownership, to be ensured by placing an upper limit on land holdings, exemptions from the upper limit to be granted to modern and intensive large-scale farms under owner-cultivation.

Tax-farming and similar titles have been abolished, for which compensation is paid.[14] Land cultivated by the zamindars became their property.[15] Share-cropping was prohibited by law. An unknown number of tenants were evicted when modern farm equipment became available. Other share-croppers formally became farm workers with remuneration in kind. In certain regions, tenants could pay off the capitalised rent and become independent smallholders. Frequently, though, share-cropping continues, even in those federal states, where communist-led governments are or were (temporarily) in power (Kerala, West Bengal).

The upper limit on landholdings varies greatly from state to state and according to land quality. The extremes are 18 and 324 acres.[16] Some states have fixed lower ceilings for purchased than for inherited land. – There are, however, many generally known ways of circumventing the already generous laws. The Hindu extended family was and is one of the many pretexts. Most of the states allowed big landowners to subdivide the extended family's property *pro forma*, and to allocate land up to the ceiling to each member of the family. Thus, in reality the holding could be a multiple of the legal ceiling.

If the new smallholders are able to pay the compensation for land distributed in a land reform, this implies mobilisation and transfer of capital funds from a productive group to strata which in the past were not investment-minded, but rather given to luxury consumption. This raises an additional obstacle to capital formation in the agrarian sector. Yet, there can be no industrial development or technical improvement and intensification of farm production without capital formation in the farming sector. Furthermore, the administration is seen by the new owner-peasants as debt-collector for the former landlords. The twofold impulse provided by a radical agrarian reform – economically by the remission of old debts, psychologically by creating a new sense of economic and social freedom – could not emerge from this gradualist approach.

One objective of agrarian reform was to stimulate big landlords to invest in farming and to promote modern capital-intensive pilot farms, which then would act as examples and starting points for wide-spread innovation. Dependence and unproductive payments were to be abolished, the titles of tenants and their status to be improved. Land distribution, the result of land reform measured in terms of distributed land, was meagre. – It is hard to say, whether reform and progress or stagnation are prevailing.

The *bhoodan* movement, initiated by Vinoba Bhave, endeavoured to obviate harsh agrarian reform laws and agrarian revolutions by appealing to the conscience of landlords to donate part of their land voluntarily. With the land donated, dwarf holdings should be enlarged and landless people be settled. From 1951 up to the end of 1970, 1.69 million ha were donated, of which 0.5 million were distributed. Bhave had envisaged procuring 20 million ha by 1957 and distributing an average of 2 ha to 10 million families. This target was set after the strong initial response. In 1957, the movement was enlarged to *gramdan*: entire villages should be donated and then be equally distributed among the inhabitants. By the autumn of 1972, 168, 108[17] villages had been "donated". – This success story, however, seems illusory. The landlords often donated the poorest soils. The settlers had no capital, the movement lacked planning and organisation. Where the land is not distributed, the owners continue as owners and replace the actual donation of land by a payment in lieu. For one fifth of the *gramdan* villages an equal distribution was reported. In the remaining 80 per cent the donors have retained a multiple of the maximum acreage stipulated by Bhave.

Bhave himself became very critical of the results of his movement. Its aims of equalisation and non-violent distribution of land holdings became increasingly diluted. When the landlords did no longer feel the pressure of the landless, land donations declined. The movement seems to have been in limbo since about 1963 and is at present without importance.

A final evaluation of agrarian reform poses some problems. The third Five-Year-Plan (1961) noted that the acreage mobilised by the reforms was substantially smaller than expected, and added:

"In recent years, transfers of lands have tended to defeat the aims of the legislation for ceilings and to reduce its impact on the rural economy." (P. 229.)

It seems, that many landowners have made the fullest use of the exceptions. The fourth plan (1970) gives the following figures:

a. About 20 million tenants were liberated from the zamindari system and brought into a direct relationship with the State;

b. 3 million tenants and share croppers have acquired titles to over 2.8 million ha (i.e. less than 1 ha per beneficiary).

c. More than 0.9 million ha land held in excess of the ceiling[18] was declared agrarian reform land and taken over by government. Yet, 23.6 per cent of all farming households were still classified as tenants.

2.2.4. *Cooperatives*

The formation of cooperatives to assist the new smallholders created by the land reform is part of the reform and therefore also an important item in the reform programmes of Congress Party and government.

Cooperative activities have so far centred on agricultural credit and the sale and processing of sugar-cane. The actual figures of cooperative societies are impressive (see Table 2.12.). The organisation and guidance of hundreds of thousands of primary societies with millions of members is in any case a huge task. But the membership still falls far short of the vast numbers of agricultural families. In 1969 it was estimated that the primary cooperatives provided about 40 per cent of all agrarian credit.

To some extent, the wealthy and influential people in the village dominate the cooperatives also, and channel the credits to their own

Table 2.12.: Number and membership of co-operatives by type of society

	Number			Membership (1000)		
	1967/68	1971/72	1973/74	1967/68	1971/72	1973/74
Credit Societies						
State and central banks	369	367	367	376	324	682
Central land development banks	19	19	19	916	1,693	2,937
Primary land development banks	731	870	857	2,447	3,906	4,117
Grain banks	6,510	5,444	5,473	823	605	609
Primary agricultural societies	171,804	157,454	153,808	28,074	32,009	34,956
Primary non-agricultural societies	13,965	16,091	17,536	7,593	8,948	12,332
Non-Credit-Societies						
Marketing	3,466	3,654	3,681	2,620	5,276	5,507
Milk supply	9,301	13,437	17,017	697	1,173	1,455
Farming	8,048	9,605	9,477	213	263	264
Irrigation	1,667	3,869	4,758	87	137	170
Sugar factories	85	144	158	352	560	750
Cotton ginning and pressing	164	171	204	116	137	157
Other processing	1,344	1,170	772	187	213	199
Weavers	12,346	12,270	12,990	1,264	1,234	1,205
Other industrial societies	35,472	33,736	34,559	1,570	1,653	1,730
Consumers stores	14,335	13,278	14,321	4,275	4,363	4,913
Fishermen	3,784	4,498	4,715	395	482	580
Supervising unions	779	648	350	45	33	30
State and district unions and institutes	224	311	323	100	104	107

Source: Statistical statements

group. Moreover, members are indebted to private moneylenders, and utilise official credits only to pay off their debts. Due to socio-economic inferiority and low educational standards, democratic participation on the part of the members is weak. Part of the credit is used for immediate consumption. These facts have led to the proposal of supervised production credits, to be given in kind (seeds, fertilisers, tools).

The cooperative movement was and is quite successful in the field of sugar-cane and sugar production. Sugar-cane is a quite recent cash crop, introduced in view of the world shortage, following the US blockade of Cuban sugar. For its marketing and processing no established links existed. The cooperative movement, mainly in Maharashtra, discovered the chance in time and in cooperation with the government established a large number of sugar refineries. Similarly, in dairy farming, another new branch of agricultural production, cooperatives have had reasonable success.

The joint and collective farming societies – about 9,500 in 1974/75 – meet the same difficulties as the other types of cooperatives. They were the subject of public and expert discussion, but their practical role in agricultural production has been insignificant. They are small – averaging 52.3 and 30.9 ha respectively for the two types of society – and account together for much less than 1/100 of the sown area. Land available per working member is less than 2 ha, an acreage insufficient, on the basis of current yields, to feed a large rural family, as pointed out above (Chapter 2.2.2.). Actually, many of the joint and collective farming societies are not genuine at all, but were formed in order to circumvent the land reform or to get government subsidies. This fact is set out in the reports of government inquiry committees. A major part of these societies is dominated by the wealthy village elite, and thus can have no integrating or equalising effect. Caste segregation between landowners and ultimate cultivators is not eliminated.

Where genuine cooperative farming societies exist, their performance in land reclamation and irrigation has been excellent. No individual smallholder would have been able to achieve similar results on his own. In new settlements these cooperatives show the effect of cooperation, which is more than the simple aggregation of individual performances. In established villages with their tightly knit social system, however, they could not succeed. – Similarly, the cooperatives were and are quite successful in the spheres of sugar-cane and sugar and of dairy farming. Here we have new farm products with a large cash economy element, in a sphere where no established and entrenched private market organisations existed before.

In *Asian Drama*, Myrdal (1968) analysed the poor success of the cooperative movement and arrived at the following conclusion:

"Unfortunately, the notion that cooperation will have an equalising effect is bound to turn out to be an illusion. While land reform and tenancy legislation are, at least in their intent, devices for producing fundamental alterations in property rights and economic obligations, the 'cooperative' approach fails to incorporate a frontal attack on the existing inegalitarian power structure. Indeed, it aims at improving conditions without disturbing that structure and represents, in fact, an evasion of the equality issue. If, as is ordinarily the case, only the higher strata in the villages can avail themselves of the advantages offered by cooperative institutions – and profit from the government subsidies given for their development – the net effect is to create more, not less, inequality. This will hold true even when the announced purpose is to aid the disadvantaged strata." (p. 1335).

2.2.5. *Features of the agrarian system*

European notions hardly fit the Indian situation. Feudalism here is not of the European but of the oriental type, modified by the need for irrigation, by the traditional division of labour and cooperation of the castes, certain social functions of the landlord, the close connection between farming and village crafts. The functions performed by the peasant or farmer in Western Europe are here divided between at least two antagonistic social strata. The absentee landlord owns the land and decides about tenancy and tenants, but does not invest. The cultivator has no assured rights to the land, but bears all risks of farming and has to provide all the active capital; economically and socially he is dependent. He cannot be called a farmer or peasant, as his operational holding is no family farm in the Western sense.

The slow progress of cooperation, for instance, cannot be attributed to the producers' individualism and lack of cooperative spirit. They are not independent and free enough to establish cooperative societies and transact their business with them; they are too poor to raise capital for their societies; they are too oppressed and deprived socially and culturally to manage them democratically. As subsistence farmers, they cannot take many economic decisions, since they are subject to economic restraints and most of their surplus produce flows to the landlord. Surplus production for the market is an exception. As a whole, the cultivators live and work in a pre-cooperative state.

2.2.6. *Break-through of the green revolution?*

Since about 1967, experts and periodicals have been writing about the "green revolution", with its high-yielding wheat, which originated in Mexico and slowly conquered parts of Asia, in particular Pakistan and India. After several harvest failures, years of catastrophic scarcity of food grain, of hunger and large-scale wheat imports from industrial countries, India saw three good harvests in a row, beginning in 1967/68. This reversal of the trend aroused strong optimism and led to a discussion about future wheat surpluses and what to do with them. When Professor Borlaug received the Nobel Peace Prize, the result of his breeding work, the miracle wheat adapted to tropical conditions, came into the focus of public attention. – What, then, are the real achievements?

The long-term development of farm production and population is presented in Table 2.13. and Fig. 2.3. – Since 1950, agricultural produc-

Table 2.13.: Growth of production and of population

Year [1]	Farm production [2]			Industrial production		Population [3]	
	acreage	yield	pro-duction	total	percapita	millions	index 1951=100
1950-51	100.0	100.0	100.0	100.0	100.0	363.4	100.0
1955-56	113.8	107.4	122.2	143.1	130.2	397.8	109.5
1960-61	121.2	117.5	142.4	201.8	165.3	442.7	121.8
1965-66	122.7	117.9	144.7	277.1	201.1	498.9	137.3
1970-71	129.6	140.6	182.2	352.5	232.8	540.0	151.1
1971-72	128.1	141.8	181.6	362.8	234.7	561.9	154.6
1972-73	128.7	141.2	181.7	388.1	246.3	573.6	157.8
1973-74	128.0	141.0	181.0	423.0	.	584.9	161.0

[1]) The agricultural years runs from July 1 to June 30
[2]) Basis: 1946/50-1951/52 = 100; moving three years averages
[3]) Estimate June 30, each year; thus first line June 30, 1951, etc.

Sources: Economic survey (1975); Brief on Indian agriculture (1975)

tion has grown slowly, with two heavy setbacks and one great leap
forward in 1967/68. That year, production was 50 per cent above the
level of 1950. Half of the increase was due to the extended acreage, the
other half to improved hectare yields. At the same time, the population
continued to grow, over some periods at almost the same rate as did
production. Since 1967/68, however, production has increased faster than
the number of people to be fed. But it remains uncertain to this day
whether the three good harvests were due to systematic and successful
efforts or to favourable weather. Since 1972/73, the country has been
beset by a new crisis of food supplies, accompanied by malnutrition of the
vast masses of the poor.

The production of rice, wheat, sorghum and jute has increased, while
barley, pulses and sugar-cane have not (see Table 2.14. and Fig. 2.4.).
The three good harvests of 1967 to 1969 were followed by a measure of
stagnation, particularly in food grains, while cash crops are on the decrease.

The "green revolution" has not touched the whole country and has not
benefited all social strata equally. It was most effective in regions of well-
organised irrigation or of normal and regular rainfall. And it is in
particular the well-to-do farmers, producing for the market, who have
been able to utilise the new high-yielding varieties, bred for Indian
conditions. It is they again who stand to benefit most from industrial
inputs, government subsidies, increased institutional cheap credit
facilities and the heavily increased producer prices.

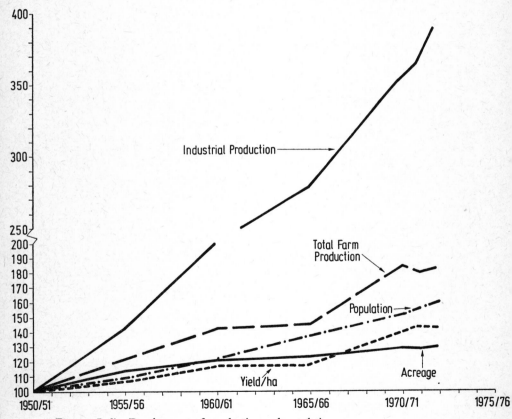

400
350
300 — Industrial Production →
250
200
190 — Total Farm Production →
180
170
160 — Population →
150
140
130
120
110 — Yield/ha
100
Acreage

1950/51   1955/56   1960/61   1965/66   1970/71   1975/76

Fig. 2.3. India: Development of production and population

Table 2.14.: Acreage, production and yield of selected crops

	Rice	Wheat	Food-grain	Ground-nut	Cotton [1]	Jute	Sugar-cane
Acreage mln. ha							
1950/51	30.8	9.7	97.3	4.5	5.9	0.6	1.7
1967/68	36.7	14.9	121.5	7.6	8.0	0.9	2.0
1969/70	37.7	16.6	123.6	7.2	7.7	0.8	2.7
1970/71	37.6	18.2	124.3	7.3	7.6	0.7	2.6
1971/72	37.8	19.1	122.6	7.5	7.8	0.8	2.4
1972/73 [2]	36.7	19.5	119.3	7.0	7.7	0.7	2.5
1973/74 [3]	38.0	19.1	126.1	7.0	7.6	0.8	2.7
Production mln to							
1950/51	20.6	6.5	50.8	3.5 [4]	2.9 [5]	3.3 [6]	7.1 [7]
1960/61	34.6	11.0	82.0	4.8	5.3	4.1	11.4
1964/65	39.0	12.3	89.0	5.9	5.7	6.1	12.5
1965/66	30.7	10.4	72.0	4.2	4.6	4.5	12.8
1967/68	37.6	16.5	95.1	5.7	5.5	6.3	9.8
1969/70	40.4	20.1	99.5	5.1	5.2	5.6	13.8
1970/71	42.2	23.8	108.4	6.1	5.7	4.9	13.0
1971/72	43.1	26.4	105.2	6.2	7.2	5.7	11.6
1972/73 [2]	39.2	24.7	97.0	4.1	6.3	5.0	17.8
1973/74 [3]	43.7	22.1	103.6	5.8	6.4	6.2	14.0
Yield q/ha							
1950/51	6.7	6.6	5.2	7.7	1.0 [7]	10.4	33.4 [8]
1960/61	10.1	8.5	7.1	7.4	1.3	11.8	46.1
1970/71	11.2	13.1	8.7	8.3	1.3	11.8	49.6
1971/72	11.4	13.8	8.6	8.2	1.5	12.5	48.6
1972/73 [2]	11.7	12.7	8.1	5.9	1.4	12.8	52.0
1973/74 [3]	11.5	11.6	8.2	8.4	1.4	14.0	51.5

[1] Ginned
[2] Revised official estimates
[3] Unrevised official estimates
[4] Nuts in shell
[5] Million bales à 180 kg
[6] Production and yield expressed in gur = marketable brown sugar, processed in the village
[7] Based on trade estimates of production and official estimates of acreage

Sources: Annual report (1975), Brief on Indian agriculture (1975), Economic survey (1975), Statistical abstract (1967)

It may well be that the substantial increases in the producer prices of some basic commodities have improved the supply situation. Stocks hoarded by speculators were mobilised, while small producers perhaps reduced consumption to the physiological limit. Increased supply and

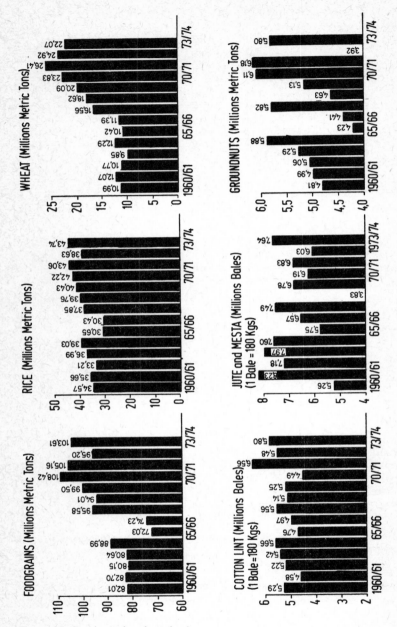

Fig. 2.4. India: Agricultural production

price rises diminish demand and consumption among the poorer rural and urban strata, who suffer most from the price increases.[19] There are many, many millions of them. A basic ration is sold in about 137,000 fair-price shops at fixed and to some extent controlled prices, but this service fails by a long way to reach all those in need.

Rising prices have a different effect in a developing country than in a modern society with a modern marketing system and an expanding productive capacity. In India, the marketed quantities constitute a relatively small proportion of total production, and that proportion is marketed for the most part not by the producers themselves, but by the landlords who receive land-rent in kind. The rest is consumed without ever entering the monetised economic circuit. Here, very little influence would be brought to bear by official action. Price rises thus benefit in the first place not the producers but the middlemen. The stimulating effect of higher prices on production is therefore weak, its socially polarising effect on the other hand quite marked.[20] Only when capitalist entrepreneurs are willing to invest in agricultural production rather than in land purchase will government assistance be able to stimulate production.

Even as regards crops, the success of the green revolution remained partial and sectional, as did its regional and social impact. High-yielding varieties are practically available and in use only for wheat and millets, while for rice, the country's most important food grain, the development of suitable varieties has not yet been completed. It is probable that some farmers have increased their wheat acreage on suitable land at the expense of rice and cash crops. A significant imbalance between wheat and competing crops has resulted, stimulated in part by the price incentive for wheat. While improved seeds have been delivered, other inputs – like water, fertilisers, machinery, tools – have been supplied in insufficient quantities. Certainly, the improved seeds give a chance for better harvests, but they are far from being high-yielding. Hitherto, they have hardly improved the level of average yields. The most important limitation of the green revolution, however, is the social one. The vast majority of cultivators and dwarf holders and all the land they cultivate are still excluded from technical progress and from public subsidies.

It seems that at least for some of the experts the green revolution is meant to replace and obviate a red revolution or an agrarian reform. This approach rests on several errors.

1. It ignores the very narrow limitation of biological-technical progress (seeds, fertilisers, pesticides, feed etc.) in isolation. The dynamic force of mechanical-technical progress (pumps, tractors, threshers) and its multiplier effect on bio-technical progress is ignored. Both forms of

technical progress in farming are closely interlinked, mutually dependent and cannot be separated with impunity.

2. Bio-technical progress, unlike mechanical progress, is divisible. Thus, bio-technical progress can technically be applied to the smallest plot or holding. But economically, this size-neutrality does not exist. Small and marginal producers are mostly unable to utilise the new inputs.

3. The active participation of the millions of underprivileged is lost. Their production potential remains unutilised for economic and social development.

4. The feelings and wishes of millions of small producers, which are tangible facts in politics, are not taken into account.

5. It is assumed that the existing social framework is sufficient to raise production and productivity. But this assumption negates the interdependence of the means of production and the productive forces, on the one hand, and the production relations on the other.

If this explanation is correct, it shows that some of the advocates of the green revolution may blind themselves, but not the hungry cultivators. In reality, green revolution and radical agrarian reform are not opposites or alternatives, but belong together and are mutually dependent for their efficiency. Without agrarian reform the technological innovations – which do not constitute a revolution – cannot be adopted quickly and widely. A radical agrarian reform, on the other hand, has to utilise and apply all available technological advances, in order to assure an optimum material and psychological result of the social transformation.

2.2.7. *Effects of social polarisation*

Growing social tension in the villages is apparent everywhere. Unrest and discontent of cultivators and share-croppers are expressed in very different forms. Landlords' houses, mansions and property are looted, sometimes put on fire. Landlords are murdered. Debts and interest are not paid. The harvest is carried away before the share due to the owner is levied. Land is occupied – sometimes symbolically – as a protest against non-implementation of agrarian reform laws (land-grabbing movement). An internal survey,[21] undertaken by the Home Ministry in New Delhi, described the situation by the end of 1969 in certain rural regions as explosive.

Increased productivity of labour and land provide new opportunities for the farmworkers to put forward their demands and fight for higher wages and a better standard of living. In a predominantly agrarian country emotions and discontent of the rural masses must affect the political institutions and authorities. It was the deep agrarian unrest that formed the background to the split in the Congress Party in 1970. This has accelerated several government decisions on economic policies, above all the nationalisation of the 14 large banks. Private banking had entirely neglected agricultural credit needs, particularly the needs of the small producers, because that would have entailed much work, expense and risk. The banks preferred to leave that function to the village money-lenders and usurers. Neither were the rural credit cooperatives able to allocate their scarce credit funds according to real needs and social urgency. This inequality of opportunities was further aggravated by the green revolution.

The central government therefore launched two new agencies for supporting the rural poor. This programme, too, is implemented by the state governments. Small Farmers' Development Agencies (SFDA) have been established in 46 districts. They are to assist viable smallholders farming 1-3 ha with supervised credits.[22] By June 1975, these agencies had identified 3.29 million small-holders, of whom 1.79 million were brought into primary credit cooperatives. Agencies for marginal farmers and landless labourers were organised in 41 districts. They seek to help cultivators with marginal holdings of up to 1 ha as well as farmworkers who own a house and who derive more than 50 per cent of their income from paid employment in agriculture.[23] By June 1975, 1.47 million marginal farmers and labourers had been identified. This latter programme will "increase the income capacity of these people by improved technology, subsidised credit for the purchase of selected inputs and create additional employment opportunities through a rural works programme". In the framework of the two programmes wells were dug, irrigation pumps were installed, dairy cattle was purchased and short and medium-term credit was given. (For further details see Table 2.15.). In 1975, the central government considered the merger of these two agencies with other rural aid projects – such as a programme for drought-prone areas, a crash scheme for rural employment, tribal development projects, etc. – into one single organisation.

The assistance to the weaker sections has not touched the broad masses of the rural poor as yet, and it seems doubtful, whether such programmes can solve the basic problems. But the programmes clearly show that earlier activities had not touched those numerically important strata.

2.3. *Industrialisation*

While the farming sector dominates the economy and society, India occupies an exceptional position as one of the few developing nations where a measure of industrial development was achieved even before

Table 2.15.: Special programs for the weaker sections of the rural population

	Small farmers' development agencies		Marginal farmers' + landless labourers' development agencies	
	upto June 1972	upto June 1975	upto June 1972	upto June 1975
1. Number of projects	46	46	41	41
2. Small farmers + labourers identified (1000)	1,684	3,290	788	1,470
Thereof brought into cooperatives (1000)	818	1,790	194	610
3. Finance released to agencies since start (mln. Rs.)	123.6	370	73.8	246
thereof utilized (mln. Rs.)	65.9	381 [1])	29.2	235
4. Shortterm production loans issued during the year (mln. Rs.)				
by cooperatives	122.3	302.0	9.2	29.6
by commercial banks	–	10.3	–	2.4
5. Investment loans (mln. Rs.)				
by cooperatives	148.6	629.2	10.4	131.4
by commercial banks	3.8	106.4	2.8	79.2
6. Physical achievements				
Wells constructed	34,146	136,782	2,573	24.254
Pumpsets installed	8,081	36,195	1,279	9,111
Cattle units set up [2])	11,047	66,130	5,776	54,735
Poultry units set up	2,113	5,883	2,583	3,770
Rural artisans trained	600	8,553	463	4,923
Labourers employed on rural works [3])	8,476	92,739	12,756	216,638

[1]) Expenditure exceeds funds; agency could utilize funds received under "other sources"
[2]) Number of milk animals distributed or purchased not given; in most cases probably one milking animal
[3]) Total employment created (mandays) not given

Source: RBI Report on currency... (1975)

political independence. After 1947, development was able to build on these foundations.

2.3.1. *The starting point*
During British rule, a comprehensive railway system and an educational system catering for the needs of civil administration were created and irrigation was extended and improved. Development of industry, how-

ever, was permitted only to a limited extent. The profit interests and monopoly position of metropolitan industries and commerce had to be given full consideration and protection. Thus the construction of factories was sanctioned only in industries that offered no competitive threat to British business, or in which large profits could be expected for British investors. Thus industrialisation was hindered in two ways, economically by the draining away of the Indian surplus into the metropolis[24] and administratively by the exercise of Britain's political domination. There were internal factors as well that were working in the same direction, including on the one hand the reluctance of the comprador bourgeoisie to invest, and on the other the after-effects of a misunderstood Gandhian philosophy. These external and internal factors combined to bring about a delayed, unequal, restricted industrial development, so that industry succeeded neither in meeting domestic demand nor in offering employment to those redundant in agriculture.

In 1947, India had a weak extractive industry for raw materials, with large parts of the country not sufficiently explored; there was one steel plant in Jamshedpur, plus substantial textile factories, mainly in Bombay, Ahmedabad and Calcutta, in which British capital played a major part. The metal-processing and engineering industry had one stronghold in Calcutta and some factories in Madras, but was little developed over-all. Large docks and engineering industries, located in and around Bombay, may also be mentioned.

The manufacture of cheap consumer goods had rapidly become a disastrous competitor for millions of village artisans (weavers, potters etc.), who used to produce their goods in the villages as a main occupation or as a side-line. Their activities were largely integrated in the framework of a non-monetary division of labour, with very simple tools and equipment, without any energy source except their and their families' muscle. In spite of their low wages and the living standard of coolies, they could not stand the competition of cheap industrial large-scale production. The destruction of the traditional village crafts, the retardation of industrial development and the simultaneous population explosion have increased the pressure on the land, the fragmentation of the fields, the partition of "holdings", the increase in the land-rent. Owing to the vast reserves of manpower, industrial wages remained low. The internal market could not expand.

2.3.2. *Two concepts*
In the face of this situation, two different concepts had been developed. M. K. Gandhi advocated a revitalisation of rural crafts both as a means and as an end in the struggle of resistance to British rule and the Anglo-

Indian textile industry. The Indian village, seen in an idealised and somewhat mystical way, was to become economically self-sufficient again and
at the same time strike a blow at foreign-owned industry. The workless
should find employment. Thus, the hand-operated spinning wheel (*ambar
charkha*) became the symbol of resistance and struggle for freedom, which
presented Gandhi to the villagers as a leader who knew and shared their
way of life and their work.

Slowly, this idea became an ideology, and its ambiguous tenets had
their effect. Like Gandhi himself, supporters of this ideology visualised
a return to the simplicity of rural life and to the village community, the
time-honoured fortress against foreign invaders for hundreds of years.
Industrialisation with its concomitants – social mobility and change,
social tensions and class struggle – was seen as an acute or latent threat to
the very unity of the independence movement. On social and humanitarian grounds it was felt that cottage industries or village crafts and those
active in them ought to be protected against unemployment or the lower
status of industrial workers. Gandhi's utterances on this issue were
ambiguous. But it seems that his statements against modern industry
predominate; at any rate, they have proved to be dominant in the minds
of his followers and ideological heirs.[25] Up to the 1970s, the government has been maintaining institutions for training teachers in the
manual skills of cottage industries. Thus Gandhi's personality cult
perpetuates outmoded techniques and ideologies.

Jawaharlal Nehru, Gandhi's political heir and at the same time his
opponent, was close to British socialism in his thinking (Harold Laski,
Stafford Cripps), and an enthusiastic supporter of the Russian revolution
of 1917 and of economic planning. He fought for independence as a
means to modernise his country economically and socially and to overcome its mass poverty. These goals could not be achieved without
industries. In order to build them quickly and catch up with the development lag, planning was vital. India provides a sufficient domestic market
for a diversified and independent expansion of all industries. Mineral raw
materials, to be prospected, extracted and processed at home, were to be
the base. On that base, capital goods industries were to be established,
producing complete factories, heavy machinery and other means of
production. These, in turn, were to be followed by consumer goods
industries, first for the essentials, later for sophisticated non-essential
durable goods. Such a build-up necessitates a technological infrastructure
(energy from different sources, railways, roads, communications) and a
cultural infrastructure (schools at all levels, elimination of illiteracy, etc.).

The draining away of economic wealth, which appeared in the European metropolis as colonial extra-profit, had deprived the country of its

economic power and funds, which otherwise would have permitted a quick formation and mobilisation of capital. The dominant position of the agrarian sector and of subsistence farming imply even today a slow and dispersed formation of agricultural surpluses, which under the prevailing conditions cannot easily be utilised. Nehru and his economic advisers therefore wanted to boost the slow rate of internal capital formation during the early phases of development by foreign assistance, thus accelerating economic take-off. In that way, the agrarian sector was to be spared a painful blood-letting and enabled to increase its production in parallel with industrial development. The most modern technology suitable for India's specific conditions was to be introduced. The transformation was to be speeded up by the importation of experts and the training of local personnel. – The natural resources are only partly explored and put to practical use. Some raw materials, particularly for oil refineries and fertiliser factories, are still being imported.

In spite of the general underdevelopment, industry today produces a wide variety of goods, including sophisticated weaponry, nuclear devices, jet aircraft, space research equipment, etc. A new dualism seems to emerge in the non-food sectors: a highly developed technology in some fields – mostly those judged by the ruling authorities to be of strategic importance – contrasting with a relatively primitive technology and slow progress in the fields of mass consumer goods and basic food production. In the productive industries – mining, large-scale and small-scale industries, construction, electricity, gas – 20.7 million persons were active in 1971, i.e. 11.5 per cent of the economically active population (see Table 2.4.). They produced 22 per cent of the gross national product. Some finished goods are processed from imported semi-finished materials.

There were several old industrial centres (Madras, Bombay, Ahmedabad, Calcutta, Jamshedpur). New ones have developed, e.g. Bangalore (metal-processing and engineering), Coimbatore (textiles), Poona (metal-processing, engineering, industrial installations), Baroda (tractors etc.), Canpur (textiles, metal-processing), Vizagapatnam (ship-building), Rourkela, Bhilai and Durgapur (steel), Ranchi (heavy engineering), Bhopal (electrical equipment), Barauni (oil), Faridabad-Delhi (various industries). Close to the old centres of industrial activities, satellite centres or sub-centres have been established, e.g. Nasik near Bombay, Ludhiana in the Punjab. Growth centres of industrial development have so far been Bombay-Poona, Orissa, West Bengal, Western Uttar Pradesh and the Punjab. The states always fight hard for central government aid for their regional developments.

The producing sector of the national economy is divided into three main subsectors:

public sector – predominantly modern industrial enterprises,

cooperative sector ⟨ modern factories (e.g. sugar), manufacture, traditional crafts ⟨ cottage industries,

private sector ⟨ modern factories, small workshops, where manual work prevails.

The three subsectors are not always competitive, but rather complementary, and a certain division of functions can be seen between them.

2.3.3. *Quantitative achievements*

During the 28 years since independence a substantial industrial capacity has been established in spite of technological, cultural, natural, social and economic obstacles. (See Table 2.16.). Setbacks were caused by droughts, harvest failures, lack of energy and of raw materials, import difficulties due to lack of foreign currency, economic crises and other factors; nevertheless, substantial growth of capacity and production has been recorded. (Looking at statistical data, a distinction is necessary between effective production, licensed capacity, installed capacity and production target.) Progress has been sizeable, measured against the low point of departure, but it must also be related to the size of the population. Such an assessment gives a clearer idea of achievements and needs, even if per capita production and availability of goods in India cannot be compared with the record of the Netherlands or Sweden.[26]

The rise in industrial production has slowly changed the composition of the gross national product and the structure and direction of exports. The share of industrial goods is growing. At the same time, the direction has moved towards more sales to socialist countries. They are less demanding as regards the finish and sophistication of the goods they import; they accept non-convertible currencies and barter deals; and in fact their demand for typical Indian products substantially exceeds India's ability to deliver.

The "village industries" produce a wide variety of goods, mostly from agricultural or local raw materials. Most important among these cottage industries are weaving, processing of coconut-husk into coir, production of brown sugar (*gur*) and a few more crafts. Rural non-agricultural production has enjoyed comprehensive government protection and has given employment to a vast bureaucratic administration. This traditional

Table 2.16.: Production of selected commodities 1950/51-1973/74

Item	Unit	1950/51	1960/61	1970/71	1973/74 [1])
Mining					
Coal	mln to	32.8	55.7	74.3	81.2
Iron ore [2])	mln to	3.0	11.0	22.5	34.4
Metallurgy					
Raw iron	mln to	1.7	4.3	7.0	7.0
Raw steel	mln to	1.5	3.4	6.1	5.8
Steel ingots	mln to	1.0	2.4	4.5	4.5
Steel castings	1000 to	–	34	62	55
Aluminium	1000 to	4.0	18.3	166.8	147.9
Copper	1000 to	7.1	8.5	9.3	12.1
Engineering					
Machine tools [3])	mln Rs.	54	224	877	1,439
Railway wagons	1000	2.9	11.9	11.1	12.2
Cars and trucks	1000	16.5	55.0	87.9	99.4
Motocycles etc.	1000	–	19.4	97.0	124.0
Motorpumps	1000	35	109	259	331
Diesel engines	1000	5.5	55.5	68.9	139.8
Transformers	1000 kVa	179	1,413	8,086	11,631
Electric motors	1000 h.p.	99	728	2,721	2,908
Electric fans	1000	199	1,059	1,716	2,230
Electric light bulbs	mln	14.0	43.5	119.3	133.2
Radio receivers	1000	54	282	1,794	1,776
Bicycles	1000	99	1,071	2,042	2,581
Sewing machines	1000	33	303	235	258
Chemicals					
Nitrogenous fertilisers [4])	1000 to	9	98	830	1,060
Phosphatic fertilisers [4])	1000 to	9	52	229	323
Paper and paper board	1000 to	116	350	755	722
Tyres	mln	?	1.4	3.8	4.6
Cement	mln to	2.7	8.0	14.4	14.7
Refined oil products	mln to	0.2	5.8	17.1	19.7
Electricity generated [5])	md kWh	5.3	16.9	55.8	64.6
Textiles					
Cotton cloth	md m	4.2	6.7	7.6	8.0
mill sector	md m	3.4	4.6	4.1	4.1
decentralised sector	md m	0.8	2.1	3.5	3.9
Food					
Sugar	1000 to	1,134	3,029	3,110	3,967
Tea	1000 to	277	322	430	467
Coffee	1000 to	21	54	96	87
Peanutbutter	1000 to	170	340	594	449

[1]) Estimates
[2]) In 1973/74 production in Goa included: 11.8 mln to
[3]) Machine tools, machines for cotton, sugar, cement factories, first figures for 1955/56
[4]) Pure nutrients
[5]) Government power stations only

Sources: Economic survey (1975); Statistical outline (1975)

sector, however, has no large employment or growth potential. If growth of production is the aim, subsidies could be utilised more effectively. In their actual form, they can at best be a passing remedy for social evils. It seems quite improbable that this ailing sector can be revitalised so as to make a significant contribution to economic progress. For all the subsidies, those active in these crafts suffer from hidden unemployment and stark poverty.[27] In several instances, totally obsolete, bankrupt private manufacturing enterprises were bought by government and formally transformed into cooperative societies. Thus, the cooperative sector is burdened with workshops that cannot develop further and is held responsible for their inevitable failure.

2.3.4. *Plan targets*
The qualitative objectives of the plans and their priorities have changed over the four five-year-plan periods, in line with the cycles of internal and economic policies. The main objectives are:
1. Creation of a modern industrial sector and of a modern infrastructure;
2. increase in agricultural production;
3. self-reliance and economic independence;
4. radical agrarian reform;
5. employment, reduction in unemployment;
6. elimination of illiteracy;
7. family planning, substantial reduction in population growth;
8. abolition of poverty;
9. lessening of social inequality;
10. a socialist commonwealth.

These main objectives are not without inherent contradictions, and they compete for the allocation of scarce resources. The priorities laid down have varied greatly in the course of the different phases of development, following discussions, rectifications and interventions by social pressure groups. Some have only declamatory value, reflecting – it is true – the desire of the masses as expressed by a few leaders, but decidedly at variance with the intentions of the ruling class and the administration.

From 1947 or 1951, the start of the first five-year plan, substantial quantitative gains have been achieved. The physical targets till 1978/79 are given in Table 2.17. They foresee a sizable increase in crop production, 22 per cent for food grains, 40 per cent for sugar. The production of nitrogen fertilisers, alumina, sulphuric acid, newsprint shall be increased twofold or more; iron, coal, steel, oil, by 90-62 per cent. Consumer goods production is to grow at a slower pace. But the targets for 1973/74, which are the basis for further planning, have not been reached. The gap

Table 2.17.: Estimated targets of production: Fifth Five-Year-Plan 1974/75-1978/79

Commodity	Unit	1973/74 base year	1978/79	Planned increase %
Foodgrains	mn. to	115.0	139.9	22
Sugar	mn. to	4.2	5.9	40
Nitrogenous fertiliser (pure nutrients)	mn. to	1.6	3.9	144
Coal	mn. to	80.0	141.2	77
Oil	mn. to	7.7	7.8	–
Oil products	mn. to	20.5	36.0	76
Electricity Production	1000 mn. kWh	78.0	129.3	66
Electricity Consumption	1000 mn. kWh	62.4	106.0	70
Iron ore	mn. to	42.0	66.5	58
Iron	mn. to	2.0	3.8	90
Steel	mn. to	5.8	9.4	62
Steel alloys and special steels	mn. to	0.4	0.5	25
Aluminium (ingots)	mn. to	0.2	0.4	100
Sulphuric acid	mn. to	1.5	3.3	120
Cement	mn. to	18.0	26.8	49
Paper and board	mn. to	0.9	1.3	44
Newsprint	mn. to	0.07	0.16	129
Jute (processed)	mn. to	1.3	1.6	23
Cotton cloth (mill)	mn. m	8,500	10,703	26
Synthetic rayon cloth	mn. m	1,200	1,513	26
Wool cloth	mn. m	17	24	41
Electric motors	mn. HP	3.4	5.6	65
Radio receivers	mn	3.25	3.85	18
Watches	mn	1.58	2.19	39

Source: Eastern economist (1974)

between planned and actual points of departure varies for the different items, as shown in Table 2.18. Only for special steels was the target exceeded, while for paper, cement, bauxite, jute and electrical motors it was barely reached. For all other products the gaps are significant. The statistics show the giant tasks ahead of the country.

The plan figures are no rigid directive, with the force of law and for the fulfilment of which all energies are mobilised. They present no more than a loose guide-line, a vision of desirable development, sometimes no more than a verbal device to please specific political groupings.

Industrial production as a whole is to grow between 1973 and 1978 by almost 50 per cent with an annual growth rate of 8.3 per cent. Since 1950, this rate has been reached or exceeded on nine occasions. With the general upward trend it will naturally become more difficult to maintain this pace.

Table 2.18.: Lag of industrial production behind plan targets in 1973/74

Commodity	Mn. units	Target	Probable output	Lag
		official estimates		
Sugar	to	4.7	4.2	0.5
Nitrogenous fertilizer (pure nutrient)	to	2.5	1.6	0.9
Coal	to	93.5	80.0	13.5
Oil products	to	26.0	20.5	5.5
Iron ore	to	51.4	42.0	9.4
Iron	to	3.8	2.0	1.8
Steel	to	8.1	6.2	1.9
Steel alloys and special steel	to	0.22	0.35	+ 0.13
Aluminium	to	0.22	0.21	0.01
Sulphuric acid	to	2.5	1.5	0.1
Cement	to	18.0	18.0	–
Paper and board	to	0.85	0.85	–
Newsprint	to	0.15	0.07	0.08
Jute (processed)	to	1.4	1.3	0.1
Cotton cloth (mill)	m	5,100	4,500	600
Synthetic rayon cloth	m	1,500	1,200	300
Wool cloth	m	20	17	3
Electric motors	h.p.	3.4	3.4	–
Radio receivers	sets	3.80	3.25	0.55

Source: Eastern economist (1974)

2.3.5. *Allocation of resources*

Besides central government outlays for development, which are by far the largest part, those of the States have to be taken into account. Table 2.19. shows the following main facts.

1. Total annual outlays have increased from the third plan (ending in in 1965/66) to 1971/72 from 17,150 to 31,450 million Rs, i.e. nominally by 84 per cent.

2. Transport and communications remains the most important sector in development planning, with an allocation of 20 per cent of total plan outlays.

3. Promotion of modern industry remains a priority with 19.4 per cent.

4. The share of the agrarian sector rose from 12.7 to 17.6 per cent. Moreover agriculture has benefited from a large proportion of the allocations for irrigation and flood control. Agriculture has so great a political and economic weight, that it cannot be ignored or neglected in the allocation of public funds.

Table 2.19.: Plan expenditures ¹) by sectors of development

Development sector	Third plan 1961/62-65/66 mln Rs	%	Plan interval 1966/67-68/69 mln Rs	%	Fourth plan 1969-74 mln Rs	%	Fifth plan (1974-79) mln Rs	%
1. Agriculture and allied	10,890	12.7	11,071	16.7	23,535	15.0	47,300	12.6
2. Irrigation, flood control	6,637	7.7	4,710	7.1	17,722	8.1	26,810	7.2
3. Power	12,523	14.6	12,215	18.3	29,118	18.5	61,900	16.6
4. Village + small industries	2,408	2.8	1,261	1.9	2,447	1.6	89,640 }	24.0
5. Industry + mining	17,263	20.1	15,104	22.8	28,736	18.3		
6. Transport + communications	21,117	24.6	12,224	18.5	30,620	19.5	71,150	19.0
7. Education	5,887	6.9	3,068	4.6	7,822	5.0	17,260	4.6
8. Scientific research	714	0.8	471	0.7	1,307	0.8	4,190	1.1
9. Health	2,259	2.6	1,391	2.1	3,367	2.1	7,960	2.1
10. Family planning	249	0.3	715	1.1	2,779	1.7	5,160	1.4
11. { Water supply, sanitation Urban + regional development	2,332	2.7	1,760	2.7	7,207	4.6	21,650	5.8
12. Welfare of backward classes	991	1.2	736	1.1	1,675	1.1	7,260	1.9
13. Social + labour welfare, artisan training	752	0.9	460	0.7	992	0.6	2,860	0.8
14. Other programs	1,750	2.1	1,158	1.7	4,931	3.1	10,680	2.9
15. Total	85,772	100.0	66,254	100.0	157,420	100.0	372,500	100.0

¹) Central government, state governments, union territories

Sources: Economic survey (1972, 1975)

5. As regards education, the percentage of allocated funds has decreased compared with the third plan, except for family planning, which shows a marked increase.

6. Expenditure for social assistance and protection remains very limited. To this should be added as an item of social assistance the outlays for village industries, accounting for 1.5 per cent of the total, as against 2.8 per cent in the earlier period.

The nominal growth of expenditure for the different development tasks would have to be adjusted by the rate of inflation to get a true picture of allocations of public funds. Moreover, the substantial difference between planned outlay and effective fund utilisation ought to be taken into account, but the extent of this gap is hardly known. For the fourth plan, this is shown in Table 2.20. During both years the gap was about a quarter of the planned amounts.

Table 2.20.: Planned and actual expenditure of public sector industries during Fourth plan (million Rs.)

	Approved outlay	Estimated expenditure	Difference in percent
Iron and steel	10,530	8,670	− 17.7
Non-ferrous metals	2,480	2,090	− 15.7
Fertilizers	4,930	3,780	− 23.2
Petroleum exploration and refining	3,030	3,070	+ 1.3
Petrochemicals	770	820	+ 6.5
Coal	1,100	890	− 19.1
Iron ore	880	800	− 9.1
Other industries [1]	6,780	6,880	+ 1.5
Total	30,500	27,000	− 11.5

[1] Here are included: electric power stations, paper, cement, plantations, textiles, shipbuilding, atomic energy and loans to financing institutions

Source: Draft Five-Year-Plan (1974-79)

The central government is, no doubt, financially the largest investor. This, however, does not imply the same amount of influence on the direction of total investment. A large part of public investment funds is channelled via the private sector.

2.3.6. *The workers and salaried employees*

For a modern structure of society and for the development of a monetary economy, the class of wage and salary earners is of prime importance. This class is growing very slowly. Table 2.21 gives full data only for

Table 2.21.: Employment (millions, March each year) [1]

A. *Public sector*	1956	1966	1971 [1]	1974 [2]	1956-74 mln	%
I. by employer						
1. Central government	1.86	2.64	2.77	2.94	+ 1.08	
2. State governments	2.27	3.72	4.15	4.69	+ 2.42	
3. Quasi governmental	0.37	1.32	1.93	2.93	+ 2.56	
4. Local bodies	0.74	1.70	1.88	1.93	+ 1.19	
II. by industry						
1. Plantations, forestry etc.	0.01	0.23	0.28	0.32	+ 0.31	
2. Mining and quarrying	0.05	0.16	0.18	0.61	+ 0.56	
3. Manufacturing	0.21	0.67	0.81	1.03	+ 0.82	
4. Construction	0.42	0.77	0.88	1.00	+ 0.58	
5. Electricity, gas, water etc.	0.08	0.30	0.44	0.53	+ 0.45	
6. Trade and commerce	0.04	0.16	0.33	0.45	+ 0.41	
7. Transport and communications	1.39	2.09	2.22	2.34	+ 0.95	
8. Services	3.03	5.00	5.61	6.21	+ 3.18	
Total	5.23	9.38	10.73	12.49	+ 7.26	+ 138.8
B. *Private sector*						
1. Plantations, forestry [3]	0.67	0.90	0.80	0.80	+ 0.13	
2. Mining and quarrying	0.55	0.51	0.41	0.14	− 0.41	
3. Manufacturing	3.02	3.86	3.97	4.17	+ 1.15	
4. Construction [4]	0.24	0.25	0.14	0.12	− 0.12	
5. Electricity, gas, water etc.	0.04	0.04	0.05	0.04	± 0	
6. Trade and commerce	0.16	0.33	0.30	0.31	+ 0.15	
7. Transport and communication	0.08	0.12	0.10	0.08	± 0	
8. Services	0.28	0.80	1.00	1.11	+ 0.83	
Total	5.04	6.81	6.76	6.77	+ 1.73	+ 34.3
Total A + B	10.27	16.19	17.49	19.26	+ 8.99	+ 87.5

[1]) Includes employment data for the Union Territory of Goa, Daman & Diu from March 1970 onwards
[2]) Provisional
[3]) This includes most of the plantations excluding coffee; here the coverage is inadequate.
[4]) Coverage in construction particularly on private account is known to be inadequate.

Source: Economic survey (1975)

those employed in workshops employing over 25 workers. For firms with 10-24 employees, statistics are incomplete, since the relevant information is supplied on a voluntary basis, while the large number of seasonal or casual workers and of those working in workshops employing up to 9 people or with no motive power is not yet covered in official statistics.[28]

In the public sector the number of employed people rose during the 15 years 1956-71 by 105 per cent, in the private sector by 34 per cent. The increase in the number of regularly employed workers – 70 per cent – exceeds the rate of population growth, but is still far too low to offer employment to the vast army of rural and urban unemployed and under-employed, if the present development strategy remains unchanged.

Next to administration proper, the largest group in the public sector are the railway workers and postal services, while construction and manufacturing industries employ smaller – but at 1.68 million still substantial – numbers. This contrasts with the picture of employment in the private sector, where processing industries employ about 59 per cent of the total. These figures, on the whole, confirm that complementarity rather than competition prevails between the public and private sectors.[29]

A total of 19 million workers and employees receiving money wages and salaries is not very much in a total population of almost 600 million.

In spite of favourable conditions for investment, large parts of the upper class are hardly willing to invest in long-term projects or to take any risks. A merchant or comprador bourgeoisie, they are not a class of entrepreneurs prepared to accept risks, as the ideal type is seen through West European eyes. They are used to regular high returns from modest investments and given to conspicuous consumption.

The labour exchanges, with 429 offices spread over the country in 1970, cannot efficiently serve either the whole country or all applicants for employment. Of more then 4.5 million registered unemployed in 1970 under 450,000 were offered employment. Moreover, the registered numbers are only a small proportion of all those seeking work.

As regards factory wages (Table 2.22), only state averages are given in the statistics. Thus, the stratification of incomes cannot be discerned. Nominal wages rose substantially between 1961 and 1973. The real growth rate is unknown. Annual wages ranging from 1,695 Rs in Jammu and Kashmir to 3,242 Rs in Orissa are close to the subsistence minimum. In the more industrialised states of Gujarat, Maharashtra and West Bengal annual wages vary between 2,961 and 3,157 Rs. Industrial wages are incomparably lower than middle-class incomes.[30] The workers' ability to finance trade unions of their own or to afford lengthy strikes is very limited. In such circumstances it happens not infrequently that employers or agile lawyers, who manage several small "independent" local trade unions simultaneously, acquire considerable influence. The conditions of the labour market keep wages at a very low level.

In 1968, there were 584 national and 15,128 state-wide trade unions

Table 2.22.: Average wages ¹) and number of factory workers by states

	Per capita annual earnings (Rs)				Daily average employment 1971	
	1961	1969	1971	1961–71 %	1000	in percent of population
Andhra Pradesh	1,149	2,088	2,349	104.4	221	0.5
Assam	1,599	2,340	2,481	55.2	66	0.4
Bihar	1,856	2,486	2,767	49.1	285	0.5
Gujarat	1,702	2,643	2,961	74.0	410	1.5
Haryana	–	2,436	2,569	–	77	0.8
Himachal Pradesh	1,288	2,521	2,849	121.2	9	0.3
Jammu & Kashmir	–	1,805	1,695	–	5	0.1
Karnataka	1,375	2,088	2,656	93.2	149	0.5
Kerala	1,152	2,467	2,730	137.0	116	0.5
Madhya Pradesh	1,816	2,939	3,013	65.9	137	0.3
Maharashtra	1,775	2,903	3,157	77.9	953	1.9
Manipur	–	–	–	–	1	0.1
Orissa	1,180	2,143	3,242	174.7	54	0.2
Punjab	1,174	2,070	2,219	89.0	82	0.6
Rajasthan	761	2,003	2,503	228.9	66	0.3
Tamil Nadu	1,465	2,442	2,670	82.3	431	1.0
Tripura	–	2,010	2,790	–	1	0.1
Uttar Pradesh	1,264	2,200	2,471	95.5	380	0.4
West Bengal	1,410	2,675	3,028	114.8	745	1.7
Delhi	1,655	2,860	3,042	83.8	85	2.1
Total	1,540	2,588	2,852	85.2	4,296	0.8

¹) Workers earning less than Rs. 400 per month

Source: Indian labour statistics

with 2.5 million members, according to official statistics. They were in part affiliated to 5 nation-wide trade union congresses of differing political allegiance. The trade union congress with the widest membership is ideologically close to the CPI, another is close to the CPI(M); two congresses have links with the socialist parties; one cooperates with the Congress Party and largely follows M. K. Gandhi's philosophy of no class struggle, but social partnership. – Sometimes, the government uses all its power, including police and army, against strikers and strikes, which then are declared illegal.

In accordance with the low degree of economic development, social security is not very comprehensive. In regularly working factories with more than 20 employees and which apply motive power, employees earning below 500 Rs per month are included in a government social security scheme, which in February 1971 covered 4.1 million persons and their families in 323 towns. The scheme pays sickness and maternity benefits, compensation for accidents and death grants. Furthermore, there is an old-age insurance for enterprises which have been operating for three years or more and employ more than 50 people. It covers employees of at least one year's standing up to an earnings limit of 1,000 Rs per month. Altogether 5.7 million persons are covered by this scheme, a large proportion of them presumably the same people as are covered by the former scheme.

2.4. *The educational system and its achievements*

Apart from material production, the plans also formulate objectives for education (see Table 2.23. and Fig. 2.5.). At the end of the fifth plan, i.e. after 25 years of planning and 31 years of independence, all children shall have at least five years of primary schooling, 76 per cent are to complete 6 to 8, 41 per cent 9 to 11 years of schooling, while 7 per cent of the relevant age group – 5.2 million young people – are to attend universities. Expenditure on education is to grow in the decade up to 1978/79 by 165 per cent to 22,500 million Rs, which will be 4.5 per cent of the national product.

Even if the targets of the plan are achieved, it will have taken 30 years to enrol all children of school age in primary schools with five forms, a demand formulated by the constitution of 1949. The gradual approach is valid for the educational sector, too, though in this field hardly any foreign currency expenditure is involved and no foreign aid is necessary or feasible. It will, then, take even more time to wipe out illiteracy.

On the other hand, the quantitative results are impressive. The number of boys enrolled in the primary schools (first to fifth form) increased from 13.8 to 34.0 million, of girls from 5.4 to 19.9 million over 18 years. Here, again, expansion is hard put to it to outpace the rapid growth of the population. While the actual numbers rose for boys by 146 per cent, for girls by 269 per cent, yet only half the girls of school age were actually able to go to school. For a number of reasons, partly religious and socio-cultural, partly due to sheer poverty, girls are severely disadvantaged. It is also doubtful, whether the targets of 1978/79 can be reached, which would call for a much greater effort and more rapid progress in the enrolment of girls during the last few years. The disparity between the sexes is even more acute at the higher levels of education.

Table 2.23.: Development and plan targets in education

Class	Age	1950/51	1960/61	1968/69	1973/74 Estimate	1978/79 Target
I-V	*6-11*					
Boys	mln.	13.8	23.6	34.0	41.3	45.5
	% [1])	60.8	82.6	92.7	99.6	109.2 [2])
Girls	mln.	5.4	11.4	19.9	27.3	42.5
	%	24.9	41.4	56.6	70.1	109.2
Total	mln.	19.2	35.0	53.9	68.6	88.0
	%	43.1	62.4	75.1	85.3	109.2
VI-VIII	*11-14*					
Boys	mln.	2.6	5.1	8.7	12.2	18.2
	%	20.8	32.2	45.6	54.3	75.8
Girls	mln.	0.5	1.6	3.4	5.9	17.0
	%	4.3	11.3	18.3	27.7	76.2
Total	mln.	3.1	6.7	12.1	18.1	35.1
	%	12.8	22.5	32.1	41.3	76.0
IX-XI	*14-17*					
Boys	mln.	1.1	2.5	4.9	7.1	9.1
	%	9.3	17.5	28.3	36.6	41.1
Girls	mln.	0.2	0.5	1.6	2.6	4.6
	%	1.5	4.3	9.5	14.1	22.0
Total	mln.	1.3	3.0	6.5	9.7	13.7
	%	5.5	11.1	19.1	25.6	31.9
University	*17-23*					
	mln.	0.1	0.6	1.8	3.2	5.2
	%	0.4	1.2	3.0	4.5	7.0
Total expenditure mln.Rs.		1,144	3,444	8,500	12,500	22,500
% of national income [3])		1.2	2.4	2.8	3.3	4.5

[1]) Percentages refer to the total number of the respective group
[2]) 109.2 p.c. means probably, that part of the children shall be recruited into pre-school institutions
[3]) At current prices

Source: Eastern economist (1974)

The whole educational system is well organised and offers a wide variety of courses and options. Standards of teaching are reasonable in the lower forms and good in the higher ones. This is a creditable performance, achieved against heavy odds (variety of languages, poverty and physical condition of pupils and teachers, overcrowding of classes etc.). Compared with the achievements of 250 years of British colonial rule,

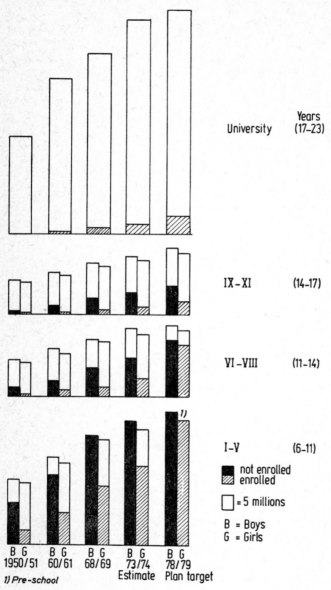

University   Years (17–23)

IX – XI   (14–17)

VI – VIII   (11–14)

I – V   (6–11)

■ not enrolled
▨ enrolled

☐ = 5 millions

B = Boys
G = Girls

B G   B G   B G   B G   B G
1950/51   60/61   68/69   73/74   78/79
                         Estimate   Plan target

1) Pre-school

Fig. 2.5. India: Development and targets in education 1950/51-1979

performance and pace are enormous and impressive, but in terms of the development expectations of the people, one generation is felt to be a long time.

Education moreover seems to be a key sector for cultural and social uplift and mobilisation, which to a certain extent could influence work performance in industry, innovations and production growth in farming, family planning etc. Slow progress in education thus affects and retards general progress.

Some drawbacks can be recognised in education. There is a bias against technical and natural sciences and a certain over-emphasis on philosophy, Hindu culture and similar curricula. In spite of special protective measures for the scheduled castes, the upper castes are heavily privileged and strongly over-represented at the higher levels of education. Thus, one basic target of expanded education, that is, mobilisation of the mental potential and greater equality of opportunity, is not achieved. The caste bias of society is reflected in education and in academic careers, and social inequality is aggravated.

2.5. *Development problems and strategy*

2.5.1. *Reasons for the development lag*
The student of Indian affairs knows the country's famous history, its cultural achievements and the prolonged development efforts. The question, then, is inevitable: what are the factors making for a long period of stagnation, and paralysing the ability to cope with the urgent quantitative and qualitative demands of society? Different explanations are offered.

a. Climate and nature – so it is argued – are the reasons for the living conditions. Easy growth of vegetation and energy-draining heat call for a minimised input of human effort, induce low effort, even laziness. – Nature, of course, is the basis of all human life and activities, and the different climates are the prerequisites influencing human labour and its approach to the actual problems. Yet, nature is largely neutral, i.e. it poses difficulties everywhere on earth, though different ones in different regions. Man faces nature and tries to shape and subordinate it to his needs in culture and agriculture by his genius and resourcefulness. Southern Japan, Southern China, the Southern parts of the USA, Israel have climatic conditions similar to those of India, but their living standards are different.

b. Character and mentality of the individual and the nation are then said to be wholly different from "normal" standards in highly developed countries. The people are not able to think rationally, to grasp the discoveries of natural science, to adapt themselves to the use of techno-logical innovations. – This looks more like a veiled expression of obsolete white self-conceit than a serious scientifically based argument.[31] There are no known genetic factors particular to any nation, which bar the development and utilisation of science and technology. Statements about the national character of 600 million human beings are non-scientific generalisations.

c. Non-adaptation and inadaptability of an old culture and social system seem in reality to be the main reason for near-stagnation and a growing development lag. But internal and external factors can be discerned here.

2.5.1.1. The Asian mode of production

The peculiar features of Indian and Asian society and economy aroused early on the interest of Karl Marx, who analysed the material available in England. Marx recognised both the modernising effects of British rule and its exploitative and oppressive character. In his sociological analysis he tried to understand the special combination of utter mass poverty and social stability of the system, which again is linked to social immobility. He saw the main and specific causes of those conditions in the age-old village organisation, the decisive role of irrigation, the division of labour in a largely non-monetary system, the combination of agricultural production and village crafts or, in his words, "the domestic union of agricultural and manufacturing pursuits".

Marx describes the internal village structure and its effect on Indian society:

"However changing the political aspect of India's past must appear, its social condition has remained unaltered since its remotest antiquity, until the first decennium of the nineteenth century. The hand-loom and the spinning wheel, producing their regular myriads of spinners and weavers were the pivots of the structure of that society... [The] Hindu, on the one hand, leaving, like all Oriental peoples, to the central government the care of the great public works, the prime condition of his agriculture and commerce, dispersed, on the other hand, over the surface of the country, and agglomerated in small centres by the domestic union of agricultural and manufacturing pursuits – these two circumstances had brought about, since the remotest times, a social system of particular features – the so-called *village system*, which gave to each of these small units their independent organisation and distinct life." (Karl Marx, 'British Rule in India', *Selected Works*, Moscow-London 1942, vol. 2, pp. 653f.)

But it is the sombre constraints of village life to which Marx attributes the immobility of society:

"[We] must not forget that these idyllic village communities, inoffensive though they may appear, had always been the solid foundation of Oriental despotism, that they restrained the human mind within the smallest possible compass, making it the unresisting tool of superstition, enslaving it beneath traditional rules, depriving it of all grandeur and historical energies.

We must not forget that these little communities were contaminated by distinctions of caste and by slavery, that they subjugated man to external circumstances, instead of elevating man the sovereign of circumstances, that they transformed a self-developing social state into never changing natural destiny..." (*Ib.*, pp. 655f.)

An important feature of the Asian mode of production is the combination of manufacture and agriculture in the small community, which thus can cater for its own needs, and within which all the requirements for production and the creation of surpluses are present. This unity of village crafts and farming cultivation provides an assured basis of economic independence for each village and gives to the Asian mode of production a singular capacity to resist social change. Of all primary forms, the Asian one "of necessity survives for the longest period and is particularly hardy."

Later, in *Capital*, Marx explained the stagnation of Asian societies as a consequence of the stubborn survival of the village and its internal organisation, while at the same time profound political changes occurred on the Asian political scene:

"The simplicity of the organisation for production in these self-sufficing communities that constantly reproduce themselves in the same form, and when accidentally destroyed, spring up again on the spot and with the same name – this simplicity supplies the key to the secret of the unchangeableness of Asiatic societies, an unchangeableness in such striking contrast with the constant dissolution and refounding of Asiatic States, and the never-ceasing changes of dynasty. The structure of the economical elements of society remains untouched by the storm-clouds of the political sky."

(*Capital*, vol. I, translated by Samuel Moore and Edward Aveling, London 1909, p. 352).

The special societal formation, which combined some forms of communal land-ownership, and communal work organisation with a despotic central administration, did not fit into any one of the three main modes of production categorised by Marx: the archaic, the feudal and the capitalist.[32] These modes of production can be understood as phases of economic development over a period of time. The different phases still exist side by side in various societies today. In view of its specific traits, Marx defined the Asian mode of production as a separate category, characterised by an original, genuine and ancient network of socio-economic conditions and relations, exposed to little or no change – up to a certain point.

British rule initiated the destruction of the old social balance. New paths were cautiously opened to prepare for the urgently needed social change. But that, in the main, was left for the time after independence, and it will come in the course of hard social struggles between the small privileged minority and the vast exploited majority.

2.5.1.2. Caste, class and society

The caste system largely determines everybody's life and status. Profession, social environment and social life, participation in family festivities, community and religious life, choice of marriage partner are predetermined by birth, i.e. inherited. Marriage partners are selected by the parents within their caste and sub-caste, though only in specified villages some distance away, so as to avoid inbreeding. Members of a caste know this geographical delimitation. It was not necessary, it was even unthinkable, to choose an occupation, since that was inherited. Mental capacity or interests of a child could have no influence on its future occupation. Vocational training was not called for, because the son learned the working methods from his father and took over his tools. That again militates against the introduction and adoption of innovations. Thinking and working, land-ownership and cultivation are clearly separate functions of distinct castes. A landowner does not cultivate his land. This behaviour is maintained and is not changed even after division and fragmentation of the hereditament, leading to the growing pauperisation of the landowners.

A man is known by his caste: this is true in a double sense.

a. Everybody can recognise the caste of a person from the last part of his or her name, the caste-name. Brahmins are the highest caste, originally in charge of religious services and teaching. Patels are landowners. The lowest caste are the harijans, the untouchables; in reality they do not belong to the caste society. They used to be called pariahs. Mahatma Gandhi changed their name and wanted to integrate them into Hindu society.

b. The members of a caste or sub-caste know all those who are part of their caste or sub-caste. They are approached by the people of the same caste in matters of employment, assistance or support.

Caste gave its members a measure of social security within a limited group and thus promoted nepotism and office patronage in public services and in the private economy.

Orthodox Hindus of the upper castes would look upon physical or manual work as a diminution of their social status. Substantial privileges in education, employment and living standards are attached to caste and status. These privileges are strongly defended by the high castes.

British colonial domination was based on indirect rule by a relatively small group of officers and civil servants, who favoured, strengthened and consolidated the caste system by a number of measures.[33] Nehru, India's first Prime Minister after independence, claimed that the nation would have rid itself of the caste system, had it been independent and not a colony. While such an historical hypothesis can never be tested and verified, it seems in this case to be quite reasonable. On the other hand, the continuity and strength of the system almost 30 years after independence proves the strength of the internal social forces acting to enforce and maintain it.

Some members of low castes have tried to escape from the oppressive system by conversion to Christianity, particularly in Kerala and Orissa. In Kerala, for instance, the statistical percentage of the population belonging to scheduled castes and tribes[34] is very low (9.6 per cent against the national average of 21.5 per cent). The Christian churches became institutions for the most oppressed social strata and were viewed as such, too, by the upper castes in these states.

The caste system implies a high degree of social immobility, which puts heavy barriers in the way of social change and progress. It assigns to each individual his place and position in society, not to be questioned under any circumstances, thus creating a very stable framework, able to neutralise a large amount of social tension and unrest. To destroy or even to question this framework, then, is a sin to be punished in later lives, after reincarnation. Fatalistic acceptance of the system and of one's own low position in it, on the other hand, will be rewarded in subsequent lives by promotion to a higher caste. This basic belief, which is still widely accepted even by the low castes, contributes substantially to the perpetuation of the system. Low educational standards as well as socio-religious beliefs which came to be internalised as an innate inferiority feeling, inhibit the harijans from raising from their own ranks a leadership able and willing to challenge and topple the old social order.

The Constitution and laws have formally dissolved the caste system. Protective measures in several fields (education, employment in public services, representation in parliament, welfare, housing) were legislated. The plan was to abolish these protective regulations at an early stage after full equality and integration had been achieved. The protective measures, however, have established a new group of vested interests determined to defend their minor privileges and to fight against abolition.

The villages appear outwardly as socially well-organised and balanced systems, with clearly defined social roles assigned to each citizen and accepted by him. Under the surface, however, strong social tensions are at work. Frequently they lead to heavy riots, fighting, strikes, unrest and murder, regularly and frankly reported in the press.

Apart from its hold on the countryside, the caste system is still very effective in small and large towns, where people live separated by caste in their housing blocks. The old social order, the most solidified class society of our time, is closely knit. In ancient times, perhaps, it had its functions and achieved a high cultural level, naturally for a small minority. But, its solidity and durability only reflect the inability to adapt to new societal needs.

The social functions in the old society were performed in return for payment in kind or services – the typical phenomenon of a non-monetary economy. But, Indian society has changed enormously in numbers, and at the same time it modified and expanded its public and social services. While thus the functions of the castes were eroded, the corresponding privileges tend to be maintained and defended.

Hindu religion and caste are religious and social expressions of the same phenomenon and are inseparably interlinked. Caste society is distinguished from "normal" stratification in other class societies by three features. (1) In its archetypal form it is 100 per cent immobile, with no physical or cultural communication between the strata (= castes). (2) Behaviour and attitudes are so deeply rooted, so well internalised and transferred by tradition and social control, that even pauperisation and social degradation cannot influence the actual habits and customs. (3) Social inequality and rigid stratification are sublimated by religion and accepted by the oppressed, while in a modern class society the defence of social group interests is seen and accepted as a normal expression of social development and social change.

The sacredness of the cow is closely connected with the Hindu belief in reincarnation and with the caste system. Because a human soul might live in a cow, cows may not be slaughtered and their meat is forbidden. Zebu-cows and bullocks may be used as draught animals for ploughing and other field operations and for milk production. This taboo implies, that no active breeding, i.e. eradication of genetically undesirable animals, is possible. The taboo is valid only for zebu-cattle, not for water-buffaloes. It concerns Hindus alone, and is of no relevance to Muslims and followers of other religions. The taboo is strictly observed in the northern, western and central regions, much less in the south and east. It is only logical, that the Hindu priests (saddhus) and the two Right-wing parties (Swatantra[35] and Jana Sangh Hindu Mahasabha) should be campaigning for the total prohibition of cattle slaughter.

2.5.1.3. Colonial domination and economic exploitation
Foreign rule, as stated above, has systematically consolidated an anachronistic social structure, which otherwise might have been adapted or removed. – Economically, India was taken as complementary to the metropolis: industrial development, a harmonious development of the economic and cultural infrastructure, was barred. Enormous funds were diverted to Great Britain for
a. monopoly profits of commerce, banking and other activities;
b. British wars at India's frontiers;
c. high salaries and pensions of British officials and soldiers.[36]
On the other hand, the strength of internal factors is demonstrated by the fact, that almost 30 years after political independence the development process is still very slow.

2.5.1.4. Cumulative factors of depression
The different factors are not isolated, but rather interact and compound the difficulties. Considered on its own, no single factor is decisive or beyond control. A few examples will explain this statement.
a. Low yields per hectare, combined with population growth and the lack of industrial inputs to raise production lead to hunger, diminish labour productivity and efficiency and militate against the efforts to bring about change.
b. The immobility of the social strata (caste system) causes the segregation of science, the separation of theory and practice. Because scientists and researchers are distant from practical execution and experience, they are scarcely in a position to reflect on the removal of old social deficiencies and on new proposals.
c. Generally, cooperative societies are intended to assist the poor cultivators. But owing to the backwardness and feelings of inferiority of the poor, it often is landlords, moneylenders or middlemen who are elected chairmen of cooperatives, and then the loans will go mainly to the affluent groups in the villages.

The self-image of the system is reflected in the Hindu vision of the world, in the submission to destiny, predetermined by the deities and by a man's earlier lives. Good deeds and the toleration of evil in this life will then be rewarded in later lives.
Khusro (1968) and Thorner (1962) speak about the system's built-in

factors of depression. Rothermund (1967) about "negative dynamics",
Bobek (1961) about economy of minimum input:

> "Wisdom commands each participant to limit his input to the
> minimum he can tolerate".

Myrdal (1957) analyses the "mechanism of circular causation of cumulative processes". Boserup (1964) sees the socio-psychological blockage of development:

> "Even if the view were correct, that there exists a surplus of manpower, the widespread belief in it is in itself a force, that contributes to bar a rationalisation of agrarian structure. Such considerations did not exist in Europe. But in South Asia today (and in developing countries generally) the fear of a worsening employment situation blocks the formulation and implementation of clear-cut targets for structural reform and technical change of its agriculture."

Mandal (1961) shows the effect of dwarf-holdings and of subsistence producers: these two elements bar an increase in production. K. N. Raj (1966) hints at the counter-productive effects of some forms of development aid, the advice tied to it and the interests of importers. Thus, we find a whole series of socio-economic factors, which between them slow down or impede the development process.

2.5.2. *Macro-economic results of development*

To an observer looking back and comparing the present position with that of 1947, the results are impressive. The net national product has risen gradually (see Table 2.24), though with setbacks and varying

Table 2.24.: Development trend of net national product

| Year | At current prices | | | | At 1960/61 prices | | | |
| | Rs. 1,000 mln. | Rs. per capita | 1960-61 = 100 | | Rs. 1,000 mln. | Rs. per capita | 1960-61 = 100 | |
			NNP	NNP per capita			NNP	NNP per capita
1950/51	87.0	232	66	76	90.8	253	68	83
1955/56	91.2	242	69	79	108.6	276	82	90
1960/61	132.7	306	100	100	132.7	306	100	100
1965/66	206.4	426	156	139	150.8	311	114	102
1970/71 [1])	346.3	640	261	209	190.4	352	143	115
1972/73 [1])	395.9	698	298	228	191.3	337	144	110
1973/74 [2])	492.9	850	372	278	197.2	340	149	111

[1]) Provisional
[2]) Quick estimates

Sources: Economic survey (1975); Choudhury and Narain (1975)

Table 2.25.: Net national product by industry of origin – percentage distribution (at 1960-61 prices)

	1960-61	1965-66	1970-71 [1])	1973-74 [2])
1. Agriculture, forestry, fishing, mining, quarrying	52.5	44.2	46.2	43.2
2. Manufacturing, construction, electricity, gas and water supply	19.2	23.6	22.3	22.6
3. Transport, communication, trade	14.1	16.4	15.8	16.3
4. Banking and insurance, real estate, ownership of residential housing, business services	4.2	4.4	4.0	4.3
5. Public administration, defence, other services	10.5	12.4	12.6	14.5
6. Net domestic product at factor cost	100.5	101.0	100.9	100.9
7. Net factor income from abroad	—0.5	—1.0	—0.9	—0.9
8. Net national product at factor cost	100.0	100.0	100.0	100.0

[1]) Provisional
[2]) Quick estimates

Source: Economic survey (1975)

growth rates. The objectives envisaged for the fifth five-year plan demand an average annual growth rate of 5.5 per cent, which is a high target under the given conditions, and it remains doubtful, whether it can be attained. The net national product rose nominally by 271.5 per cent during the 13 years 1960/61 to 1973/74, but by much less in real terms. Per-capita income increased much more slowly owing to rapid population growth, about 12-13 per cent in each decade. Up to 1978, per-capita income is due to grow by 3 per cent annually. These global figures provide no information about the distribution of total macro-economic growth, another very important indicator of socio-economic progress.

A comparison of the figures relating respectively to current and to constant prices reveals the gathering speed of inflation in the sixties and seventies. In the sixties, the net national product increased by 135 per cent nominally, but only by 35 per cent in real terms. The table also illustrates the negative effects of population growth under the given conditions. If the NNP is computed per capita, the growth dwindles to 11 per cent for the last 13 years. The sectoral composition of the net national product (Table 2.25.) shows that in 1973/74 the agrarian sector still contributed 43 per cent, or in other words that agriculture has retained its key position. Its share declines very slowly. The share of industrial production rose very moderately, while the contribution

Table 2.26.: External trade (mn. US $)

	1965	1968	1970	1972	1973
Export					
Total	1,821.6	1,753.7	1,957.7	2,335.3	2,935.0
Farm commodities	696.2	659.2	700.9	787.0	1,013.4
Farm commodities in %	38.2	37.6	35.8	33.7	34.5
Imports					
Total	2.990.1	2,487.5	2,170.3	2,225.8	3,176.8
Farm commodities	903.9	788.6	603.2	456.5	919.0
Farm commodities in %	30.2	31.7	27.8	20.5	28.9
Agricultural production inputs	114.7	262.9	110.0	150.0	247.6
Negative trade balance	1,168.5	733.8	212.6	— 109.5	241.8

Source: FAO trade yearbook

of the tertiary sector, i.e. services, grew substantially from 28.8 to 35.1 per cent. In this sector, defence probably shows the highest growth rate. Since this sector is unproductive in part, the hypertrophy of services may in itself become an obstacle to the effective growth of production and the satisfaction of basic needs.

The balance of foreign trade seems more favourable (see Table 2.26.). Total exports rose from $1,800 million to $2,900 million. The gap in the balance of commercial goods was gradually narrowed and by 1970 almost eliminated. The share of agricultural produce in total exports

Table 2.27.: Inflow of external assistance (1,000 mln. Rs)

Item	1967/68	1969/70	1970/71	1973/74	1974/75 [1]
1. Gross disbursements	11.96	8.56	8.34	8.49	10.81
a. food aid	3.30	1.47	1.53	0.82	0.20
b. other aid	8.66	7.09	6.81	7.67	10.61
2. Total debt service	3.33	4.12	4.79	5.95	6.01
a. amortisation	2.11	2.68	2.99	3.99	4.01
b. interest	1.22	1.44	1.80	1.96	2.00
3. Net inflow of aid	8.63	4.44	3.55	2.54	4.80
4. Net inflow without food aid	5.33	2.97	3.02	1.72	5.81
5. Total debt service in % of gross disbursements	27.8	48.1	57.3	70.1	55.6

[1] Estimates

Source: Economic survey (1975)

decreased from 38 to 34 per cent. Even so, the agrarian sector remains an important earner of foreign currency, although the varying imports of agricultural produce, mainly wheat and oil – still more than one quarter of all imports – have to be taken into account.

Foreign aid decreased rapidly in recent years from about 12,000 million Rs in 1967/68 to 7,000 millions in 1973/74. During the same period the Rupee was substantially devalued (see Table 2.27.). On the other hand, total debt payments rose by 53 per cent. In 1971/72 these repayments absorbed more than half (54.3 per cent), in 1972/73 more than two thirds of all foreign aid. Net aid declined nominally by 76 per cent, in real terms even more. If foreign aid is compared with Government investment for development (Table 2.19.), the relations between internal effort and development aid become clearer still. The major part of the effort comes – and must come – from India herself. Foreign aid, even if given generously, can be no more than a small additional impulse to an already moving engine.

3. SOVIET UNION – MODEL OF A SETTLED REVOLUTION

3.1. *The prerequisites*

3.1.1. *Historical-political factors*

1904-05   Russo-Japanese war – Russia is defeated by Japan. Geographically and militarily a big imperialist power, she is socially backward and economically dependent on Western Europe's industrial nations.

1905   First attempt at a bourgeois revolution is crushed.

1906   Second agrarian reform by Stolypin, dissolution of the rural communes (*Mir*).

1914   Russia enters the first world war on the side of the Western allies, but suffers heavy military defeats.

1917   February/March: The Tsar is overthrown, democratic revolution.

1917   October: Second phase of the revolution, victory of Social-Democratic Workers' Party (Bolshevik). Decree introduces land nationalisation, abolition of peasants' payments to the landlords; peasants seize and distribute the land.

1917-21   Civil war, massive military intervention of several foreign powers. Under the leadership of Leo Trotsky, the Red Army is formed and wins the civil war.

1921   End of war communism, New Economic Policy (NEP): private initiative is permitted and promoted, foreign capitalists are invited to invest.

1924   After Lenin's death, J. V. Stalin seizes the leading positions in the Communist Party and in Government.

1929   First five-year plan for accelerated industrialisation.

1929-33   Collectivisation of agriculture throughout the country.

1933   Hitler is allowed to take power in Germany.

1936-38   Civil war in Spain ends with the victory of Franco, who was openly and decisively supported by the military intervention of Hitler's Germany and Mussolini's Italy. Hard factional struggles in the CPSU develop into a large-scale purge, the physical liquidation of the old guard of leading communists, who were critical of Stalin's methods in all fields of social, economic and political activities.

1939 August: Stalin-Hitler pact.

1939 September to 1945, May: Second world war.

1941-1945 War between Germany and Soviet Union ends with Soviet victory. The Red Army marches into Bulgaria, Rumania, Hungary, Czechoslovakia, Poland, East Germany. The gradual transformation of the social systems of these countries begins.

1944 The Yugoslav communists win the guerrilla war and form a communist government.

1948 Conflict between Yugoslavia and the Soviet Union and its allies – first open split in the communist system of states. Yugoslavia is excommunicated from the community of socialist states and from the Cominform.

1949 The Chinese communists finally win power after 20 years of changing fortunes in the civil war.

1949 Comecon – Council for Mutual Economic Assistance – is formed by the European socialist countries.

1953 February: Stalin dies and G. Malenkov succeeds in the leading position.

1953 June: Workers' rising in the German Democratic Republic.

1954 N. S. Khrushchev takes over the most important political functions.

1954-58 Virgin lands campaign in Kazakhstan.

1955 Warsaw Treaty: military coordination of the communist states in Europe.

1956 20th CPSU Congress – official de-Stalinisation begins.

1956 Risings in Hungary and Poland.

1958 Dissolution of the machine-and-tractor stations.

1959 Victory of the Cuban revolution.

1960 First signs of tension between China and the Soviet Union.

1961 Albania withdraws from Warsaw Treaty and Comecon.

1964 Khrushchev is removed; L. Brezhnev and A. Kossygin take over the leading political positions.

1965 Break between China and USSR.

1968 August: The armies of Soviet Union and four of its allies occupy Czechoslovakia and stop the Prague Spring. – Rumania dissociates herself from Soviet foreign policies.

1969 November: Third Congress of kolkhoz-peasants.

| 1970 | Soviet-Chinese tension rises, armed fighting at the border river Ussuri. Efforts begin for detente with Western capitalist nations after failure of the attempts at reconciliation with China. |
| 1973 | Brezhnev visits the USA after Nixon's visit to Moscow in 1972. |

3.1.2.   *Geographical and natural factors*

The country, geographically by far the largest on earth, covering an area of 22 million sq. km., contains contrasting climatic and agricultural zones, which, however, are averaged out in all-Russian global statistics. A regional subdivision reveals wide differences in density and structure of settlement, size of farm holdings, farming intensity, cropping patterns, animal production, size of household plots, degree of development and industrialisation, incomes (see Table 3.1. and Fig. 3.1.). Thus the description is of necessity very summary. The Soviet Union stretches west to east from 21° eastern to 170° eastern longitude and from 82 to 35° northern latitude. From north to south seven natural geographical zones can be distinguished: tundra, taiga (boreal coniferous forests), mixed forests in European Russia, forest steppe, steppe, semi-desert, desert. Mainly in Transcaucasia and to a minor extent on the southern slopes of the Crimean coast there are small regions of subtropical climate. The main mountain ranges are the Urals, Greater and Lesser Caucasus, mountains at the edge of Central Asia and in Southern and Eastern Siberia. The Soviet Far East is predominantly covered with mixed forests.

The tundra does not lend itself to agricultural utilisation, except for nomadic reindeer husbandry. In the taiga belt, the only substantial productive areas are in the western part of the region's southern fringe, and beyond the Yenisey only in river basins, owing to the severity of the continental climate, which becomes progressively more extreme from west to east. In the north the boundary of the land suitable for cultivation is pushed southwards by the low prevailing temperatures and the shortness of the growing season. Proceeding from north to south, the next three zones – mixed forest, forest steppe and steppe – make up the big agriculturally important regions; they constitute the so-called agrarian triangle. This is bordered in the south by a broad fringe (Volgograd, Uralsk, Tselinograd, Semipalatinsk), which marks the transition to the arid and desert regions. Other agriculturally important areas are the Caucasus region, the oases in Central Asia, and the zone of mixed forests found in the foothills and highland basins, along the desert rivers and in the Far East. The mixed forests of the Far East are affected by monsoons. The winter in that zone is similar to that in Central Siberia, with tem-

Table 3.1.: Geographical, agricultural, economic data for Soviet republics

Republic	Area ('000 sq.km)	Population ('000) 1975	Inhabitants per sq.km 1975	No. kolkhozes 1940	No. kolkhozes 1974	Household plots 1940	Household plots 1974	Sown area [3] per kolkhoz 1940 ha	Sown area [3] per kolkhoz 1974 '000 ha	Cattle [4] 1940	Cattle [4] 1974
RSFSR	17,075.4	133,741	8	167,291	13,058	66	377	474	4.5	72	1,669
Armenia	29.8	2,785	93	1,030	374	169	232	398	0.5	280	553
Azerbaijan	86.6	5,607	65	3,416	911	105	287	311	0.9	173	551
Belorussia	207.6	9,331	45	10,237	2,099	75	385	283	1.7	75	1,532
Estonia [1]	45.1	1,429	32	2,213	209	55	306	263	2.1	100	1,507
Georgia	69.7	4,923	71	4,256	1,020	112	356	184	0.4	134	415
Kazakhstan	2,717.3	14,168	5	6,639 [2]	428	87	497	724	10.8	257	2,168
Kirghizia	198.5	3,298	17	1,732	222	106	768	534	3.2	106	1,847
Latvia [1]	63.7	2,478	39	1,776	462	128	293	644	1.9	231	1,262
Lithuania [1]	65.2	3,290	50	4,500	1,157	73	217	330	1.3	34	799
Moldavia [1]	33.7	3,812	113	1,636	472	284	992	899	2.6	140	1,386
Tajikistan	143.1	3,387	24	3,093	245	64	876	248	1.8	37	1,343
Turkmenistan	488.1	2,506	5	1,540	334	83	519	245	2.1	44	680
Ukraine	603.7	48,817	81	28,374	8,069	141	614	784	3.0	122	1,854
Uzbekistan	447.4	13,689	31	7,499	966	106	838	365	1.8	66	875
USSR	22,402.2	253,261	11	236,900	30,026	79	463	492	3.3	85	1,543

1) 1950 instead of 1940 throughout
2) 1945 instead of 1940
3) Without collective farmers' household plots
4) Kolkhoz-owned, at year end

Table 3.1.: (*continued*): Geographical, agricultural, economic data for Soviet republics

Republic	Population 1975	Sown area 1974 (as percent of total for USSR)	Urban population 1975	Wage and salary earners (percentage of population) 1972	Gross product per inhabitant				Per capita national income (RSFSR=100)
					Industry Roubles	1968 Index	Agriculture Roubles	1965 Index	
RSFSR	52.8	59.0	67	38.4	1,430	100	218	100	100
Armenia	1.1	0.2	63	29.8	1,047	73	146	67	75
Azerbeizjan	2.2	0.6	51	22.8	633	44	122	56	68
Belorussia	3.7	2.9	51	29.3	990	69	346	158	72
Estonia	0.6	0.4	68	44.5	1,839	128	381	179	112
Georgia	1.9	0.4	50	27.2	852	59	180	82	68
Kazakhstan	5.6	14.5	53	33.8	721	50	228	104	72
Kirghizia	1.3	0.6	38	23.5	731	51	227	104	60
Latvia	1.0	0.8	65	41.2	1,877	131	353	161	123
Lithuania	1.3	1.1	56	32.7	1,235	86	387	177	89
Moldavia	1.5	0.9	52	21.0	843	58	387	177	69
Tajikistan	1.3	0.3	38	17.8	527	36	206	94	51
Turkmenistan	1.0	0.4	49	20.7	473	33	208	95	62
Ukraine	19.3	16.2	59	30.4	1,405	98	300	137	87
Uzbekistan	5.4	1.7	38	20.5	524	36	205	94	58
USSR	100.0	100.0	60						
USSR less RSFSR					1,073	75	269	123	78
USSR less RSFSR and Ukraina					822	57	245	112	71

Source: Narodnoe Khozyaystvo

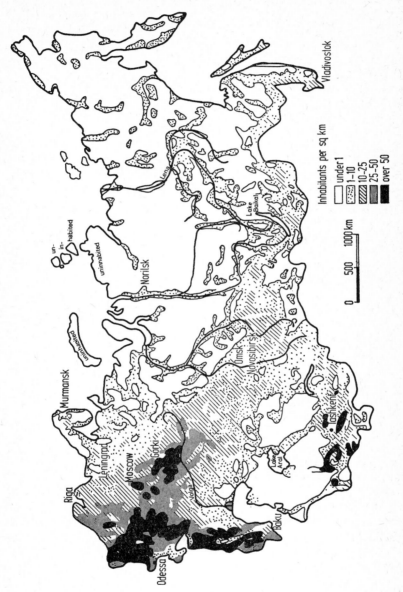

Fig. 3.1. Population density in the Soviet regions. 1965 (Source: Mellor)

peratures unusually low for those latitudes (January mean –15 to –20°C). The summer is humid and warm, moderated by the influx of Pacific sea air (July mean 20°C). In Trans-Caucasia climatic conditions are completely different from those in the rest of the country. On low ground, the climate is warm and humid, with torrential rainfalls (upwards of 600 mm per annum).

Natural conditions influence the regional cropping patterns. Optimum regional specialisation, however, is unattainable, because the territories within which natural conditions favour uniform production schedules are enormous self-contained zones, ranged consecutively from north to south. It follows that goods not produced in a particular specialised region would have to be brought in over very long distances, involving high costs and long haulage times, an arrangement which moreover might overtax the capacity of the transport system. Thus, transport problems are among the main reasons for the diversified cropping patterns to be noted in nearly every region.

The basic ecological data have influenced industrial development as well. Even the prospecting of mineral deposits is hampered by the climate and by the vast distances, and new methods have to be found from the beginning. Extraction and processing, then, demand new settlements, infrastructure (railways, energy, water, roads), secondary installations and supply enterprises of all types. New industrial centres had to be established, partly in very inhospitable regions, which necessitated high initial investments in infrastructure. Until 1920, industries were located mainly in the settlement centres of European Russia. After that, the utilisation of domestic raw materials, colonisation and opening up of the interior, as well as decentralisation for strategic reasons called for an eastward migration of industries.

3.1.3. *Development and structure of population*

The population has grown substantially – from 159.2 million in 1913 to 253 million in 1975, i.e. by 59 per cent (see Table 3.2.). The growth rate has decreased slowly in recent years. The heavy losses during the wars have been made good. Population density varies widely as between the republics.[37] The population is concentrated in the western and north-western parts of the country. Generally, population density still follows closely the intensity zones of farming.[38] Attempts have been made to promote eastward migration and to settle the distant eastern regions. They call for heavy investment, and the success so far has been moderate.

The new agrarian structure together with rapid industrialisation have changed the population structure in a relatively short span of time. The proportion of the agricultural population declined from 75 per cent in

74

Table 3.2.: Population growth and changes – urbanization

Year	Population (millions)	Agricultural population (as percentage of total)	Village population
1897	124.6	.	85
1913	159.2	75	82
1939	170.6	62	68
1940	194.1	54	67
1956	200.2	43	55
1961	216.1	35	50
1966	231.9	28	46
1969	238.9	25	44
1970	241.7	25	43
1971	243.9	.	43
1973	248.6	.	41
1975	253.3	24 [1])	40

[1]) 1974

Sources: Informationen zur politischen Bildung; Narodnoe khozyaystvo

1913 to 25 per cent in 1969. The proportion of the rural population declined simultaneously, though less radically.[39] Rapid urbanisation has caused a troublesome urban housing shortage, since the allocations for housing construction were very small.

The proportion of workers and employees in factories and offices, including State farms, grew from 17 per cent before 1913 to 83 per cent in 1975. The collective farmers account for 17.1 per cent of all economically active persons. Their share was highest in 1939 and has steadily decreased since then (see Table 3.3. and Fig. 3.2.). – Unfortunately, the figures of Table 3.3. give no clue to social stratification and income differentiation in the two main social groups or non-antagonistic classes.

Table 3.3.: Social change: the social strata in percent of economically active population

Class	1913	1928	1939	1959	1970	1975
Factory and office staff	2.4	5.2	16.7	18.8	22.7	22.0
Factory and office workers	14.6	12.4	33.5	49.5	56.8	60.9
Co-operative peasants and artisans	–	2.9	47.2	31.4	20.5	17.1
Independent peasants and artisans	66.7	74.9	2.6	0.3	–	–
Bourgeoisie, landowners, merchants	16.3	4.6	–	–	–	–
	100	100	100	100	100	100

Source: Narodnoe khozyaystvo (1975)

75

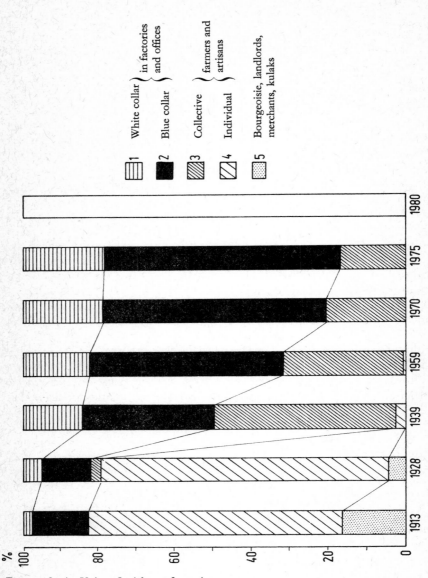

Fig. 3.2. Soviet Union: Social transformation

This seems to be a significant gap in the otherwise consistent and reliable statistics of the Soviet Union.

Four closely interlinked demographic processes were thus taking place simultaneously:

a. Population growth;
b. decline in the rural and agrarian population;
c. social changes from independent to collective farmer, liquidation of the capitalist class and of the "independent" middle class, increase in the number of salary earners;
d. urbanisation and emergence of a large industrial working class.

The country includes a number of different nationalities; in 1962, 54.5 per cent of the total population were Russians. Further important national groups are: Ukrainians – 17.7 per cent; Belorussians – 3.7 per cent; Uzbeks – 3.0 per cent. The nationalities differ in language and culture, as well as in the level of economic development.

Government policies towards the national groups have passed through different phases: (1) Russification till 1917; (2) Lenin's rejection of Greater Russian chauvinism; self-determination, including the right to secession from the Union; (3) Stalin's line of cultural autonomy, combined with centralisation and subordination in politics and in economic planning, and accompanied by a policy of assimilation and the settlement of Russians in regions of different ethnic character; (4) preventive oppression and resettlement of national minorities in strategically exposed regions; (5) limited liberalisation and rectifications in the post-Stalin era.

3.1.4. *Administration and political set-up*

By its constitution, the Union of Socialist Soviet Republics is a federal State. The municipalities (communes) elect village or town soviets to guide, and check on, the administration. For the *rayons* and *oblasts*, the next level of administration, soviets are similarly elected. The 15 Soviet Republics composing the USSR are free to form autonomous republics, regions or national districts for special regions and smaller ethnic groups. This has been done above all in the RSFSR, the federal State with the largest area (17 million sq.km. or 76 per cent) and population (133.7 million, or 52.8 per cent of the total). All the 15 Republics and their subdivisions have their governments, two of which – the Ukraine and Belorussia – have their own foreign ministries as well as seats and votes in the UN. All assemblies (soviets), including the federal assembly (All-Union Soviet), are elected by direct and equal franchise. Two houses of parliament – the directly elected federal assembly and the soviet of nationalities – control the central government. Formally, the parliaments enjoy all the prerogatives characteristic of bourgeois-parliamentary democracy: election of the premier, vote on budget and economic plan, legislation, supervision of Government activities. The central Government has a strong position vis-à-vis the State Governments.

Decisive proposals and initiatives stem mostly from the Communist Party and its Central Committee. The General Secretary of the Party actually has more political weight than the Prime Minister. The Party is organised in a centralised fashion from the basic cells upwards, with political and professional secretaries at each level of public administration. The Party secretary mobilises the administration and checks whether and how far it has fulfilled the obligations laid upon it. During the first years after the revolution of 1917, several truly independent political parties existed, which were gradually dissolved. When Stalin took over as CPSU Secretary General, all political currents, groups or factions within the Party were banned, and the Party was politically unified, "bolshevis-ed". Genuine political votes were replaced by unanimity and acclamation. If there are different opinions in basic issues, they are probably discussed in the Central Committee and a decision is arrived at before the new proposals and targets are divulged to parliament and public opinion. The Central Committee is probably the highest effective decision-making body. On it the most important power factors (army, administration, industry, agriculture, science) are represented.[40]

3.2. *Planned economy, its development and methods*

Planning of the main spheres of a whole national economy was introduced in the Soviet Union for the first time in human history. Economic planning, unthinkable and unbelievable in the capitalist rest of the world, was without precedent and had no experience to fall back on. The main features of this basic method, which characterises a socialist as distinct from a capitalist economy and society, shall be briefly described.

3.2.1. *Periods of economic development*
In the course of the first world war and four years of civil war, factories and the infrastructure were largely destroyed or worn out; the farming sector received no inputs; rural-urban trade was dislocated; and the industrial proletariat – in any case a relatively small section of the population – was severely reduced in numbers, since many workers joined the Red Army or the new administration, while others were driven by famine conditions in the towns and the breakdown of factories to return to the countryside. The first task was to reconstruct the foundations of industry with physically exhausted manpower. Thereafter, the developing coun-

try had to catch up with international industrial, technological and cultural developments.

All industrial means of production were expropriated without compensation and taken over by the State. During the period of war communism, commodities in short supply were rationed and officially distributed. While all industrial nations boycotted the Soviet Union politically and economically, socialists from all over the world and humanitarian institutions tried to alleviate emergencies and famine by international solidarity. First attempts at planning ("electrification plus planning equals communism") failed, since the economy had lost too much blood. In 1921, the State Planning Commission was formed. That step was followed by the New Economic Policy, which permitted and encouraged private enterprise, both from within and from foreign capitalist sources. Foreign capitalists and large firms were granted concessions for limited periods, with the transfer of profit assured. After the treaty of Rapallo in 1922, Germany was the first nation to stop the blockade. Speculation and black market were tolerated, so as to stimulate domestic trade and food supplies for the cities. To get food to the towns in spite of inflation, a tax in kind was levied on the peasantry. The "commanding heights" of the economy (large-scale industry, construction, transport, foreign trade) remained under the State's control. Bukharin, adapting a famous historic slogan, exclaimed: "Peasants, enrich yourselves!"

During the period of slow economic recovery, intellectual preparations were made for the introduction of a planned economy. In 1929, the first five-year plan was promulgated with immediate effect. Relying chiefly on domestic resources, an independent basic and heavy industry was to be created in the shortest possible time in order to provide a foundation for consumer goods industries to be established later, for defence, and for the safeguarding of the country's political and economic independence. A high factor contribution exacted from the agrarian sector, combined with a low level of consumption of the new working class, was designed to accelerate primary capital accumulation. In allocating the scarce investment resources, the highest priority was given to heavy industry; consumer goods industries and housing received a low priority. Farming was compelled to disinvest, to wear out, and live on, its substance. The official slogans were: "to catch up with and overtake capitalism"; "to fulfil and overfulfil the five-year plan in four years".

By the end of the second five-year plan period, the Soviet Union had built up its own heavy industry and a stock of basic modern armaments for its red army. Stalin exploited the rising tensions in world politics to rid himself of his internal opponents and critics and of the foreign experts.

The second world war interrupted the normal development. Many factories were moved into the interior of the country, the remainder were destroyed by Hitler's scorched earth policy. All the same, a basic potential was preserved, which – in combination with US lend-lease deliveries – assured military victory.

After 1945, a second phase of reconstruction began, boosted by reparations from the GDR and by cheap deliveries from other socialist countries. Priorities remained unchanged until the death of Stalin. His successor, G. Malenkov, tried for the first time to lay emphasis on the two grossly neglected sectors, agriculture and consumer goods. Khrushchev, who succeeded Malenkov, pursued the same objective: investment in industries providing farm inputs, increase in agricultural production by intensification and wasteland reclamation, expansion of consumer goods manufacture and housing construction. But once production had become diversified and the most acute deficiencies had been overcome, the old planning methods and rigid centralisation ceased to be a help and instead became a hindrance, an obstacle to development. Economic accounting, profitability, liberalisation, decentralisation, new system of planning, economic incentives – these are the new watchwords.

3.2.2. *The Soviet planning system*
The point of departure in economic and social policy was an underdeveloped country, with a vast majority of the population living on the land and illiterate. There were few industrial centres, most of them of recent origin. But the country had rich deposits of various raw materials. The general objective was to attain the level of industrialised and literate nations. To this end, all available (physical and intellectual) energies had to be mobilised in a planned way, so as to concentrate on the strategically decisive sectors. Planning all development aspects of a vast society was a completely new and unique venture, with no historical precedent and no previous experience to learn from. This historic experiment aroused in some quarters the greatest enthusiasm, in others the deepest suspicion, alarm and revulsion against the destroyers of the god-given capitalist society.

Further aims were: elimination of illiteracy, expansion of the educational system, construction of heavy industries. The development lag was to be overcome in the shortest possible time and to this end some less crucial sectors were to be neglected. Abolition of all unproductive payments and of all unproductive social classes, expropriation and nationalisation of all means of production and of profits were the most important first steps taken to get hold of the decisive levers of economic development. The order of economic priorities was established as follows:

1. Extraction of raw materials;
2. construction of heavy industries (steel works, oil refineries, power stations);
3. construction of industries for investment goods;
4. consumer goods industries;
5. the agrarian sector.

The low priority accorded to consumer goods and farming compelled the consumers – who, of course, are identical with the producers – to forego consumption or improved consumption for a long period. The motives were political as well as economic. In social reality both aspects are closely interlinked. In politics, internal and external factors have to be considered. The internal revolutionary steps – expropriation of capitalists, liquidation of their political machinery – aroused the hostility of almost all world powers. This led to military intervention, economic blockade, cultural isolation, non-recognition. That again forced the political leadership to rely entirely on domestic resources. The wide variety of available resources and the country's size favoured self-sufficiency (autarky) and the "construction of socialism in one country".[41] The vast internal distances and the difficulties experienced in developing the infrastructure strengthened the desire to regionalise planning and economic life. But even within the regions and in the large-scale projects, vast distances must still be overcome if different raw materials have to be combined for processing in one place. The costs and psychological barriers to planned migration and resettlement on a mass-scale must also be taken into account. – The political opposition of the former ruling classes was broken in step with the social transformation, which liquidated the capitalist class (see Table 3.3.).

Planning implies the concentration of maximum efforts and resources on limited and well-defined economic goals, irrespective of short-term micro-economic profitability. Clear priorities are set. In this way the economic take-off is to be accelerated.

In the first phases of planning and general scarcity, physical targets are fixed (measured in tons of steel or oil, number of tractors and trucks etc.). As diversification and production capacities increase, producers and consumers become more demanding, and then planning methods must change. Modern techniques (computers, cybernetics) and the availability of far more comprehensive data call for a new style of more general and indicative planning, with targets fixed in monetary units (measured and indicated in million roubles per production unit). Instead of the direct allocation of raw materials and semi-finished goods, indirect guidance and indirect control by financial instruments can be adopted (measured by the scale of interest payments to public financial institutions or in terms of the profitability of an enterprise, and paid in the form of a profit tax).

Planned efforts allow rapid economic material results to be achieved in the take-off phase. But planning, on the other hand, implies a series of problems, e.g.:

1. Establishment of a cohesive planning bureaucracy with sectional interests of its own;
2. supervision of the planning mechanism;
3. setting of objectives and priorities;
4. early recognition of planning errors by an operative monitoring and feedback mechanism, followed by transition to new methods;
5. participation of the producers in the planning process and its democratisation;
6. consideration of the needs and demands of the consumers-producers;
7. material incentives and their socially reasonable distribution;
8. ensuring the producers' whole-hearted support for the objectives of planning;
9. income distribution, degree of social differentiation.

3.2.3. *Changes under the new economic system*

Since the early sixties, work on the discussion and elaboration of a new system of planning and economic stimulation has been in progress, but no clear definitions or comprehensive descriptions have so far been forthcoming.

Central planning of the original type was suited to the initial phase of economic development characterised by a few large, centrally implemented projects and by a scarcity of consumer goods. Diversification of production and consumption tends to aggravate the difficulties of detailed central planning, but at the same time renders it largely superfluous. While planning methods and controls are refined, they are elevated to the level of outline planning and long-term trend planning. The rigid five-year plans give way to a three-tier system of "perspective plans", drawn up for longer periods (10 or 20 years), in conjunction with increasingly specific five-year plans and one-year production plans. Feedback from the latter provides the basis for continuous adjustments of the long-term plans. Decisions of detail, e.g. production plans, are delegated to the industrial and agricultural enterprises, and left in practice to the discretion of the managers, with their first-hand knowledge of capacities, constraints, local markets etc. New prices and basic indices are introduced. The number of indices is being reduced, and their strict observance is no longer as rigidly enforced as it used to be. Indices of physical planning are replaced by those of indirect, financial planning, defined in monetary terms. The flow of raw materials and inputs becomes more regular and steady. Limited liberalisation of prices and production increases the material incentives of management and workers. Fixing of wages is decentralised and becomes more flexible.

Market factors are allowed a limited influence. The market is no longer regarded as running counter to socialist economic planning, but as a complement and corrective. Rational planning cannot achieve its objectives unless the market is satisfied, at least in the long term. Indeed, it was the original idea of planning to ascertain and satisfy the aggregate needs of consumers and society. Since over a long period the supply of goods and services is bound to fall short of demand, fierce controversy and social pressures will inevitably focus on the problem of setting priorities, of singling out the most vital and essential demands, of deciding to what extent the various needs shall be met, and what should be accepted as social norm at each point in time.

In the long run at least, goods and services offered have to satisfy needs and demand. If they do not, the planning was faulty and not up to its task. Guidance and supervision are exercised chiefly by economic and financial instruments, while administrative measures are being dropped. The new economic system builds on the material foundations of the earlier achievements, but supersedes obsolete methods.

3.3. *Quantitative results in the industrial sector*

The physical achievements of accelerated industrialisation are shown in Table 3.4. From its starting point as a very backward country, the Soviet Union has developed into one of the leading industrial nations of the world in terms of quantity and variety as well as quality of production. All industrial goods, including the most sophisticated, are manufactured. In some technologies, Soviet industry is in the front ranks, which is not inconsistent with a development lag and poor quality in other fields. Vast amounts of steel, coal, oil are produced. Some commodities, e.g. fertilisers, show both the planned neglect up to 1950 and the results of a planned effort, which led to a considerable increase in output over a short period. The economy has wiped out the development lag, and has overtaken, or caught up whith, most other economies in a much shorter time than was needed by the other industrially advanced nations for their process of industrialisation. The priorities and the corresponding allocation of investments are easily discernible, if the results in the individual sectors are considered. It must be borne in mind, however, that an international comparison of output of individual commodities does not give a true picture, owing to different social customs, patterns of con-

Table 3.4.: Production of selected raw materials and industrial goods 1913-1974

Item	Unit	1913	1917	1928	1940	1945	1950	1960	1970	1974
Electricity	1,000 mln. kWh	1.9	2.6	5	48	43	91	292	740	975
Oil	mln. tons	10	9	12	31	19	38	148	353	459
Gas	1,000 mln. cu m	0	?	0.3	3.0	3.4	6	47	200	243
Coal	mln. tons	29	31	36	166	149	261	510	574	684
Iron	mln. tons	4	3	3	15	9	19	47	86	100
Steel	mln. tons	4	3	4	18	12	27	65	116	136
Lathes + machine tools	1,000	1.5	0.2	2	58	38	71	156	202	207[1]
Turbines	mln. kW	0	?	0	1.2	0.2	2.7	9.2	16.2	16.8[1]
Tractors	1,000	•	•	1.3	32	8	117	239	459	531
Cars + trucks	1,000	0	•	0.8	145	75	327	524	920	1,846
Fertilisers	mln. tons	0.1	?	0.1	3	1	6	14	55	80
Synthetic fibres	1,000 tons	•	•	0.2	11	1	24	211	623	887
Synthetic resin, plastics	1,000 tons	•	•	•	11	21	67	312	1,673	2,300[2]
Textiles (all types)	1,000 mln. sq m	2.1	1.2	2.2	3.3	1.4	3.4	6.6	8.9	9.8
Leather shoes	mln. pairs	68	50	58	211	63	203	419	676	684
Radio-sets	mln	•	•	?	0.2	0	1.1	4.1	7.8	8.8
Refrigerators	mln	•	•	•	0	0	0	0.5	4.1	5.4

[1] 1971   [2] 1973

Sources: Sowjetunion – Land und Wirtschaft; Länderberichte; Narodnoye khozyaystvo; BfA; SSSR ve cifrach

sumption and consumer preferences, which are integrated into planning. The figures show clearly, how late in the day consumer goods industries were discovered by the planners. Particularly harmful was and is the long-standing neglect of housing, even though attempts are currently being made to fill the gap.

Growth rates show marked changes over the years. During the early phases spectacular growth rates were achieved, thanks partly to the low level at the outset. In the later stages the curve is flattening. Destruction by war has had its effects also. Disproportions between various commodities and industries slow the growth temporarily. But at the same time it must be recognised that such disproportions are an essential part of the growth process itself. It was necessary, therefore, to interpose intervals between the regular five-year plan period, in order to overcome the bottlenecks in the annual plans. Certain signs of economic cycles can be discovered, which are determined by factors dissimilar to those influencing the cycles of boom and crisis characteristic of profit-oriented capitalist economies. These factors may be:

a. Excessive disproportions between industries and between main sectors;
b. lack of essential consumer goods, which affects the working capacity of the employees and causes sickness and absenteeism;
c. deficient planning and insufficient feedback mechanisms;
d. backwardness of technological infrastructure, particularly transport.

3.4. *The educational system*

The point of departure in 1917 was: 60 per cent of the population were illiterate; 50 per cent of all children of school-age attended school. In less than 15 years the situation changed profoundly: general school attendance and the elimination of illiteracy through adult education were achieved simultaneously. Eight years of compulsory general education provide a broad basis for the effort of secondary and academic educational institutions. Together with vocational training, they benefit 80 per cent of all primary school leavers. By 1980, compulsory education is to be extended to 10 years. Adult education is provided for those with regular employment in evening and correspondence courses. Quantitative achievements are shown in Table 3.5.

The main distinctive features of the educational system are:
1. Heavy emphasis on natural and engineering sciences;
2. broad access to secondary and academic education;
3. importance of evening and correspondence studies accompanying regular work;

Table 3.5.: Development of the educational system

	1960/61	1965/66	1970/71	1972/73	1974/75
Institutions					
Primary schools ('000)	169.0	156.8	128.3	116.1	102.6
Secondary education ('000)	29.2	31.9	44.2	46.7	49.9
Vocational schools	3,328	3,820	4,223	4,270	4,286
Universities and other institutions of higher education	739	756	805	825	?
Teachers ('000)					
Primary and secondary education	1,933	2,366	2,510	2,562	2,593
Vocational schools	?	134	?	?	?
Institutions of higher education	128	201	?	302	?
Attendants					
Primary schools (mln)	16.4	20.4	14.9	13.0	10.9
Secondary education (mln)	16.9	22.7	30.2	31.4	32.2
Vocational schools ('000)	2,060	3,659	4,388	4,438	4,523
thereof					
day instruction ('000)	1,091	1,835	2,558	2,690	2,762
evening + correspondence classes ('000)	969	1,824	1,830	1,748	1,716
Polytechnics ('000)	1,113	1,672	2,411	2,442	2,297
Institutions of adult education('000)	10,909	14,381	18,881	20,150	20,200 [1])
Universities ('000)	2,396	3,861	4,581	4,630	4,751
thereof					
day classes ('000)	1,156	1,584	2,241	2,386	?
evening + correspondence classes ('000)	1,240	2,277	2,340	2,244	?

[1]) 1973/74

Sources: Länderberichte; Narodnoye chozjajstvo; SSSR ve cifrach

4. social structure of students, better representation of workers and peasants;
5. separation of teaching and research between universities and colleges on the one hand and research institutions (academies) on the other hand.

Whether all the features mentioned are advantageous and permanent is open to discussion. Some might be seen as transitory measures in a crash programme to raise the general educational level. Thus it appears, that the academics themselves are not always satisfied with the institutional separation of teaching and research and try to overcome these barriers.

3.5. *The agrarian sector*

The Soviet experiment in agriculture was as radical in terms of social change as it was in the fields of industry and education, perhaps more so. It affected from 1929 onwards the majority of the nation.

3.5.1. *Revolutionary transformation of the agrarian structure*
When Stolypin introduced the second agrarian reform in 1906, there was a huge number of dwarf and smallholdings, accounting for only a small proportion of the agricultural land. There was a polarisation of land ownership, with wide-spread semifeudal bondage and unproductive payments to the landlords. The agrarian reform was largely abortive, except for the dissolution of the communes. After the first world war the number of smallholdings continued to rise. In 1917, all feudal relics – obligations and unproductive payments – were abolished, and in a radical agrarian reform the land of the landlords was distributed among the cultivators, tenants, smallholders, landless labourers. The landlords were forbidden to reside in "their" former villages or to visit their former properties. All titles to the land were nationalised and placed at the disposal of the cultivators rent-free. No further steps were taken by the Government.

Voluntary communes and artels – in 1925 there were about 22,000 of them, with a combined area of 3.25 million ha – were formed mainly by 300,000 formerly landless labourers and enthusiastic communists. By the end of 1928, the number had risen to 33,000 with about 400,000 families, cultivating on average 96 ha each. The communes thus had little impact on an agrarian sector dominated by individual holdings. These experiments were tolerated, but not encouraged by Party and Government.

From 1929 to 1960, the agrarian structure was characterised by four institutions:
1. Collective farms (kolkhozes);
2. individual or household plots;
3. state farms (sovkhozes);
4. machine and tractor stations (MTS).

3.5.1.1. The collective farms
Collectivisation was launched simultaneously with the accelerated industrialisation in 1929. Attempts at persuasion and propaganda campaigns by the Party were followed in the end by coercion and the use of force against the reluctant independent peasants, whereas in theory peasants were to have joined the collective farms of their own free will. Within four years 24.6 million peasant households were enrolled and organised in 237,000 collective farms. In the primary phases of collectivisation, fields and the main crops only were pooled. Vegetables, fruit

and particularly animal production remained the strongholds of the household plot.

The rational economic motives of collectivisation are:

1. Organisation of the amorphous and atomised peasantry, utilisation of economies of scale, while avoiding the disadvantages of the big agricultural estates, since cooperatives should appeal to the members' self-interest;
2. promotion of production and procurement of cereals, assuring supplies of staple foods for a growing urban population at low prices (production contribution);
3. movement of labour into the emerging industries – voluntary or involuntary (kulaks) (factor contribution I);
4. rationing and macro-economically optimal utilisation of farm machinery via machine-and-tractor stations;
5. simplified planning and organisation of agricultural advice, optimum use of scarce expert manpower;
6. reducing direct and indirect investment in agriculture (production of inputs) to a minimum, while concentrating industrial development on raw materials, investment goods, and on the technological, social and cultural infrastructure;
7. providing capital for economic development from the proceeds of the agricultural sector (factor contribution II).

The accelerated and forcible enrolment of many million smallholders in the collective farms without offering economic or technological incentives aroused their resistance, expressed in

a. non-delivery of farm produce;
b. hiding away of grain;
c. slaughtering of cattle;
d. chasing away, sometimes assassination of Government or Party officials visiting the villages.

The silent, sometimes armed resistance of the peasantry on the one hand, and the pressure brought to bear by the authorities on the other, led to a reciprocal escalation, until in the end police and army were called in to enforce collectivisation.

After the second world war the 237,000 collective farms were merged into large-scale agricultural enterprises, of which there were 30,000 in 1974. On average they comprised 463 families, as compared with 80 in 1940 (see Table 3.6 and Fig. 3.3). Agricultural land per farm increased from 1,400 to 6,400 ha, of which about half was arable, the rest pasture, meadows and fallow. The number of actively working collective peasants fell from 29 million to 15.7 million, a decline of 46

Table 3.6.: Collective farms

	1940	1950	1960	1965	1970	1974
Collective farms ('000)	235.5	121.4	44.9	36.9	33.6	30.0
Members' household plots (millions)	18.7	20.5	17.1	15.4	14.4	13.8
Families per kolkhoz	81	165	391	426	435	463
Collective farmers engaged in agricultural work (average over year, millions)	29.0	27.6	21.8	18.6	16.7	15.7
Arable land (million ha)	117.7	121.0	123.0	105.1	99.1	98.4
Arable land per kolkhoz ('000 ha)	0.5	1.0	2.7	2.9	3.0	3.4
Agricultural land per kolkhoz ('000 ha)	1.4	3.1	6.6	6.1	6.1	6.4
Cattle per kolkhoz	85	224	826	1,056	1,258	1,556

Sources: Rochlin and Hagemann (1971); Narodnoe khozyaystvo; SSSR ve cifrach

per cent.[42] These figures reflect the normal development of industrialising economies. But the ratio of agricultural population to agricultural land is still very high, although labour productivity has increased. The total cropland of the kolkhozes declined by 19 million ha. On the other hand, kolkhoz cattle stocks increased substantially, from about 20 million head in 1940 to 45 million head in 1973. The average per unit thus rose from 85 to 1,550 head of cattle. The gradual transition to large-scale animal husbandry has been made possible by new developments in technology, genetics, and veterinary medicine, but it calls for heavy investment in construction, equipment, feeds and other inputs.

Remuneration was initially paid according to day-work units, a combination of payment for the physical effort and the qualifications involved. Wages due to the working member were paid partly in advance, partly at the end of the year, after the balance-sheet had been drawn up. In fact, these year-end payments were only made after the machine-and-tractor station had been paid for its work, compulsory deliveries to the State had been completed. statutory contributions to the joint funds of the collective farm duly made, etc. Under that system – in force for an extended period – the members' remuneration was a residual payment, ranking last after all other obligations of the kolkhoz. It was a distribution of the variable remainder, after all fixed dues had been paid. Wages are in cash and in kind. Produce received in kind is converted into animal products on the household plots.[43]

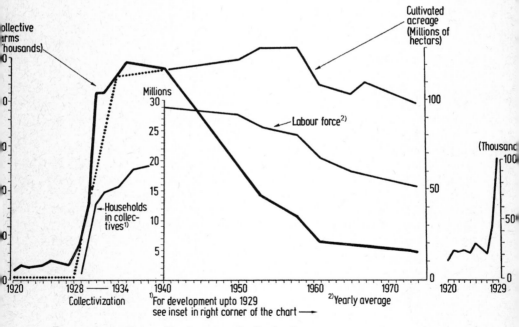

Fig. 3.3. Soviet Union: Development of collective farms

In some socialist countries there are three or even four types of producer cooperatives, distinguished by the degree of integration of production and varying payments for the land brought into the cooperative by each member. In the Soviet Union there is only one type, since all the land was nationalised in 1917.

Formally and according to its statutes, the collective farm is a fully fledged cooperative institution: all members are working, all its workers are members.[44] A high degree of equality is established by two provisions: big peasants with holdings above a certain limit are not allowed to join, at least not during the first years, and landless labourers are invited to join and are (formally) equipped with land from land reform funds to be brought into the collective farm. The identity of workers and members and the equality of all the members provide a good basis for the smooth functioning of cooperative production. Decisions on tillage, work plans and assignments, election of all councils and office-bearers and distribution of profits rests with the members.

If all these provisions were applied in practice, the kolkhoz would represent an ideal form of large-scale enterprise adapted to the specific conditions of agricultural production: maximum economies of scale combined with the producers' self-interest, which ought to obviate the need for expensive supervision. – What actually happened was that the collective farms were totally integrated with the centrally planned economic system, in which all directives were issued by the central authorities, leaving no room for objections, or even consultation. The fulfilment of the plan was overseen by the appointed chairmen and by officials, who often enough came from outside the village and were controlled by the Party. Thus, the plan was fulfilled and the supply of basic foodstuffs and commodities assured by administrative action, but the cooperative atmosphere, the identification of the members with the enterprise, and incentives to high performance, initiative and supervision at local level – vital ingredients of economic success in a socialist unit of production – were destroyed.

The collective farm places a large proportion of the risks of farming on the members' shoulders. It is a convenient way of exacting the factor contribution of the agrarian sector. As long as this sector comprises the vast majority of the population, that is economically unavoidable. Were it otherwise, the Government would lose its capacity to finance industrial development.

Despite the relatively high level of mechanisation of tillage, labour productivity remains low, because the private sector (see 3.5.1.2.) does not work efficiently and the peasants spend much time on their trips to market. As is invariably the case before the introduction of intensive animal husbandry, the agricultural population is underemployed. Thus, in January 1959 18 million persons were employed in the collective farms, as against 30.7 million in July of the same year. Employment levels vary according to region and sex. Where there is more animal production, more even employment can be offered, and more women are employed. In 1967, men were employed for periods ranging from 158 days during the whole year in the central black-earth region to 254 days in the north-west. For women the corresponding figure varied from 184 to 262 days.

3.5.1.2. The household plot
Beside the main, large-scale cooperative production unit, the household plots of the collective farmers continue to play a part. They range from 1/4 to 1/2 ha, supporting 1-2 cows, 2 calves, 12-25 sheep, a few pigs, etc., the size varying according to regional conditions.

The private sector is of substantial importance. The collective peasants market their produce in part themselves, sometimes in places thousands of miles away, and for the rest they sell to state purchasing enterprises, which pay higher rates for voluntary deliveries than for quota deliveries exacted from the kolkhoz.

The collective peasants and their family members work partly in the collective farm, partly on the household plot. In 1959, 9.9 million family members worked on those plots.

The household plot fulfils the following functions:
1. It supplements the production of the large-scale units by sypplying commodities that cannot, or cannot yet, be produced by mechanised methods;
2. it diversifies market supplies by deliveries to local and regional markets;
3. it utilises surplus manpower at times when the seasonal demand for labour is lowest;
4. it converts surplus fodder crops (roughage) produced by the collective farm;
5. it provides additional income for the members' families, so as to improve and safeguard their living standards.

By utilising the factors of production and contributing food supplies for the population, the household plot complements the large collective farms, with which it lives in a sort of symbiosis, even while competing with them for the factors of production, in the first place for manpower, but also for fertilisers and the use of the collective tractor. If remuneration for work in the kolkhoz is low, the individual member will seek to concentrate more on farming his household plot, and to supplement his store of feeding stuffs from the collectively grown fodder crops. Thus the household plot is the last refuge of the members in their confrontations with a strict and unscrupulous planning bureaucracy and an unfeeling kolkhoz chairman.

The attitude of the Government and the Communist Party towards the household plot has varied widely from period to period. At times the prevailing tendency favoured the total abolition or at the very least a severe curtailment of the household plot. At other times it was in official favour and its extension was encouraged. At present the latter view is predominant. Today the economists and planners understand and recognise that the household plot is not a capitalist relic, but that it can discharge functions complementary to basic planning. Its abolition would create difficult economic problems. Important factors of production (farm buildings, areas of marginal land) would be devalued at a stroke. Large new public investments would become necessary. Underemployment would turn into unemployment, or the wage funds of the collective farms would have to be substantially increased. If the household plot is to be abolished at some distant future stage, it can only be done step by step, to an extent depending on the parallel development of technological progress, accompanied by the production of more agricultural machinery and the supply of more, as well as more varied, goods to the urban and rural markets.

The ruling official view has been formulated as follows in the theoretical journal of the CPSU:

"In its decision on the household plot the Congress of Collective Farmers has taken account of the actual conditions and recognised the household plot as useful. It was decided not to break with a practice established over decades and to take the peculiarities of the individual republics and of the various ecological and economic zones into account. Now and in the future the collective farmer's household plot has an important part to play in expanding the general resources governing the country's food supplies. It would be a great mistake to ignore this fact. The model statutes of the kolkhozes have set a standard for the delimitation of the household plots, which will effectively prevent their unchecked growth on the one hand and their decline on the other" (*Kommunist* 17, 1969).

Collective farming, then, does not involve the complete integration of all the elements of production – as it does in the kibbutz, for example – but a symbiosis between co-operative and private-enterprise elements. The co-operative, however, matters most, with the household plots playing no more than an auxiliary part.

In view of this mutual dependence and complementarity the productivity of Soviet collective agriculture does not lend itself to comparisons with agricultural productivity in the USA or West Germany. In assessing productivity per unit area, consideration must be given to the climate, the use of chemical fertilisers and the supply of fodder crops to the household plots. In assessing labour productivity, the factors to be considered are: intermittent employment owing to the predominance of arable farming, with full-year working feasible only for small groups on both climatic and operational grounds. The relative shares of the co-operative and private components in the total income of the collective farmer cannot be disentangled, since the produce supplied to the household plot by the kolkhoz by way of remuneration in kind enters into the home consumption of the individual household as well as into its stock-raising activities and its private marketing efforts.

3.5.1.3. State farms

The third element of the communist agrarian structure is the state farms. They require no special explanation or comment in terms of rural sociology. Within the framework of general agricultural policy they fulfil several tasks:

Breeding of plants and animals;
experiments in all spheres of agricultural science and in the application of its results;
supplying staple foods to urban centres under direct State supervision, so as to safeguard regular deliveries and maintain price levels.

The figures relating to development are given in Table 3.7 and Fig. 3.4. The number of state farms increased from about 4,000 in 1940, with a total of 11.6 million ha of arable land, to 17,700 in 1974, farming 105.8 million ha. The acreage increased most rapidly during and immediately after the virgin lands campaign, from 1956 to 1962. After that, expansion slowed down substantially, while the number of units continued to grow. Animal husbandry grew at a higher rate than crop farming. The total cattle population on state farms went up steadily from 2.5 to 34.6 million head during the 34 years ending in 1974. During the same period the labour force increased from 1.37 to 9.95 millions.[45]

Certain internal developments are worth noting. On average, the area of cropland held by each state farm reached a maximum of more than 10,000 ha in 1962, since when it declined to 6,000 ha. This indicates a measure of decentralisation, accompanied by the formation of smaller units. The average cattle stocks per farm have also declined to some extent since 1962. Arable farming increased ninefold in terms of acreage

Table 3.7.: Development of state farms

A. *Absolute values*

Year	Number	Labour force ('ooo) [1]	Arable land (million ha)	Cattle (million)	Tractors ('ooo)
1940	4,159	1,373	11.6	2.5	.
1953	4,857	1,844	15.2	3.4	.
1958	6,002	3,835	37.1	8.2	.
1960	7,375	5,800	67.2	14.4	403
1962	8,570	6,893	86.7	20.9	.
1965	11,681	8,230	89.1	24.5	681
1970	14,994	8,888	91.7	29.1	803
1972	15,747	9,328	96.6	31.4	865
1974	17,717	9,947	105.8	34.6	984

B. *Average per state farm*

Year	Labour force	Arable land ('ooo ha)	Cattle	Pigs	Tractors [2] (at 15 HP)
1928	134	0.8	97	31	2
1940	330	2.8	592	459	24
1950	334	2.6	562	500	26
1953	380	3.1	700	.	.
1958	639	8.7	1,370	1,355	90
1960	786	9.0	1,957	1,715	41
1962	804	10.1	2,439	.	.
1965	705	7.6	2,098	1,073	58
1970	613	6.2	1,944	1,116	54
1972	592	6.1	1,996	1,143	55
1974	562	6.0	1,955	1,157	56

[1] Annual average
[2] From 1960 onwards physical units

Sources: Strauss (1969), Rochlin and Hagemann (1971), Narodnoe khoyaystvo, SSSR ve cifrach 1973

from 1940 to 1974, while the cattle population rose by a factor of 14. The stronger emphasis on animal production is evident.

Labour productivity has improved substantially. Acreage per worker increased from 8.4 ha in 1940 to 10.6 ha in 1974, while the ratio of cattle to worker rose from 1.8 to 3.5 head.

The two principal forms of large-scale agricultural enterprise – the

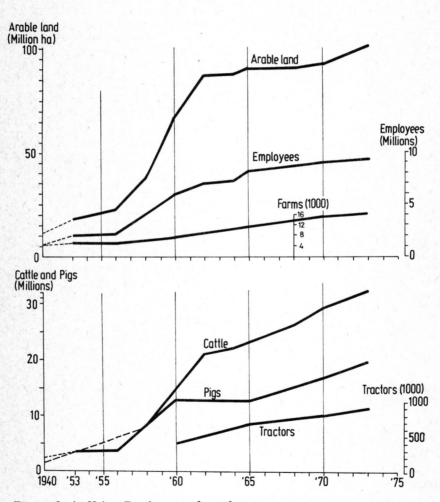

Fig. 3.4. Soviet Union: Development of state farms

kolkhoz and sovkhoz – vary greatly in relative importance from region to region. The kolkhozes predominate in the long-settled densely populated and intensively exploited lands, whereas sovkhozes hold the major share of agricultural land in, above all, the recently settled regions, where the prevailing ecological and economic conditions are marginal.

The relative shares of the three sectors have slightly shifted over the years (see Table 3.8). In absolute terms, the kolkhozes have retained almost their entire agricultural area, but their share declined owing to the vast tracts of virgin lands brought into cultivation by the state farms. The share of the private sector in the total agricultural land is very small, but its share in animal production is still important, declining in the case of cattle and pigs, increasing in respect of sheep and goats. Its share in industrial crops (sugar beet, cotton) is negligible; in crops reaped with combine harvesters very small; in the case of labour-intensive crops still relatively high. While declining, the share of the private sector in animal production still represents a significant contribution to market supplies, and is at any rate substantially higher than its share in agricultural land. There is in fact no correlation between acreage and livestock holdings. This is a case of production independent of acreage, supported by supplies of fodder and concentrates from the large-scale enterprice.

3.5.1.4. The machine and tractor stations (MTS)

Collectivisation went hand in hand with the establishment of the machine and tractor stations. The entire technical equipment assigned to the collective sector, as well as the staff of tractor drivers, mechanics, etc., were concentrated there. The collective farms had to negotiate with the machine and tractor stations about every tillage job. The payment for contract work was in kind. In that way the scant material was used to the best advantage, the few technically qualified people were deployed according to plans drawn up at higher levels, and staple products were collected for the state. The MTS also had advisory and planning functions. In 1958 all the stations were disbanded, the bulk of their equipment was sold off to the kolkhozes and their personnel was integrated with the collective farms. A limited number of stations was retained to cope with special tasks, such as repair of heavy machinery, hiring out of, and contract work with, new machines designed for operating over vast areas. The winding up of the MTS had become possible at this stage, as more agricultural machines were now being manufactured and could be bought by the collective farms, thus dispensing with the need for administrative allocation. Moreover the collective farms had more experienced and trained manpower than in the past.

Table 3.8.: Percentage shares of the social sectors in farm inputs and production 1950-1970

Items	1950				1968				1970			
	K¹	S	SS	H	K	S	SS	H	K	S	SS	H
Land												
Agricultural	79	19	98	2	40	58	98	2	37	62	99	1
Sown	83	11	94	6	50	47	97	3	48	51	99	1
Livestock												
Cattle	49	7	56	44	42	30	72	28	44	29	73	27
Pigs	50	15	65	35	44	30	74	26	47	26	73	27
Sheep	74	11	85	15	40	39	79	21	–	–	–	–
Goats	46	1	47	53	11	6	17	83	–	–	–	–
Vegetable products												
Grain	82	11	93	7	53	45	98	2	53	46	99	1
Sunflower	91	5	96	4	80	18	98	2	–	–	–	–
Potatoes	23	4	27	73	24	14	38	62	21	14	35	65
Sugarbeet	97	3	100	–	92	8	100	–	–	–	–	–
Cotton	96	4	100	–	80	20	100	–	77	23	100	–
Vegetables	45	11	56	44	26	33	59	41	26	36	62	38
Fruit²	20	13	33	67	29	26	55	45	–	–	–	–
Grapes²	51	25	76	24	37	43	80	20	–	–	–	–
Animal products												
Meat	22	11	33	67	32	30	62	38	34	32	66	34
Milk	19	6	25	75	35	27	62	38	36	28	64	36
Eggs	9	2	11	89	14	26	40	60	14	33	47	53
Wool	67	12	79	21	39	41	80	20	–	–	81	19

¹) K – Kolkhozes, S – Sovkhozes, SS – Socialist sector (K + S), H – Household plots
²) 1959 instead of 1950

Sources: Länderberichte; Wädekin (1967); SSSR ve cifrach

The liquidation of the MTS had four main consequences:
1. Improved internal organisation and operational planning of the collective farms;
2. streamlining and rationalisation of public administration;
3. abolition of compulsory deliveries in kind from the kolkhoz to the MTS in payment for work done;
4. increased opportunities of social advancement for the members.

3.5.1.5. Main features of the new production relations
The emerging new agrarian structure is clearly distinguished from all hitherto existing agrarian systems. The new structure is based chiefly on large-scale production units capable of utilising the most up-to-date technology, benefiting from economies of scale and introducing industrial techniques where applicable, provided the relevant inputs are available. The majority of the new large units are collective farms, which by definition ought to offer the chance of the full identification of all working members with their co-operative enterprise.

The specific features of Soviet collectivisation under Stalin were:
1. Radical change of production relations;
2. compression of the change-over into a minimum time span;
3. absence of all material and technological incentives;
4. no breathing space allowing the peasants to adjust to the new socio-economic set-up;
5. economic and technical management governed by rigid mandatory directives;
6. no membership participation in running collective farms;
7. no attempt to persuade or convince the peasantry during the transformation;
8. opposition and alienation[46] of the majority of the peasantry.
Three reasons may be singled out as most decisive in alienating the peasants: (a) All basic decisions were taken from above and by external agencies. What counted was the planning directives, not the wishes of the members, who at best were allowed to formally acclaim the decisions imposed upon them. (b) For a long time the remuneration of the members was a residual claim on the resources of the kolkhoz, after all its other obligations had been met. (c) Annual wages were assessed and paid at the year-end, which was far too long after the work had been performed, so that the connection between greater effort and higher reward was scarcely discernible. This acted as a disincentive and led to absenteeism and the neglect or theft of collective inputs. – However, as will be shown later, these conditions belong to the past.

3.5.2. *Problems of production*

3.5.2.1. The inputs

Over large sections of agricultural land in the Soviet Union the value of production cannot be compared with conditions in Western Europe. Marginal production conditions necessitate extensive exploitation. Yields are correspondingly low.

Of the country's total land surface less than half – about 1,043 million ha – is held by agricultural enterprises (see Table 3.9). Only 551 million ha are in agricultural use, of which 41 per cent is cropland, the rest meadows and pasture. Collective and state farms have almost the same acreage of cropland, while the state farms hold 235 million ha pastures and meadow-land as against 84 million ha held by the collective farms.

Table 3.9.: Land use November 1, 1974 (million ha)

	Land area	AL	Arable less permanent fallow	Meadows	Pastures
Kolkhozes	316.5	193.0	106.1	13.4	70.9
collectively farmed	311.8	188.5	102.2	13.2	70.9
privately farmed	4.7	4.5	3.9	0.2	–
Sovkhozes and other	723.8	355.0	116.7	24.5	210.9
Privately farmed outside kolkhozes	3.8	3.5	2.5	0.4	–
Total used by agricultural production units	1,044.1	551.5	225.3	38.3	281.8
State forest and land fund	1,122.8	37.3	0.4	5.6	31.0
Other areas	60.6	19.0	0.5	1.1	17.3
Total area 1971	2,227.5	607.3	224.6	46.5	328.2
1974	2,227.5	607.8	226.2	45.0	330.1

Source: Narodnoe khozyaystvo (1975)

Irrigable land totalled in 1968 about 10.2 million ha, of which 9.8 million ha was actually irrigated (i.e. 4.6 per cent of cropland). By the end of 1972 the irrigated area had increased to 12 million ha. Open-ditch draining systems operated in 1968 on 7.1 million ha, tile-line drainage on 2.6 million ha, together 1.8 per cent of the agricultural land.

Fertiliser production was neglected for decades, and it was only under Khrushchev that the development of the fertiliser industry was begun. Output has risen, but so far not enough to fulfil plans and meet requirements (Table 3.10). The use of fertilisers per unit area is correspondingly

Table 3.10.: Fertiliser production (thousand tonnes [1]))

	Nitrogen	Phosphate	Potassium	Nitrogen + Phosphate + Potassium
1940	789	1,844	526	3,159
1950	1,497	2,838	1,015	5,350
1960	3,749	5,795	1,842	11,386
1965	11,132	11,290	4,547	26,969
1970	22,463	16,943	6,187	45,593
1972	27,436	19,497	7,784	54,717
1974	32,934	24,003	8,917	65,865
1974 (pure nutrients)	6,746	4,496	3,708	14,958

[1]) Produced quantity, not pure nutrients

Sources: Narodnoe khozyaystvo; SSSR ve cifrach; Länderkurzberichte

low: 15.1 kg pure nutrient per ha agricultural land, 37.7 kg per ha cropland in 1968, rising to 65.5 kg in 1974. Since land is abundant and population density is low, a comparison with Western Europe seems unreasonable. Use of fertilisers at a level of intensity comparable to that of, say, the Netherlands would be economically wasteful.

Mechanisation was started as early as 1930, but its progress was held up by the needs of the arms industry and by the Second World War. After 1958 large investments were made to increase the production of agricultural machinery (Table 3.11). Production (in thousand units) rose as follows:

	1962	1965	1970	1971	1974
Tractors	287.0	239.5	309.3	472.0	347.4
Tractor ploughs	146.6	158.5	207.2	217.0	203.4
Seed drills	162.5	259.5	187.0	170.1	209.8
Combine harvesters	79.8	79.4	97.1	99.0	83.4

The volume of production is high – more than 470,000 tractors were manufactured in 1971 – but not yet sufficient to meet genuine needs, i.e. the numbers required to complete all field operations at the proper time. Tractors and other equipment can be utilised with higher economic efficiency in a farming structure characterised by large enterprises. But it seems, that the optimum of tractor and equipment density has not been attained yet. Scarcity of spare parts and lack of repair facilities may add to the difficulties regularly reported in the Soviet press.

Table 3.11.: Machinery stock (thousands)

Year	Tractors		Combine harvesters	Trucks
	No.	Nominal 15 hp units		
1928	27	.	2	0.7
1940	531	684	182	228
1950	595	933	211	283
1960	1,122	1,985	497	778
1962	1,329	2,400	520	875
1962 [1])	–	2,696	845	1,650
1965	1,613	3,543	520	945
1970	1,977	4,343	623	1,206
1970 (Plan)	2,490	5,470	530	1,012
1971	2,046	4,530	639	1,243
1974	2,289	5,068	673	1,336

[1]) Number required to ensure completion of work on schedule

Sources: Narodnoe khozyaystvo; Länderkurzberichte

Manpower in farming was 26.7 millions in 1974 (see Table 3.12), a slow decline – 15 per cent – since 1940. But there was a shift in the composition of the labour force. Those active in collective farms declined from 29 to 16 millions, i.e. by 45 per cent, while the share of the state farms increased.

Great efforts have been made in the general and vocational education of the agricultural labour force, resulting in improved skills and qualifications.

Table 3.12.: The agricultural labour force (seasonally adjusted average) in millions

	1940	1950	1960	1970	1974
Kolkhozes	29.0	27.6	22.3	17.0	15.9
directly engaged in agriculture	26.1	25.1	26.1	15.2	14.2
All agricultural production units	31.3	30.9	29.4	26.8	26.7
directly engaged in agriculture	28.1	27.9	26.1	23.8	23.6
Kolkhoz labour as percentage of total agricultural labour	92.6	89.3	75.8	63.6	59.6
Kolkhoz workers directly engaged in agriculture as percentage of total work force so engaged	92.8	90.0	74.0	63.9	60.2

Source: Narodnoe khozyaystvo; SSSR ve cifrach

The share of agriculture in the country's total manpower is still relatively high for an industrialised economy. But the following points have to be made for a better understanding of differences between industrialised nations and between different social systems:

1. Owing to the climate and the insignificant part played by high-grade animal husbandry in the large-scale enterprises, there is high seasonal unemployment or underemployment.
2. The functions of the agricultural sector are different and more comprehensive than in the agriculture of capitalist societies (construction brigades, repair work, advice services). All the services for agriculture are carried out by the large-scale enterprises for themselves. There are hardly any non-agricultural enterprises undertaking contract work or providing services for agriculture.

3.5.2.2. The virgin lands campaign: socio-economic problems

Efforts to raise agricultural production resulted only in slow progress in the long-settled areas. That is why the decision was taken in 1954 to bring vast tracts of virgin land in Kazakhstan under cultivation. The intention was to assure a rapid increase in grain production by extending the acreage. Young people, equipped with new machines, were sent into the region with the task of establishing new settlements and vast new state farms. After several good harvests, the yields fell owing to the vagaries of natural conditions. The campaign achieved a limited success at best. Investments were high, but the results were uncertain and mediocre.[47] Everything had to be built from scratch: roads, farm buildings, dwelling houses, schools, hospitals, silos, storage depots. Tractors and equipment had to be brought in. The extension of the cultivated acreage beyond the limits of established settlements meant that, while agricultural land had been gained, marginal soils had now to be tilled under marginal ecological conditions.

The cultivation and settlement of the virgin lands was not abandoned, despite the difficulties and obstacles; but a certain policy change was introduced after the overthrow of Khrushchev and his group: once again measures were taken to advance and intensify production in the regions with established settlements by the increased use of machines, fertilisers and plant protection agents, and by expanding animal production, introducing drainage schemes, and so on. In the course of the virgin lands campaign the area of the state farms was substantially increased. This was due above all to the cultivation of new lands, and only to a lesser extent, if at all, to the liquidation of collective farms and their conversion into state farms. Yields in the virgin land regions were lower than in the rest of the Soviet Union, and thus depressed the average.

But the total cultivated acreage was expanded within five years by more than 38 million ha, an increase of almost 25 per cent, while grain production rose by 71 per cent from 82.5 to 141.2 million tonnes.

Despite the large investments and the tremendous human exertion involved, this campaign can be justified macro-economically, at least in the long run. In the regions with old-established settlements, planning can to a certain extent draw on existing assets – farm buildings, dwelling houses, drainage installations and the whole infrastructure – accumulated by peasant investment over the centuries. But it is in most cases difficult to extend the agricultural area, because of the shortage of land and existing user rights. In order to modernise and intensify production, an administrative and advisory apparatus is required, and this finds itself face to face with the peasant masses who are attached to their ancient customs and age-old experience and who resist rapid innovation and quick changes. If production rises, the additional produce reaches the market only slowly and in part, the remainder being diverted to higher local consumption, and partly to the household plots. In the virgin land territories, on the other hand, new planning cannot benefit from the fruits of former investment, but neither is it hamstrung by old-established user rights and the rigidity of an established social structure. Once the large investments have been made, production can be rapidly increased, and there is no difficulty in ensuring that all of it reaches the market. Thus the 'incubation period' from new investments to increased market deliveries can be considerably shortened, though at some economic cost. Cultivation of new lands, therefore, is a venture more easily embarked upon in rich and highly developed economies. But, in near-emergencies it seems a reasonable strategy to achieve a quick breakthrough in production.

3.5.2.3. The output

As shown in Table 3.13., the cropped acreage was substantially increased – from 118 million ha in 1913 to 216 million in 1974, a rise of 83 per cent. The increase in acreage was below average for cereals, above average for cash crops and fodder crops. Production rose at a higher rate, the grain crop from 86 million tonnes in 1913 to no less than 222.5 million tonnes in 1973, only to drop back to 195.6 million tonnes in 1974, followed in 1975 by a truly disastrous harvest, estimated officially to have fallen short of the target by about 75 million tonnes. 1976 again gave excellent results, passing all earlier years: an example illustrating the range of annual fluctuations and the degree of dependence on the vagaries of nature. In general, grain production has more than doubled since 1913. Sugar-beet recorded eight times 'the harvest of 1913, while the

Table 3.13.: Trends of agricultural production and use of means of production

	1913	1940	1950	1960	1970	1971	1973	1974
1. Crop farming (million ha)								
Grain	104.6	110.7	102.9	115.6	119.3	117.9	126.7	127.2
Commercial crops(total)	4.9	11.8	12.2	13.1	14.5	14.3	14.7	14.7
cotton	0.7	2.1	2.3	2.2	2.8	2.8	2.7	2.9
sugar beet	0.7	1.2	1.3	3.0	3.4	3.3	3.6	3.6
sunflower	1.0	3.5	3.6	4.2	4.8	4.5	4.8	4.7
Potatoes	4.2	7.7	8.6	9.1	8.1	7.9	8.0	8.0
Fodder crops	3.3	18.1	20.7	63.1	62.8	65.2	63.4	64.4
All crops	118.2	150.6	146.3	203.0	206.7	207.3	215.0	216.5
2. Gross production (million tonnes)								
Grain	86.0	95.6	81.2	125.5	186.8	181.2	222.5	195.6
Sugar beet	11.3	18.0	20.8	57.7	78.8	72.2	86.8	76.4
Potatoes	31.9	76.1	88.6	84.4	96.8	92.7	107.7	80.7
3. Yields (q per ha)								
Grain	8.2	8.6	7.9	10.9	15.6	15.4	17.6	15.4
Sugar beet	168	146	159	191	237	219	244	212
Potatoes	76	99	104	92	120	117	134	101
4. Animal production								
Meat (mn. tonnes)	5.0	4.7	4.9	8.7	12.3	13.3	13.5	14.5
Milk (mn. tonnes)	29.4	33.6	35.3	61.7	83.0	83.2	88.3	91.8
Eggs ('000 mn.)	11.9	12.2	11.7	27.4	40.7	45.1	51.2	55.0
Milk yield per cow (kg per year)	982	1,185	1,370	1,779	2,110	2,105	2,186	2,255
5. Main inputs								
Fertilizers kg/ha bulk	0.2	3.2	11.4	11.4	45.6	50.5	60.0	66.0
pure nutrients	0.03	3.7	12.2	12.2	10.4	11.5	13.8	15.0
Tractors ('000)	27 [1])	531	595	1,122	1,977	2,046	2,188	2,289

	1916	1941	1951	1961	1966	1971	1972	1973	1974
6. Livestock (millions)									
Cattle	58.4	54.8	57.1	75.8	93.4	99.2	102.4	104.0	106.3
cows	28.8	28.0	24.3	34.8	39.3	39.8	40.0	40.6	41.5
Pigs	23.0	27.6	24.4	58.7	59.6	67.5	71.4	66.6	70.0
Sheep	89.7	80.0	82.6	133.6	129.8	138.0	139.9	139.1	142.6
Horses	.	.	13.8	9.9	8.0	7.4	7.3	6.8	.

[1]) 1928

Sources: ADSL, after "Ökonomik der Landwirtschaft" no. 11, 1967; Kolesnikow (1970); Schinke (1967); Narodnoe khozyaystvo; SSSR ve cifrach

potato crop increased threefold. Here a distinction is necessary between the long-term trends, which are clearly rising, and the marked fluctuations from year to year, shown in Table 3.13.[48]

Yields per hectare have also developed favourably; they have doubled for grain, almost doubled for potatoes and risen by 26 per cent for sugar-beet. Even so, yields are still much lower than those obtained in capitalist Western Europe, or in socialist Eastern Europe for that matter.[49] But average yields for the Soviet Union as a whole are little revealing. In the densely populated zones of the agrarian triangle[50] yields are probably much above the national average. It can be assumed, that the intensity of farming varies widely in various demographically and economically determined zones. Regional data would probably confirm this conjecture. Differences in yields are no doubt as wide within the Soviet Union as they are between Western Europe and the Soviet Union as a whole.

In animal husbandry progress has been slow in overcoming the consequences of collectivisation (1929-1933), when stocks were depleted by large-scale slaughter. The cattle population has increased again – by 51 million head (46 per cent) over a period of almost 60 years (1916-1975). Dairy cows in particular have increased by 45 per cent. As for pigs, marked fluctuations occurred even a long time after collectivisation owing to reasons such as availability of feeds, more sensitive response of production to various economic factors, better adaptability of the pig population due to rapid reproduction. The long-term trend, however, shows a strong increase – from 23 to 72 million pigs, a rise of more than 200 per cent. Sheep have similarly increased. Only horses have declined numerically, and must be expected to decline still further as mechanisation is extended and improved. The fact that there are still more than 7 million horses on the farms highlights the deficiency in mechanical equipment.

Animal production shows a good record in actual performance: meat production has increased by 190 per cent, milk by 210 per cent, eggs by about 350 per cent. But in terms of output per head of population, the quantity of animal products has changed much less since 1913, while demand and social customs have come to require a diet with a higher proportion of animal products. Production per animal has improved substantially, but has not reached the levels of more intensive farming.

Finally, the Table shows the close correlation between the main inputs and output.

Development of production and demand. The development of production can barely keep up with the population growth and the qualitative changes in demand. Production is still largely dependent on natural conditions.

Table 3.14.: Demand for, and production of, selected agricultural products

	Total demand				Domestic production			
	1961-63	1975 (high)	(low)	Average percentage increase per year	1961-63	1975 (high)	(low)	Average percentage increase per year
Grain [1])	95.4	126.3	124.6	2.1	98.5	137.2	127.7	2.3
Sugar	8.0	12.3	11.7	3.2	6.3	12.0	12.0	5.1
Cotton	1.33	1.61	1.53	2.8	1.59	2.37	2.28	6.5
Fats and oils	3.7	6.3	5.9	4.1	3.75	6.2	5.8	3.7
Meat [2])	7.46	11.6	11.0	3.2	7.46	10.9	10.4	2.8
Milk [3])	62.0	85.2	85.2	2.5	63.3	87.1	87.1	2.5
Eggs	1.63	2.4	2.3	2.8	1.62	2.4	2.3	2.8
Wool	0.25	0.38	0.38	3.3	0.23	0.42	0.39	4.6

[1]) Including rice
[2]) Not including offals
[3]) Not including butter (recorded under "fats and oils")

Sources: Agricultural projections (1968)

Owing to the low capital intensity of agriculture, harvests are fluctuating from year to year by wide margins. From time to time foodstuffs are imported on a large scale, then again food is exported. According to earlier FAO estimates (Table 3.14), demand was expected to increase considerably up to 1975, especially in respect of products with a high conversion factor. This suggests the need for a steep long-term increase in production.

3.5.3. *Evaluation of long-term performance*

A picture of the long-term production trend of Soviet agriculture as compared with population growth is presented in Table 3.15 and Fig. 3.5.

After a period of great upheavals and severe crises – the First World War and its aftermath, collectivisation, the Second World War and its aftermath – production rose steeply, considerably faster than the population. Whereas from 1913 to 1974 the population rose by 57.6 per cent, total agricultureal output increased by 234 per cent; in other words, output per inhabitant more than doubled. Crops and animal husbandry have on the whole moved in parallel, but a faster increase of the latter is desirable. The setbacks to animal production were much more severe and lasted longer than those affecting arable farming. In the livestock sector it took a long time to overcome the consequences of the mass slaughter of

Table 3.15.: Trends of agricultural production and population of Tsarist Russia and Soviet Union (1913-1974)

Year	Crops	Animal products	Agricultural production	Population
1913	100	100	100	100
1917	81	100	88	103.0
1921	55	67	60	–
1923	84	88	86	–
1925	107	121	112	92.3
1927	113	134	121	–
1929	116	129	121	96.1
1933	121	65	101	–
1935	138	86	119	–
1937	150	109	134	117.6
1938	120	120	120	119.9
1939	125	119	121	–
1940	155	114	141	120.4
1942	–	–	54	–
1945	93	72	86	–
1946	100	87	95	–
1947	140	89	122	–
1948	158	96	136	–
1950	151	118	140	114.1
1952	148	129	142	118.0
1954	153	153	153	122.0
1955	175	160	170	124.1
1960	226	219	224	133.4
1962	229	235	233	–
1964	270	217	247	142.1
1965	247	254	252	144.0
1966	281	264	274	145.9
1970	313	302	309	151.8
1971	309	313	312	153.2
1973	341	340	339	155.4
1974	329	347	337	157.6

Sources: Strauss (1969); Informationen zur polit. Bildung: Narodnoe khozyaystvo

cattle that had been the peasants' response to collectivisation. Productivity in the livestock sector is being improved, but performance so far is still indifferent. The effect of internal and external factors seems to be more lasting. Rises and falls in animal production naturally occur within a certain time after the corresponding development in plant production.

Table 3.15 and Fig. 3.5 clearly illustrate the positive and negative effects which some measures of agricultural policy had on production. Lenin's

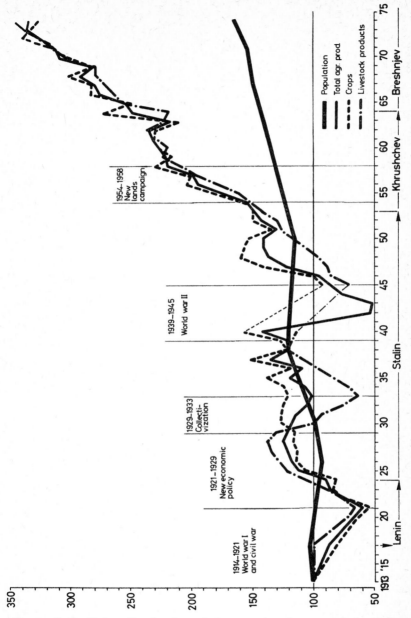

Fig. 3.5. Soviet Union: Trends of population growth and gross agricultural production 1913-1974 (1913 = 100)

NEP, Khrushchev's virgin lands campaign and the priorities recently laid down for industries serving agriculture all show up in the production curves. The negative short-term effect of collectivisation on production is also manifest.[51]

Every social transformation is painful and exacts social costs. If it is gradual, spread over a long period of time, and if the price is exacted from individuals, the cost is not readily discernible. It may also happen that production losses incurred as a result of the transformation are outbalanced by a general trend of rising production. The radical transformation of the agrarian structure, embracing the entire agricultural population and effected in a minimum of time, compresses all the negative social and production effects into that brief period, while the positive effects do not appear till later. Whether or not it would have been possible without collectivisation to have brought about a production increase of the same magnitude with equally low inputs in the agrarian sector is a question that will never be settled. The answer will depend entirely on the observer's point of view.

3.5.4. *Basic features of farm policies after the Stalin era*
The new era began at about the time of Stalin's death – that is to say at the end of the period of reconstruction which followed the devastation of large areas of the country in the second world war – and lasted into the early 1960s, when the introduction of the new economic system may be considered to have marked the opening of a new chapter of Soviet economic history. Changes were effected in four spheres:
a. Structure,
b. production and its requirements,
c. market and price policies,
d. welfare policy for the collective farmers.

3.5.4.1. Structural measures
Farm size and organisation. – In the past the medium-sized farms had been amalgamated into ever larger units (gigantomania). The idea of economies of scale was transferred from industry, ignoring the distinctions. Now, scientific investigations were launched to ascertain the optimum size. Moreover, no further amalgamations were undertaken; instead, attempts were made to link numbers of collective farms through schemes of economic co-operation and the formation of kombinats (in which the powers of the central administration are limited), and decentralisation was fostered by the establishment of semi-autonomous sub-units. Large working groups were divided into smaller units. The individual workers in sovkhozes and kolkhozes were given more responsibility. All jobs

concerned with any one particular crop or livestock were assigned to particular workers on a permanent basis.

Changes in the household plot. At present, the tendency to enlarge them prevails. The function of the household plot as a factor complementing the instrument of basic central planning is now recognised and appreciated.

The machine and tractor stations were wound up in 1958 and their machines were sold off to the collective farms. (See subsection 3.5.1.4.).

The *kolkhozes* are recognised as a lasting element in the structure of a socialist agrarian system. The idea of converting them into state farms has been abandoned.

3.5.4.2. Promotion of production

In the past, agriculture was equipped with a minimum of production aids. Deliberately and methodically the scarce investment resources were concentrated on other sectors. For a long period agriculture was not only denied all development finance but actually subjected to disinvestment by the exaction of a financial contribution to the development of the other economic sectors. In the end the stagnation of agriculture endangered the expansion of the rest of the economy. On the other hand, the successful expansion of industry provides the basis for new large-scale investments for the benefit of agriculture: agricultural machines, fertilisers, plant protection agents, buildings, land improvement, supply of consumer goods to the rural population. Thus industry has paved the way for the transition from extensive to intensive agricultural production: less reclamation of virgin lands, more investments in land already under cultivation. In the first phase all the forces of society were concentrated on the transformation of the agrarian structure. The undeniable advantages of large-scale production were overrated. Indeed, as Dumont (1964) has pointed out, large-scale production without technology is not industry at all, but belongs to the pre-industrial stage of manufacture.

Communist critics of Stalin declared, 'The collectivisation of wooden ploughs is a fraud'.[52] Perhaps a virtue was made here of necessity, and a theory was devised to rationalise the shortage of productive equipment. Accordingly, the role of technology in transforming the agrarian structure and influencing the attitude of the peasants was underestimated to begin with and subsequently replaced by administrative measures and coercion. Today, the significance of machines and fertilisers is recognised and taken into account by communist planners. The same debate about the relative importance of productive forces versus production relations took place in China at a later date (see Chapter 4.2.3.).

3.5.4.3. Marketing and price policies

A liberal period (New Economic Policy) was followed by a phase of central planning, in which agriculture was disadvantaged through the price scissors, that is unfavorable relations between prices for agricultural commodities and industrial goods which were strictly maintained by rigorous price controls on goods sold through official channels, combined with the rationing of important products. By contrast, the policy now is to cheapen the peasants' productive equipment and consumer goods, but not foodstuffs. Producer prices were raised by several methods:

a. Compulsory delivery quotas were repeatedly reduced (since July 1957, the products of the household plots have been sold freely);
b. the prices for the remaining quota deliveries were brought closer to the free market prices;
c. price controls on non-staple foods sold at the kolkhoz markets were lifted.

The dual market is abolished step by step. In contrast to the former one-sided delivery obligations, the determination of quantities, delivery dates, prices and quality is now hammered out in negotiations between equal partners at regional level. Perhaps this will lead to flexible planning without market chaos, instead of the rigid planning of the past, accompanied by delivery chaos. Compulsory deliveries at prices fixed substantially below the level of market prices are equivalent to a tax levied in kind. If that method is abandoned, some other form of taxation, openly visible and subject to inspection, must be found.

3.5.4.4. Welfare policies for the collective farmers

After the prolonged period of low pay, successive improvements were made first in the assessment, then in the payment, of the *trudoden*, the work unit. In the early days remuneration for work was paid out only or predominantly after the harvest. Later that method of computing wages was abolished altogether. Gradually payments for work were made more and more frequently, till in the end the collective farmers received fixed monthly payments at roughly the level of the wages of sovkhoz workers. This development depended on an increase in revenue and greater independence of the collective farms. The aim was gradually to introduce a guaranteed remuneration for the working collective farmers. On 1 June 1966, a guaranteed minimum wage was actually laid down for all collective farms. In the past – as stated above – the wage received by the collective farmer had been a residual payment, entirely dependent on crop yields and harvest results, while all other commitments and items of expenditure of the collective farms had to be settled first in a definite order of priorities laid down by finance directives. Now wages have a higher priority; the livelihood of the collective farmer is assured.

Data about actual wages and incomes are very scanty and difficult to evaluate, since the purchasing power remains unknown.[53] The rough figures of Table 3.16. show a general rise of monthly wages for the three

Table 3.16.: Average monthly wages (in roubles)

	1965	1967	1970	1974
Workers and salaried employees	96.5	104.7	122.0	140.7
Workers and salaried employees in state Farms and similar establishments	74.6	84.4	101.1	124.0
Collective farmers	52.3	62.7	88.2	107.5

Sources: Brunner and Westen (1970); Mitteilungen BfA; SSSR ve cifrach (1975)

categories named. But there is a substantial and enduring threefold social gradient between town and country, between industry and agriculture and, within agriculture, between state farm workers and collective farmers. This fact is confirmed by Table 3.17., part b.

The composition of the wages differs. The family plot contributes 37 per cent of the family income in the kolkhoz. This figure, for a number of reasons,[54] may be an underestimate. But, income in kind and the lower cost of food in the village cannot entirely compensate for these differentials. Thus the disparity in the status of the rural population continues, though it is somewhat less acute than it used to be. Official policy strives to end this discrimination against the agrarian sector, but so far has not fully realised this aim. Perhaps it is necessary for some disadvantages to remain, in order to encourage the flow of manpower away from agriculture, a trend that is closely connected with social mobility, social change and economic development. Not until the agricultural population has dropped to about 10 per cent of the total population, as is the rule in modern countries, will society be in a position to abolish the underpayment of the villagers. The elimination of the discrepancy will then become economically possible and socially necessary.

In the early stages planning was inevitably focused on the need to mobilise the factor contribution of agriculture (labour and capital) for

Table 3.17.: Structure of family income by social categories

a. Structure of family income

	Industrial workers	Employees	Sovkhoz workers	Kolkhoz members
	Percentage			
Wages	71.5	72.5	66.0	47.6
Output of family plots	1.0	0.5	21.4	37.0
Pensions, scholarships, other allowances	26.5	25.5	8.5	
Other income	1.0	1.5	4.1	15.4
Total	100.0	100.0	100.0	100.0

b. Farm wages and income as compared with industrial labour force (1966)

	Industrial workers	Sovkhoz workers	Kolkhoz members
Wages	100	76.9	55.8
Family income	100	91.0	77.6
Family income per capita	100	69.4	66.3

Source: Sakoff (1972)

the general economic take-off. The effects of that policy are clearly visible; they are still felt by the peasant population even now.

Social insurance. The free health service was available from the outset for all inhabitants of the Soviet Union. The collective farmers also received children's allowances and maternity grants. However, they were excluded from the general old-age insurance. Instead, the kolkhozes were obliged by law to maintain funds of their own, out of which relatively low old-age allowances had to be paid. Gradually the kolkhoz members were integrated into the general old-age insurance scheme. This process began in 1965 and was completed in 1970. Now the collective farmers qualify for old-age pensions under virtually the same conditions as apply to all workers and salaried employees: men receive the old-age pension from the age of 60, women from 55, but the amount of their pensions is only 85 per cent of what industrial workers get. The 15 per cent is intended to take account of the lower cost of foodstuffs and the income from the household plots. It is the intention of the authorities to take action in the future to bring agricultural pensions more closely into line with the rest.

3.6. *Social effects and strategies of mobilisation*

The radical social transformation of society and the economy deeply affected every citizen, liquidated old social classes and created new classes with a different status and with new problems. Before 1917, there was a very tiny working class, and before 1929 there was no collective farmer, a social category that existed nowhere in the world.

3.6.1. *The new status of the collective farmer and of the kolkhoz*

In terms of rural sociology, the kolkhoz peasant represents a special category, as typical of his sphere as the West European farmers, the North American wheat growers, the share croppers of the rice-growing areas, and the plantation labourers of the monocultures are typical of theirs. This type of cultivator was created for the first time by the planned social transformation of the whole agrarian system in a vast country. He works with modern techniques in large enterprises and relatively large working groups, not so far in his capacity as an individual worker. Many opportunities of education and development are open to him. Within the limits defined by state planning and direction he has the statutory right to participate in the running of the enterprise. In his social status the collective farmer differs from the state farm workers in several ways, which are summed up in Chart 2.1.

In terms of numbers these two groups are the most important in the socialist agriculture of the collectivised economic systems. Their social status differs in many respects. A third group, numerically smaller but socially of extreme importance, is that of the technical intelligentsia: economists, agronomists, zootechnicians, engineers, administrators, etc.

Probably employment is more even at the state farms than at the collective farms. Since the effective work load in agriculture is subject to seasonal fluctuations, it means that this 'natural loss' is transferred to the state. This state of affairs provides an additional impulse for promoting the diversification of the work of the state farms by animal production, processing of crops, auxiliary industries, and so on. It is also a fiscal barrier against the transformation of collective into state farms,[55] should such a measure ever be seriously considered.

The worker at the state farm receives his regular wage, irrespective of the harvest results, in accordance with the collective agreement negotiated between his union and the Ministry of Agriculture. The collective farmer used to be much more dependent on the year's harvest and on the farm management. This changed only in recent years, when the remuneration of the collective farmer was brought more closely into line with that of the sovkhoz worker.

Soviet Union – model of a settled revolution

Chart 2.1. Social status of sovkhoz worker and kolkhoz peasant

Aspect	Sovkhoz	Kolkhoz
Employment	more regular, all the year round	more seasonal
Remuneration		
a. mode	assured, regular wage	originally: residual payment; now: assured income, more closely in line with sovkhoz wage
b. amount		
in cash	higher	lower
in kind	less	more
household plot	less	more extensive and free
Social security		
a. health service	yes	yes
b. maternity grant and children's allowance	yes	yes
c. old-age pension	yes	originally: only from local kolkhoz funds, since 1970: included in comprehensive state insurance scheme
Vocational and social promotion	more effective	originally: less opportunity; now: almost equal opportunity
Occupational representation	trade union	1935-1970: none; now: attempt in progress to establish representative bodies at all levels
Participation in decision-making	not provided for	complete, if and when cooperative democracy has been restored

As regards education, vocational training and social betterment, the state farm workers were in a somewhat more favourable position. Having all along been in charge of their technical equipment, the state farms were able to train and encourage their workers, and they were serving their own interests in doing so. The collective farms did not reach a similar position until 1958, when the machine and tractor stations were wound up, and their machines disposed of to the kolkhozes.

To begin with, social security was more comprehensive at the state farms. Their workers and salaried employees were from the outset included in the health service, old-age insurance, maternity and family allowances as well as accident insurance. The gradual narrowing of the gap in social security and social policy benefits will eventually lead to full equality.

On paper the collective farmers have greater rights to a say in the management and production programme of their farm, in the activities of the chairman and the elected committees, in the distribution of any surplus, and so on, than are enjoyed by the sovkhoz workers. Those rights, however, were substantially curtailed through central planning, the statutes and administrative supervision. The sovkhoz worker has no share in the management of his farm; but the kolkhoz peasants and their farms have no one to represent them in their dealings with the state administration, the purchasing enterprises, and so on. There is no peasant association nor any organisation speaking on behalf of the collective farms as a whole and putting forward their views, wishes and demands. Only the chairman can try to discuss the case of his particular kolkhoz with the state administration.

During the early 1930s there were beginnings of democratic organisations in this sphere. But the speed and ruthlessness of collectivisation during the Stalin era led to peasant resistance. Attempts to persuade and convince were replaced by coercion and terror. The budding shoots of cooperative democracy were stamped out very soon and drowned in the barbarities of social transformation. The official thesis was that peasants and workers were working and fighting side by side in their alliance, since their interests were identical. That may be true in the long run, but it is certainly not the case in the short run. However, on the basis of that contention the peasants were not allowed to form organisations of their own. From the point of view of macro-economics, the government's policy on this point paid off. But the social cost was, and still is, high and must not be ignored. Since the end of 1969, a new attempt has been made to re-establish some representation for the collective farmers. As for the employees of the sovkhozes, they are members of their trade union and can let the union act on their behalf in putting forward their demands.

The collective farm ought to be democratically organised, with open communication between the elected management and the working members. Official guidelines must be discussed, and the members have to be persuaded to accept them and act on them. At the same time – as stated above (Chapter 3.5.1.1.) – the members should exercise supervision over the leadership and re-elect or dismiss it. In the special case of co-operative production, the co-operative system implies the identity of members and workers: in the co-operative all members work and all workers are members. This leads to the complete identification of the co-operators with their enterprise. Such an attitude is supported and reinforced by economic incentives. But the more the free decisions of the members are circumscribed by state directives and planning regulations, the harder it is for them to identify with their enterprise and to exercise the statutory local supervision. Conversely, a more strongly developed co-operative democracy provides the members with a motivation for improved performance and intensive participation and supervision at their farm.

The dismantling of central dirigism and central controls permits and indeed demands the more active participation of the kolkhoz members, whose share in decision-making had previously existed only on paper. Originally the co-operatives were democratic bodies, and there were formal safeguards to protect that democracy. Perhaps democracy comes in the wake of rising standards of living and better education. The new generation is free of bitterness. It did not witness the grim sequence of feudal oppression up to 1917, peasant revolution and land seizure between 1917 and 1920, the New Economic Policy in 1920-1928, collectivisation and coercion in 1929-1934. It is able to demand co-operative democracy and to work it, without resentment or psychological inhibitions.

The fact that the peasants did not join voluntarily but under coercion becomes less painful and less important as time goes on. Today's members were born into the kolkhoz. The labour market, now almost free, enables them to leave the farms and forces the authorities to improve working and living conditions at the kolkhoz. Loss of manpower to the towns and the predominance of older age groups among those remaining behind have become urgent problems. In the past nobody could be expelled from a collective farm; the kolkhozes were compelled to keep their members, irrespective of economic good sense and the needs of technical development. Now, expulsion is to be permitted to promote the mobility of labour.[56]

Democratisation, thus, has a double task:
a. to give more responsibility to members and to stimulate their identification and interest,
b. putting the managers on their mettle through sharper local supervision by the rank and file.
In modern industrial states the shift of population away from the countryside is effected by the pressure of economic forces and the attraction of industry. In the developing countries it is hardly possible to exert economic coercion, nor is there any scope for offering material incentives. Political coercion acts more harshly, as it is experienced more consciously and leaves the victim no alternative. Perhaps the motivation of the kolkhoz members will now be effectively stimulated by
a. training, prospect of rising socially to the rank of qualified technician, higher responsibility, democratic management;

b. a modern wage system;
c. higher income through an increase in production and better terms of trade;
d. inclusion of the collective farmers in the state social insurance scheme.

Underemployment continues to cause concern. Establishment of industries in the village, diversification of the village economy, closer dovetailing of industry and agriculture, and extension of animal husbandry are the kind of measures that may eliminate underemployment. But sparse settlement, long distances, poor infrastructure are obstacles in the way of decentralised industrialisation.

3.6.2. *The new working class – social composition*

The agricultural population – those who remained in the collective and state farms – experienced change chiefly in terms of social status. Their homes, environment, food habits, working tasks were not affected until the new technology and production methods were introduced on a massive scale, and that happened a long time after the transformation of the social structure. The industrial workers and salaried employees are a wholly new class, numerically and qualitatively. It grew from about 3 million in 1917 to about 100 million in 1974. Quantitative development and development of social structure are shown in Table 3.18.

The number of economically active persons rose steadily from 84 million in 1960 to 115.7 million in 1974, an increase of 37 per cent. The relative growth exceeded that of the total population, so that the proportion of economically active inhabitants rose from 39.7 to 46.1 per cent. Only 14 per cent of all gainfully employed persons are described as "self-employed", which means that they bear collectively a limited risk of employment and income, the limiting factor being collective solidarity. The other 86 per cent receive their regular income from the state and its institutions as their sole employer. – The number of collective farmers has diminished, as shown above, while the branches of the secondary and tertiary sectors increased their employment. – The proportion of working women rose from 34.8 to 44.3 per cent in 1974. They supplied 85 per cent of the manpower in the health service, 76 per cent in banks and insurance, 75 per cent in trade, 72 per cent in education and 58 per cent in public administration.[57]

Unfortunately, our knowledge of income distribution and social stratification of the new working class is negligible. There are monographs about one factory or a few "typical" families, but no comprehensive statistics.[58]

Table 3.18.: Gainful employment 1960-1974

Category/Economic sector	1960	1965	1970	1974	1974 as % of 1960
	Millions				
Gainfully employed	84.3	95.8	107.2	115.7	+ 37.2
thereof kolkhoz members	22.3	18.9	17.0	15.7	− 28.7
other employment	62.0	76.9	90.2	99.8	+ 61.0
workers	45.9	55.9	64.3	70.2	+ 52.9
women	29.3	37.7	45.8	51.3	+ 75.1
	Thousands				
Workers + employees by sector					
Agriculture	6,793	8,704	9,180	10,100	+ 48.7
sovkhozes + secondary activities	6,022	8,250	8,593	9,400	+ 56.1
Forestry	359	402	433	450	+ 25.3
Manufacturing industry [1])	22,620	27,447	31,593	33,370	+ 47.5
thereof workers	?	22,350	25,631	27,050	?
Construction	5,143	5,685	6,994	7,700	+ 49.7
thereof workers	?	4,892	5,824	6,630	?
Trade + distribution	4,675	6,009	7,537	8,660	+ 85.2
Transportation	6,279	7,252	7,985	8,980	+ 43.0
Communications	738	1,007	1,330	1,500	+ 103.3
Banking + insurance	265	300	388	490	+ 84.9
Public health	3,461	4,277	5,080	5,660	+ 63.5
Education	4,803	6,600	8,025	8,960	+ 86.6
Science + research	1,763	2,625	3,238	3,900	+ 121.2
Municipalities[2])	1,920	2,386	3,052	3,660	+ 90.6
Public + economic administration	1,245	1,460	1,883	2,160	+ 73.5
Others	1,968	2,761	3,482	4,110	+ 108.8
Kolkhoz members ⎫ in % of all gainfully	26.5	19.7	15.9	13.6	
Kolkhoz + sovkhoz workers ⎬	33.6	28.3	23.9	21.7	
women ⎭ employed	34.8	39.4	42.7	44.3	
Rate of gainful employment	39.7	41.8	44.0	46.1	

[1]) Including energy and mining
[2]) Housing and communal services

Sources: Länderberichte; author's calculations; Narodnoye khozyaystvo

3.6.3. *The new working class – social problems and their solution*

The emergence of a new class of 100 million workers and employees creates a number of material and socio-cultural problems, which ought to be solved for these millions simultaneously with economic development. The main *material problems* are housing, assured food supplies (necessitating increased output from a shrinking agricultural population and the creation of adequate facilities for storage, distribution and sale), communication systems, technical infrastructure, schools of all grades. Among the main *sociocultural problems* are: a new social security scheme, an adequate system of remuneration, understanding of new working methods, factory discipline, integration into new urban environment, change of status from peasant to factory worker.

For the planners, rapid acclimatisation and acculturation of the new workforce ranked first. At first, it was possible, and necessary, to harness revolutionary enthusiasm: voluntary labour, subbotnik (unpaid weekend work). This mood was encouraged by reducing income differentials to a minimum (party maximum, levelling) and rationing basic commodities and needs. To make use of the experience, organisation and manpower of the Red Army, Trotsky in 1919 proposed the militarisation of work: simultaneously with demobilisation after the victory in the civil war, labour units were to be formed for large development projects, so as to introduce the benefits of the Army's discipline and technical know-how in the economic sphere.

Later on, attempts were made to spur the masses of still unskilled workers to higher efforts by examples of good performance (shock workers, Stakhanov and his various successors). Awards, decorations, public mention were among the many moral incentives. During the phase of accelerated industrialisation, the labour market was put under strict administrative control (labour pass, ban on changing of employment). Wide wage differentials were introduced, depending on qualifications, while quantitative performance was encouraged by the award of bonuses for fulfilment and overfulfilment of norms. Special benefits of various types further widened the income differentials (housing, holiday opportunities). Beside the material incentives the moral ones were maintained.

In the post-Stalin era, material supplies and rumuneration were improved. Income differentials were probably reduced. The labour market has been largely liberalised.

As stated in the foregoing, no statistical information is available on social stratification. There are, however, several income levels reflecting occupational differences (intelligentsia, engineers, skilled, unskilled workers), differentials between intellectual and manual work, between

Table 3.19.: National budget

	1,000 million rubles						per cent			
	1960	1965	1970	1971	1973	1974¹	1960	1970	1971	1974
Revenue										
Sales tax	31.3	38.7	49.4	54.5	59.1	63.8	40.6	31.5	32.8	31.9
Profit of state enterprises and organizations	18.6	30.9	54.2	55.6	60.0	64.5	24.1	34.6	33.5	32.2
Income tax of enterprises, cooperatives, organizations	1.8	1.5	26.0	28.2	.		2.3	16.6	17.0	.
Public loans	0.1	0.2					0.1			
Social security contributions	3.8	5.6	8.3	8.8	9.9	10.4	4.9	5.3	5.3	5.2
Direct taxes	5.6	7.7	12.7	13.7	15.8	16.9	7.3	8.1	8.3	8.4
Total²	77.1	102.3	156.7	166.0	187.8	200.3	.		.	.
Expenditure										
National economy	34.1	44.9	74.6	80.4	91.3	100.8	46.6	48.3	49.0	50.7
Socio-cultural activities	24.9	38.2	55.9	59.4	67.3	71.2	34.0	36.2	36.2	35.8
thereof										
Education, science, research	10.3	17.5	24.7	25.8	29.8	.	14.1	16.0	15.7	.
Health + sport	4.8	6.7	9.2	9.3	10.2	.	6.6	6.0	5.6	.
Social assistance + security, aid for mothers with many children, single mothers, all-union fund³	9.8	14.0	22.1	23.3	27.4	.	13.4	14.3	14.2	.
Defence	9.3	12.8	17.9	17.9	17.9	17.7	12.7	11.6	10.9	8.9
Administration	1.1	1.3	1.7	1.8	1.9	1.9	1.5	1.1	1.1	0.9
Total²	73.1	101.6	154.6	164.2	184.0	198.5	.	.	.	.
Revenue ./. expenses	4.0	0.7	2.1	1.8	3.8	1.8				

¹) Preliminary; ²) Total is larger than sum of figures, because not all items of revenue or expenditure are listed; ³) Collective farmers' social insurance fund

Sources: Länderberichte; SSSR ve cifrach

town and country, and in the village between state farm worker and
collective peasant. The revolution liquidated the old ruling class and
thus aimed at social levelling; the Stalin era aimed at differentiation.
After Stalin's death, differentials were again reduced. – A comprehensive
system of social security was created.

The trade unions represent the socio-economic interests of the new
class of workers and employees. From their angle, problems look
different, sometimes fundamentally different, than they appear to the
economic planner. Solutions that are economically highly acceptable are
frequently rejected on social grounds. But the opposition of the trade
unions and their ability freely to represent their membership was broken
by harsh measures in the 1920s.[59]

3.7. *National budget and national product*

Like all macro-economic figures, the budget figures of countries with a
planned economy are hardly comparable with similar data for capitalist
countries with a private enterprise system. In a planned economy, nearly
all investment is the government's responsibility. In 1974 investment
accounted for over half – 51 per cent – of the Soviet budget (see Table
3.19). The next important fields of expenditure are education and science
with 16 per cent (in 1971) and social security, with 14 per cent of total
Government expenditure. Defence in 1974 absorbed almost R 18,000
million, or 9 per cent. It is questionable, whether the budget figure
really covers the entire expenditure on armaments. In view of the close
links between industry, science and defence, the available evidence is
inconclusive. Total expenditure rose over 14 years by 172 per cent,
from R 73,000 to 198,500 million. On the revenue side of the balance
sheet, the largest item is the surpluses (profits) of public enterprises and
organisations. A further third of the total revenue comes from the sales
tax. Direct taxes contribute only 8.4 per cent.

In a similar way, the net national product (see Table 3.20.) is not
easily analysed with the methods applicable to a capitalist economy.
During the period 1963 to 1971, it grew at the rate of 7 to 10 per cent a
year, from 1971 to 1972 by only 2.7 per cent. The per-capita NNP rose
from R 796 to R 1,266, at an annual rate of 5.4 to 9.6 per cent, except for
the last year of the table. Two thirds were privately consumed, about 2
per cent went into social consumption, and more than one quarter was
"accumulated" (invested).

Foreign trade (see Table 3.21.) has grown rapidly in recent years after
an extended period of very restricted exchange. The balance was always
in favour of the Soviet Union. With 12 per cent of the total, farm

Soviet Union – model of a settled revolution

Table 3.20.: Net national product

	Unit	1964	1965	1968	1970	1971	1972
Net national product at current prices							
total	1,000 million rubles	181.3	193.5	244.1	289.9	305.0	313.2
per inhabitant	rubles	796	839	1,024	1,194	1,244	1,266
Annual growth rate [1])	per cent						
total		7.4	6.7	7.8	10.7	8.3	2.7
per inhabitant		6.0	5.4	6.8	9.6	7.2	1.8
Utilisation of NNP							
NNP	1,000 million rubles	181.3	193.5	244.1	289.9	305.0	313.2
thereof	per cent						
private consumption		63.7	70.3	69.4	67.1	67.4	69.0
social consumption		8.1 [2])	2.2 [2])	2.3	2.3	2.4	2.6
accumulation		27.2	16.0 [3])	26.5	29.0	28.6	27.5
Balance of foreign trade [2])	1,000 million rubles	+ 0.9	+ 1.6	+ 4.5	+ 4.4	+ 4.9	+ 2.9

[1]) Against preceding year in the table
[2]) Exports and imports of goods and productive services
[3]) Percentage calculation of utilization of NNP for 1964 and 1965 seems doubtful

Source: Länderberichte

Table 3.21.: Development of foreign trade (mln. US-$)

	1965	1967	1969	1971	1973
Export					
All goods	8,166	9,609	11,655	13,806	21,364
Farm commodities	1,179	1,684	1,696	1,652	1,824
Farm inputs	306	382	399	471	548
Farm commodities as per cent of all	14.4	17.5	14.6	12.0	8.5
Import					
All goods	8,054	8,536	10,327	12,479	21,011
Farm commodities	2,217	1,862	1,922	2,474	5,212
Farm inputs	84	111	234	274	532
Farm commodities as per cent of all	27.5	19.4	18.6	19.8	24.8
Balance exports ./. imports	112	1,073	1,328	1,327	353

Source: FAO Commerce yearbook

products play a minor role in exports, while accounting for no less than 20 per cent of all imports. As a rule, agricultural imports exceed agricultural exports in monetary terms. Main export commodities in 1971 were cereals and sugar, main import products again cereals and sugar, as well as fruit and vegetables, coffee, tea and cocoa. Annual harvest fluctuations greatly affect the balance of agricultural imports and exports. Bad harvests call immediately for large imports and vice versa. The transition from an agrarian to an industrial economy has substantially influenced the structure of foreign trade.

Imports and exports of grain are affected also by obligations towards the partners in Comecon (the Council for Mutual Economic Assistance of the East European socialist countries), who join the Soviet Union in large deals on the world grain market. Re-exports of sugar form part of a long-term agreement with Cuba. That country "pays" for substantial Soviet deliveries largely with sugar.

4. CHINA – MODEL OF THE INTERMITTENT REVOLUTION

4.1. *The point of departure*

4.1.1. *Recent history*

1840   Irruption of the European powers; the Opium War; the Peace of Nanking; unequal treaties. China's weakness leads to a scramble for privileges on the part of the powers.

1850   First attempts at anti-colonialist risings, followed by punitive expeditions and colonial wars, ending with Chinese defeat and new concessions. 1850-64 Taiping rising, accompanied by an attempt at a land reform.

1860   Treaty of Peking: establishment of European legations; removal of restrictions on trade and missionary activities.

1864-78 Muslim rising.

1900   Boxer Rising; punitive expedition under German command. Rivalry between the colonial powers preserves China from partition, hence policy of the open door. As a result of the forcible entry of Western capitalism, China's trade, customs duties and taxes pass into foreign hands; imports of cheap industrial goods destroy Chinese crafts and artisan trades; in the densely populated rural areas standards of living fall; the traditional social order decays; a proletariat and a revolutionary intelligentsia emerge in the growing ports. The Empire declines.

1905-12 Foundation of Kuomintang. 1911 Revolution of the Young Chinese; abdication of last Manchu Emperor.

1912   Establishment of Republic.

1916-26 Internal wars between the warlords.

1921   Foundation of the Communist Party of China.

1925-49 Civil war and peasant risings.

1927   Chiang Kai-shek defeats workers in Canton and other towns and quells peasant risings; expulsion of the Soviet military advisers; beginning of the confrontation between Kuomintang and communists.

1928   Foundation of the Red Army; establishment of peasant associations; expropriation of large estate owners; redistribution of land; reduction of farm rents.

1931   Central government formed in Peking; Japan invades Manchuria.

1934-35 On the Long March to Yenan the Red Army evades Chiang's superior forces.

1937-45 Sino-Japanese war; parts of China occupied.

1949   After its final defeat, the Kuomintang army retreats to Formosa and forms the National Republic of China. A communist central government is formed in Peking.

1950   China (re-)occupies Tibet.

1950-56 Agrarian reform in four stages: distribution of land, mutual aid teams, formation of cooperatives, collectivisation.

1953   First Five-Year Plan.

1957   Abortive offensive against Formosa (Taiwan). – Mao encourages criticism: "Let hundred flowers blossom", but intervenes soon against frank critics.

1958   Setting up of people's communes; Great Leap Forward, ending in failure.

1959   Liu Shao-ch'i becomes President, Mao is relegated to a second-rank position.

1960   Beginning of ideological conflict with Moscow.

1961-63 Famine, unrest, many refugees reach Hongkong.

1962   Open break with CPSU. Border conflict with India.

1964   First Chinese nuclear bomb.

1965-66 Great Proletarian Cultural Revolution, final defeat of Liu Shao-ch'i. Dissolution and reorganisation of CPC.

1969   Armed clashes with Soviet troops over a border island in the Ussuri river.

1971   Lin Piao, Mao Tsetung's chosen heir, is disgraced and probably shot down during his attempted escape to Soviet Russia. China is admitted to the UN, takes her seat in the Security Council, is recognised as a world power.

1972   US president Nixon visits Peking. Near-diplomatic relations established between Washington and Peking.

1973   Tenth CPC Congress unanimously denounces the dead Lin Piao as a traitor.

1974   Improvement of relations with the capitalist nations of Western Europe and the EEC.

1975   Rehabilitation of some survivors of the group ousted in 1965. Teng Hsiao-ping becomes Deputy Premier. Aggravation of hostility between China and the Soviet Union. President Gerald Ford visits China.

1976   January: After the death of Prime Minister Chou En-lai, his aide Teng Hsiao-ping is replaced by Hua Kuo-feng, who becomes Prime Minister.

September: Mao Tsetung dies.

October: Hua Kuo-feng succeeds Mao in all functions. The opposing group is ousted from the Party leadership.

4.1.2. *Natural conditions and population*

China extends from longitude 73° to 135° east, and from latitude 22° to 54° north. The country covers an area of 9,561,000 sq.km. In the west there are high mountain ranges, in the east vast fertile lowland plains; in the north and in Shantung there are forest soils, in the north-west steppe soils, and in the south laterite and red earths.

There are marked climatic differences between the regions: in the north areas with a cool temperate climate; in the south tropical areas; in the west a continental climate; in the east maritime influences. Precipitation is affected by the rainy south-west monsoons in spring and summer. The winters are mostly dry. In the south precipitation is more evenly distributed over the seasons, and the total volume is higher. Peking has an annual rainfall of only 300 mm, the bulk of it between June and August. In the south the figure reaches up to 1,700 mm, and the bigger volume is more evenly distributed. Large areas in the interior of the country are arid or even approaching desert character. Inundations in the great river valleys necessitate flood protection measures, in particular the construction of dykes and reservoirs.

Up to 1949, no comprehensive agricultural statistics were issued, and the computations based on the existing regional investigations and analyses bore little relation to reality. After 1949 statistics were organised on a central basis. But since the setback following the Great Leap Forward no further statistics or statistical year-books have been published by the government. Accordingly all numerical data concerning the population, agriculture and industry are highly uncertain and controversial. They are mostly taken from calculations by Japanese, Soviet and American research workers. It remains to be hoped that domestic political stabilisation and admission to the different bodies of the UN will elicit more, and more reliable, official quantitative data from China herself.

The wide variations between different estimates of basic data are evident from Table 4.1., compiled by Bhattacharya (1974) from various sources. Even official Chinese estimates contradict each other and can vary by more than 10 per cent, which is a margin of error of 80 million

Table 4.1.: Estimates of some basic indicators in 1970

Item	Unit	Official	USSR	Hungary	USA	UK
Population	Mill.	750-830	?	785	836	750
Grain	Mill. tonnes	240	205-210	240	217.5	205
Cotton cloth	1,000 mill. m	8.5	8.0-8.5	8.5	7.5	7.5
Mineral oil	Mill. tonnes	20	18-19	20	18	15
Steel	Mill. tonnes	18	15-16	18	18	15
Fertilisers	Mill. tonnes	14	10	14	7.4	7.5

Source: Bhattacharya (1974)

inhabitants. The difficulties are caused partly by technical problems. Furthermore, the radical social changes within a brief span of time lead to difficulties in assembling data about swift transformations and their disturbing effects. Another source of discrepancies stems from the planning process itself. Each planner or group of specialised planners must be seen as a pressure group, trying to get their message across, so as to fulfil their special task. Thus, figures are sometimes deliberately inflated or played down.[60]

Population estimates diverge widely. It is reasonable to assume that at the end of the 1960s, China had a population of the order of 700 million people. The 1953 census resulted in a figure of 582.6 million; an FAO estimate put the figure at 780.5 million in 1966, while German research workers came out with a figure of 740 to 800 million. The figures of Table 4.2. – derived largely from extrapolation on the assumption of certain rates of growth – indicate that the population has nearly doubled

Table 4.2.: Development of population and economic activity 1912-1969

Year	Total	Annual Growth rate p.c.	Inhabitants per sq. km	Urban popuation	Rural	total	agri-culture	Economically active share of agri-culture
	millions			p.c.		millions		p.c.
1912	430.0	–	45.0	8.5	91.5	–	–	–
1933	500.0	–	52.3	9.3	90.7	–	–	–
1950	546.8	1.7	57.2	10.9	89.1	–	–	–
1952	586.9	2.0	59.5	12.1	87.9	270.4	237.8	87.9
1960	683.0	1.8	71.4	15.5	84.5	361.0	284.6	78.8
1969	798.6	2.0	83.5	14.6	85.4	387.2	329.1	85.0

Source: Rochlin + Hagemann (1971)

since 1912. The growth rate is estimated at about 2.0 per cent per year. The relative proportion of the rural population shows a very gradual decline, while in absolute figures it has constantly increased. The same applies to the number of people working in agriculture, who still represent 85 per cent of the country's labour force. The development of the secondary and tertiary sectors is still too weak to absorb even the annual increment of people of working age.

Population density is very uneven, as illustrated in Table 4.3. and Fig. 4.1. The population is crowded into the coastal regions and the lower reaches of the river valleys, while vast tracts are almost uninhabited or only used by nomads. The Tibetan plateau, at an altitude of over 4,000 m above sea level, does not for the time being lend itself to settlement at increased densities. Other regions, in particular the arid zones of the north-west, still await internal colonisation and reclamation by irrigation and mechanisation.

Between one fifth and one quarter of today's world population are Chinese; but China has only 8 per cent of the world's agricultural land, 1,600 sq. m. per inhabitant. The agricultural population – 85 per cent of the total – contributes 60-70 per cent of all exports in the form of raw materials or goods processed from such materials.

The International Labour Office estimated those economically active, i.e. persons above the age of 10, at 299 millions in 1960 and at 352 millions ten years later. Ca. 13 per cent only were active outside agriculture and can thus be assumed to be on public pay rolls.

4.1.3. *The politico-administrative system*
In spite of its large population and a relatively low development of the infrastructure, China is a centralised nation, administratively divided into 21 provinces and 5 autonomous regions. In 1953, 94 per cent were Han, 6 per cent belonged to various ethnic or national minorities, living mostly in the sparsely populated outlying regions. The cultural uniformity permits a concentration of powers and resources and a centralised administration, that are called for by the desire of a rapid economic take-off. The minorities in the border districts enjoy a certain autonomy. Simultaneously, the "threatened" frontier regions are settled intensively (with Chinese) through a limited internal migration and establishment of (military) state farms.

The Communist Party is in fact the only political party. It has succeeded in ending the regional and centrifugal rule of warlords and military commanders. In its tasks of mobilising and supervising the Party is supported by the Red Army. During certain periods, the Army's political influence outweighed the Party's. The CPC is formally organised

Table 4.3.: Area and population 1957, 1970

Administrative unit	Capital	Area 1000 sq. km	Population ¹) millions		Inhabitants per sq. km	
			1957	1970	1957	1970
Provinces						
NE-China						
Heilungkiang	Harbin	464	15	25	34	53
Kilin	Ch'angch'un	187	13	21	72	112
Liaoning	Shenyang	151	24	29	158	192
N						
Hopei	T'ientsin	195	42.5	46	217	236
Shansi	T'aiyüan	157	16	20	101	127
E						
Anhui	Hofei	140	34	39	242	279
Chekiang	Hangchow	102	25	31	245	304
Kiangsu	Nanking	103	45	51	436	495
Fukien	Fuchow	124	15	18	120	145
Shantung	Tsinan	153	54	60	352	392
Central + S						
Kiangsi	Nanch'ang	165	19	22	113	133
Honan	Chengchow	168	49	55	291	327
Hunan	Ch'angsha	210	36	41	171	195
Hupei	Wuhan	188	31	35	169	186
Kuangtung	Canton	231	38	40	168	173
SW						
Kweichow	Kueiyang	174	17	20	102	115
Szech'uan	Ch'engtu	569	72	75	126	132
Yünnan	K'unming	436	19	24	43	55
NW						
Tsinghai	Sining	720	2	2.5	3	3.5
Kansu	Lanchow	365	13	16	37	43
Shensi	Sian	196	18	22	92	112
Autonomous regions						
Inner Mongolia	Huhehot	1,180	9	6	8	5
Kuangsi	Nanning	220	19	25	93	113
Ninghsia	Yinch'uan	66	1.8	2.5	27	37
Sinkiang	Urumchi	1,650	6	10	4	6
Tibet	Lhasa	1,220	1.5	1.5	1	1
Urban regions						
Peking		17	4,000	7.5	235	441
Shanghai		6	6,900	10	1,150	1,667
Tientsin		3	3,200	4	1,073	1,333
Total		9,560	655,000	759	68	79

¹) Rounded figures

Sources: China-Informations; Länderkurzberichte

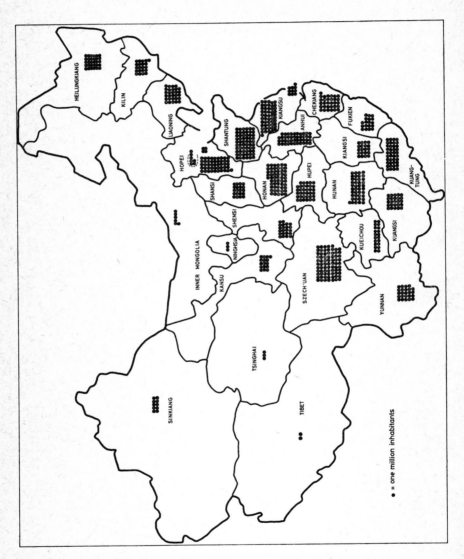

Fig. 4.1. China: Population by provinces 1970

according to the principle of democratic centralism. Party congresses were held less regularly and at longer intervals after the conquest of power than had been the case before. The struggles of the factions, representing differing political concepts, were not fought with the same ferocity as in the Soviet Union. Even so, they led to the expulsion of a large part of the political leadership, that had collectively organised and won the revolution.

On paper, other parties and political organisations do exist beside the CPC and they form the Political Consultative Conference of the Chinese nation under CPC leadership. The highest formal State institution is the People's Congress with more than 3,000 delegates (third congress 1964, fourth congress 1973), seldom and irregularly in full session. Only the local people's congresses are elected by direct ballot. These elect the regional congresses, which in turn elect the national congress. According to the new constitution of 1954, that congress elects the holders of the highest offices (President, Prime Minister, ministers, High Court judges, Attorney General) and votes the budget and the economic plan. – Since 1958, the people's communes have replaced the administrative rural communes as lowest government units in the countryside.

4.2. *The agrarian sector*

As mentioned before, the agricultural sector continues to be the most important in terms of economically active persons, factor contribution and the role assigned to it in economic development. This is emphasised by farm planning policies and resource allocation.

4.2.1. *Farm production*
In the south and east rice predominates as staple food; in the north wheat and sorghum are the preferred crops. The form of agriculture practised is mostly digging or spade husbandry and is concentrated in the densely populated river valleys and coastal marshes. The production units are very small; the land is used intensively. Draught animals are rare. The interior of the country is scarcely utilised for agriculture owing to the arid climate and the absence of tractive power. It will need irrigation and tractors to accelerate the colonisation of the interior.

Regional differences are substantial. Skibbe (1958) distinguishes the following nine zones:
1. Extensive pastoral economy in the west and north;
2. spring wheat zone;
3. sorghum-soy bean zone in the north-east and Manchuria;

4. winter wheat-millet zone;
5. winter wheat-sorghum zone;
6. Yangste rice-wheat zone;
7. south-western rice zone;
8. rice-tea zone;
9. two-crop rice zone.

Field crops

In 1969 agricultural land totalled 293 million ha, of which 112 million ha is cropland. Two crops were harvested on 50 million ha or 45 per cent of the entire cropland. Accordingly the land utilisation index works out at 145 per cent or 1.45. The irrigated area increased from 21.3 million ha in 1952 to 34.7 million ha in 1957 and 80 million ha in 1969.[61] (See Table 4.4.). The cultivated acreage was extended and utilisation intensified by irrigation and double-cropping.

Table 4.4.: Land use (mln. ha)

	1949	1960	1969	1970
Arable land	97.8	105.5	112.0	110.3
Pasture and meadows	175.0	178.1	181.0	177.0
Total agricultural land	272.8	283.6	293.0	287.3
Sown acreage [1])	135.0	145.8	162.4	–
Irrigated	16.0	66.3	80.0	80.0
Multiple cropping factor[1]), p.c.	138.1	138.2	145.0	–
Arable land ha per head of agricultural	0.20	0.18	0.16	–
Sown acreage population	0.28	0.25	0.24	–

[1]) Sown acreage = arable land multiplied by multiple cropping factor

Sources: Rochlin + Hagemann (1971); Länderkurzberichte

In spite of these efforts, the cultivated acreage per head of agricultural population declined owing to rapid population growth. It must be feared that the worsening of the man-land ratio renders an increase in labour productivity difficult or impossible. This highlights a grave problem of economic policy.

Chang (1965) believes that the utilised acreage both in arable and pastoral farming can be substantially expanded, in part by more than 100 per cent (Table 4.5.). Thus, cropland could be increased from 108 to 210 million ha, and pastures from 178 to 310 million ha. No data are given concerning the investment needed for such developments in large-scale land reclamation in terms of both finance and equipment. But, there is

Table 4.5.: Land use – present and potential

Land category	Present		Potential	
	mill. ha	%	mill. ha	%
Arable	108	11.3	210	21.9
Forests	100	10.4	250	26.1
Steppe and hill-slopes with potential for grazing	555	57.8	–	–
thereof exploited	178	18.5	310	32.3
Desert	107	11.2	100	10.4
Others	90	9.3	90	9.3
Total	960	100.0	960	100.0

Source: Chang (1965)

no doubt about the potential. The conquest of virgin lands for agriculture depends on population pressure, technical inputs and the stage of economic and technological development.

As regards particular crops, the most notable increases in acreage have been for rice, potatoes, soy beans and cotton, as shown in Table 4.6. Rice has shown the most substantial increases in production and yields over the years. It should be noted that the figures for 1958, the year of the Great Leap Forward, are most probably exaggerated. Nevertheless, the harvests of most of the basic crops can be seen to have gradually increased up to 1974.

Yields are considerably above those in India or Pakistan, but lower than in Japan. China has reached the highest level attainable on the basis of traditional technology.

Big steps forward – to the Japanese level of productivity – call for a much larger flow of industrial inputs. Supplies of staple foods seem to be assured, although certain quantities have been imported since at least 1961. Etienne (1974) gives the following figures of yearly imports.

Ø 1961-66	5.5 million tonnes wheat	
Ø 1967-70	4.3 ,, ,, ,,	
1971	3.2 ,, ,, ,,	
1972	5.0 ,, ,, ,,	
1973	7.7 ,, ,, (6.7 wheat, 1.0 maize).	

On the other hand, China exports smaller quantities of grain, mainly rice, to other countries.

The use of chemical fertilisers was initiated only after 1950 and was effectively promoted both by domestic production and by imports (see

Table 4.6.: Development of field crops

	ø1932-36	1949	1958	1960	ø1961-65	1970	1974
Acreage mill. ha							
Rice	26.8	25.8	32.9	30.5	31.0	34.2	35.2
Wheat	28.7	21.6	26.8	24.0	25.2	28.2	29.0
Maize	–	–	–	9.0 [1])	9.2	10.5	10.6
Barley	–	–	–	11.0 [1])	11.6	13.2	13.5
Sorghum	–	–	–	27.8 [1])	28.0	29.3	29.8
Other cereals	54.3	47.4	45.7	48.5	–	–	–
Total cereals	109.8	94.8	105.4	103.0	107.0	118.1	120.8
Potatoes+sweet potatoes	4.6	7.0	16.3	12.0	13.1	15.7	15.7
Soybeans	8.7	8.3	9.3	9.5	13.3	14.3	14.3
Peanuts	–	–	–	–	1.8	2.2	2.2
Sugarcane	–	–	–	–	0.4	–	0.6
Cotton	3.0	3.0	5.7	5.2	4.1	4.6	4.8
Production mill. to							
Rice (in husk)	67.8	48.7	113.7	77.5	86.0	105.2	115.3
Wheat	30.6	13.8	29.0	20.0	22.2	31.0	37.0
Maize	–	–	–	19.5 [1])	22.8	28.6	31.1
Barley	–	–	–	12.0 [1])	14.7	19.0	20.5
Sorghum	–	–	–	15.1	17.1	22.0	23.5
Other cereals	63.2	35.8	61.9	43.6	–	–	–
Total cereals	161.6	98.3	204.6	141.1	164.5	208.8	230.1
Potatoes+sweet potatoes	34.8	39.4	181.6	88.0	111.0	141.5	151.1
Soybeans	9.9	5.1	10.5	7.8	10.7	11.6	11.9
Peanuts	–	–	–	–	2.1	2.6	2.7
Sugarcane	–	–	–	–	24.7	35.7	40.0
Cotton	0.7	0.4	2.1	1.6	2.3	3.4	?
Yield q/ha							
Rice	25.3	18.8	34.5	25.4	27.8	30.7	32.7
Wheat	10.7	6.4	10.8	8.3	8.8	11.0	12.8
Maize	–	–	–	21.7 [1])	24.8	27.6	29.4
Barley	–	–	–	10.9 [1])	12.7	14.2	15.2
Sorghum	–	–	–	5.4 [1])	6.1	7.5	7.9
Other cereals	11.6	7.6	13.6	9.0	–	–	–
Total cereals	14.7	10.3	19.4	13.7	15.4	17.7	19.1
Potatoes+sweet potatoes	76	56	112	73	85	90	96
Soybeans	11.5	6.1	11.3	8.2	8.0	8.1	8.3
Peanuts	–	–	–	–	11.4	12.8	12.4
Sugarcane	–	–	–	–	563	650	685
Cotton	2.3	1.7	3.6	3.1	–	–	–
Percapita production kg					*1969*		
Rice		90	173	113	143		
Wheat		26	44	29	32		
Total cereals		183	312	207	249		
Potatoes		74	277	129	156		
Soybeans		9	16	11	14		

[1]) 1961

Sources: Rochlin + Hagemann (1971); FAO Production yearbook

Table 4.7.: Production, import and use of fertilisers [1]

Year	Production	Import	Total	Supply pure nutrients	Consumption per ha arable	sown acreage
		1000			kg	
1949	27	–	–	–	–	–
1952	181	137	318	67	0.6	0.5
1960	2,000	1,134	3,134	665	6.3	4.6
1965	5,677	2,250	7,927	1,683	15.7	10.6
1969	12,150	4,250	16,400	4,050	36.2	24.9
1970	14,000	7,000	21,000			
1973	20-21,600	6,000	26,000			

[1] All three main fertilisers aggregated

Sources: Rochlin + Hagemann (1971); Etienne (1974)

Table 4.7.). Although considerable progress has been made in this respect, the application of fertilisers still lags far behind the level customary in modern, densely populated industrial countries. However, considering the rates of growth to date and those that might be achieved in the future, it is perfectly feasible for China to catch up with the industrial nations in this respect within the foreseeable future.

Electrification and the introduction of tractors are still in their early stages. According to figures published by the Soviet Union, the output of tractors was 45,000 in 1966 and 40,000 in 1967. A different set of figures – presented in Table 4.8. – was given by Rochlin and Hagemann (1971).[62]

Table 4.8.: Inventory of modern farm equipment

Year	Tractors [1]	Harvest combines	Arable land – ha per tractor [2]
	1000		
1940	0.4	–	–
1950	1.3	–	550,300
1955	8.0	–	38,050
1960	68.0	5.7	4,250
1965	118.0	13.3	2,050
1969	203.0	23.4	850
1971	250.0 [3]	–	–

[1] Statistical units à 15 h.p.
[2] Physical units   [3] Plus 75,000 power tillers (two-wheel tractors)

Sources: Rochlin + Hagemann (1971); Etienne (1974)

Table 4.9.: Development of animal husbandry 1949-1974 (millions) [1]

Year	Cattle	of which water buffaloes	Pigs	Sheep + Goats	Horses	Donkey + mules
1949	43.9	10.2	57.7	42.3	4.9	11.0
1952	56.6	11.6	89.8	61.8	6.1	13.4
1955	66.0	12.5	87.9	84.2	7.3	14.1
1959	65.4	13.5	180.8	112.5	7.6	12.3
1960	56.5	11.8	130.0	118.0	7.6	11.8
1961	44.0	11.8	90.0	96.0	5.4	11.2
1963	61.0	28.0	198.0	119.0	8.0	13.0
1965	63.0	29.0	205.0	121.0	8.0	14.0
1967	63.0	29.0	223.0	126.0	8.0	14.0
1969	63.0	29.0	248.0	127.0	7.0	14.0
1970	63.2	30.0	223.0	127.0	7.0	14.0
1971	63.0	30.0	226.0	129.0	7.0	14.0
1972	63.0	30.0	231.0	129.0	7.0	14.0
1973	63.0	30.0	236.0	131.0	7.0	14.0
1974	63.5	30.0	239.2	132.2	7.0	14.0

[1] The different sources vary widely, particularly for buffaloes, donkeys and mules. No explanation was found.

Sources: Rochlin + Hagemann (1971); Etienne (1974); FAO Production yearbook; Statistical yearbook for Asia and the Pacific (1974)

Animal husbandry

Livestock numbers are set out in Table 4.9. and Fig. 4.2. There are only 7 million horses, which is not enough for tillage work. Since 1949 the numbers of horses, donkeys and mules have been greatly increased, though the upward trend was temporarily interrupted by a decline at the beginning of the 1960s. Virgin lands cannot be brought under the plough for lack of draught animals. Cattle stocks are low in relation to the size of the population, at any rate in terms of European levels of demand for milk and meat. Cattle stocks declined after collectivisation and the Great Leap Forward from 65.4 to 44.0 million head; that is by almost one-third. By 1969 the former level had almost been reached once again. The setback resembled the consequences of collectivisation in the Soviet Union, but on a smaller scale. The pig population has been increased substantially. Traditionally, pig and poultry keeping is of greater importance than dairy farming. The keeping of sheep and goats has also expanded. Animal production is likewise mostly on the increase (see Table 4.10.), though at a slow rate and at a relatively low level, if

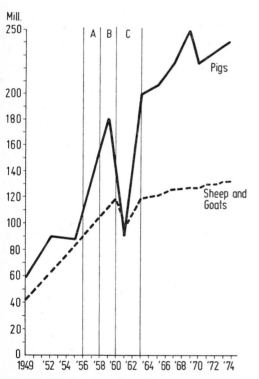
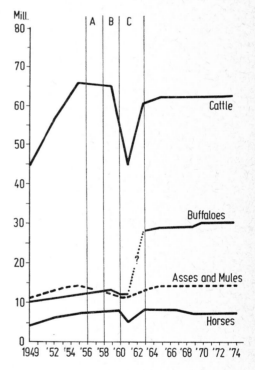

A = 1956–1958 Formation of people's communes
B = 1958–1960 Great leap forward
C = 1960–1963 Setback

Fig. 4.2. China: Animal husbandry

Table 4.10.: Development of animal production (1000 tonnes)

Item	1965	1970	1971	1974
Meat of				
cattle + buffaloes	2,050	2,200	2,230	1,969
sheep + goats	550	600	620	594
pork	9,350	8,393	8,460	9,619
poultry	2,160	2,635	?	3,085
Cow milk	2,828	3,200	3,250	3,457
Eggs (1,000 millions)	?	72.8	73.6	?
Silk cocoons	84	125	?	?
Wool (greasy)	77	60	60	61
Wool (washed)	46	36	36	37

Source: Länderkurzberichte (1974); FAO Production yearbook

compared to highly industrialised countries in moderate zones and their nutritional customs and standards. In assessing these figures it must be borne in mind that the major proportion of animal production remains in the peasants' own households for home consumption, that other parts are sold on peasant markets rather than to the official agencies (and in that case possibly not counted in statistics), that food habits in East Asia differ strongly from those in Western Europe. The above mentioned emphasis on small animals partly fed on swill and food scraps is confirmed by the data for animal production. Pork provides four times as much meat as do cattle and buffaloes, and poultry, too, produces more meat than cattle.

For the purposes of price policy, agricultural products are divided into three categories by the government. The first category comprises food grains, cotton, oil crops, important industrial crops and a number of animal products. All these products have to be delivered at fixed prices to the state trading corporations. The second category comprises 'export products', of which a fixed quota is to be delivered to the same corporations at prices fixed in the course of negotiations between the government and the producers. The third category comprises all other agricultural products, which may be freely sold at the village markets.

4.2.2. *Agrarian structure, agrarian revolution and the people's communes*
China's agrarian structure and the social set-up in the villages provided a unique starting position for subsequent developments. Owing to the highly intensive spade husbandry, landholdings in most areas were much smaller than in Europe or America. In one of his early works Mao Tse-tung defined the social groupings in the village[63] and estimated their relative numerical strength (see also Table 4.11.):

Table 4.11.: Social stratification of rural population 1934 and 1949

Class	Size of holding ha	Rural households	Cultivated land	Rural households	Cultivated land
		1934		1959	
		in %			
Landlords	11.5	3	26	4	41
Rich peasants	5.1	7	27	6	28
Medium peasants	2.2	22	25	18	21
Poor peasants + labourers	0.5	68	22	72	10
		100	100	100	100

Source: Henle (1974)

1. Landlords: they do not work, but rent their land to peasants, administer real property, and levy ground rent. Their holdings averaged 28.4 acres (11.5 ha). Usurers are classified together with landowners.
2. Big peasants: they own and/or rent land in order to farm it themselves. They take part in the work, but also employ paid labourers, and they may rent some of their land to peasants. They derived a large proportion of their income from the exploitation of the labourers employed by them. Average landholding 12.6 acres (5.1 ha).
3. Medium peasants: they own and rent land. The main source of their livelihood is their own labour. They have their own stock and working capital. Average holding 5.4 acres (2.2 ha).
4. The village poor: they own little or no land as well as little stock. They rent land, need loans, and work part of the time for others as wage labourers. Average holding 1.2 acres (0.5 ha).
5. Workers.

The polarisation of landholdings before the communist take-over was not very far-reaching. The ratio of population to land is unfavourable. The village and the agricultural land are overpopulated, with no opportunity for migration: hence the growing exploitation of tenant farmers and agricultural labourers by the landowners. The Chinese revolution and the Red Army derived their support from the peasants. Even before 1945, cautious measures of agrarian reform were introduced in the territories under communist rule: reduction of rents, limitation of landholdings, expropriation of landowners who had collaborated with the Japanese, partial redistribution of the land. During 20 years of civil war the peasants had time to adjust to the social transformation carried out step by step.

The revolutionary leaders, on the other hand, were able to gain experience in dealing with the peasantry that supported them.

Before 1949, 29 per cent of all agriculturally utilised land was tilled by tenant farmers, and only 54 per cent of all cultivators owned the land they were working. Landlords held 40 per cent of the cultivated acreage. The agrarian reform of 1949-52 expropriated the landlords and distributed 47 million ha among poor and landless cultivators, numbering together with their families 300 million.[64] – In 1954, according to official Chinese figures, 24 per cent of the acreage was cultivated by households with an average holding of 0.8 ha, equipped on average with half a draft animal and one third of a plough. Only 3.2 per cent of the acreage was cultivated by "rich" peasants with, on average, 2.3 ha, 2 draft animals and 1 plough.

From 1950 on, the, successive steps of agrarian reform led systematically in the direction of collectivisation. Here, the first stage was the setting up of mutual-aid labour teams which worked together for a season or for a whole year. From then on both the size and the scope of the co-operative units were increased progressively by the formation first of 'lower-level', then of fully socialist, co-operatives and finally of people's communes. In 1958, there were 26,400 people's communes. The number declined to 24,000 in 1960, after which it rose again to 74,000 in 1963 as the result of a further reorganisation (see also Table 4.12). In 1959, a commune on average was composed of 5,500 households and held 4,500 ha arable land. Organisationally, the communes were sub-divided into brigades and teams (see Table 4.13.).

The tasks of the various types of cooperative institutions during the phases of transformation and collectivisation are presented in Chart 4.1. The development is characterised by a progressive integration of production resources and the addition of new collective tasks. A small household plot[65] of the member of the people's commune remains exempt from the general pooling of resources and supplements the income from the collective or communal economy. The individual or household plots occupy 5-8 per cent of the co-operatively farmed agricultural land; thus they are minute in absolute terms. There are marked regional variations in the average size of household plots, depending on the intensity of land use. About 9 to 30 per cent of family incomes is derived from the private plots. Reflecting the general conditions of Chinese agriculture, the household sector is confined to the keeping of pigs and poultry and the maintenance of a vegetable plot, as a rule without dairy cattle or pasture land.

Table 4.12.: Phases of rural transformation 1950-1958

Type of institution	1950	1952	1954	1956 May	1957 June	1958 30.9	1960 estimate
Peasant households (1.000)							
Total	105,536	113,683	117,331	120,761	122,500	125,500	
In teams for							
mutual aid	11,313	45,364	68,478	+	+	++	
seasonal	–	33,916	37,765	+	+	++	
whole year	–	11,448	30,713	+	+	++	
In producer cooperatives							
total	0.2	59	2,297	110,134	118,800	++	
elementary	0.2	57	2,285	35,414	4,500	++	
fully socialist	0.0	2	12	74.720	114,300	++	
People's communes	–	–	–	–	–	121,936	
Institutions							
Producer cooperatives							
total	19	3,644	114,366	1,003,657	752,113	++	
elementary	18	3,634	114,165	700,901	72,032	++	
fully socialist	1	10	201	302,756	680,081	++	+++)
People's communes	–	–	–	–	–	26,425	24,000
State farms	1,215	2,336	2,415	–	–	–	2,500

+)   With a few exceptions integrated in producer cooperatives
++)   With a few exceptions integrated in people's communes
+++)   Until end of 1959 reduced to 24,000 by mergers, thereafter increased again to 74,000 by division.

Sources: Chao Kuo-Chün (1957); Lichnowsky (1972)

Table 4.13.: Structure of rural people's communes 1959

Units	Number	Average size	
		arable land (ha)	households
People's communes	24,000	4,500	5,500
Production brigades	500,000	220	264
Production teams	3,000,000	35	42

Source: Lichnowsky (1972)

Chart 4.1.: Forms of organized farming

Type of organization	Ownership of land, draft animals and farm implements	Average number of households and area of landholding	Type of work	Membership's income
Mutual-aid teams (both seasonal and permanent)	Private	6 to 15 households; average landholding: no estimate	Farm operations	Each member gets the produce of his own plot, sometimes plus bonus for extra work
APCs[1]	Private and cooperative	Households: 32:37 ha	Farm operations and some subsidiary occupations	Dividends from cooperative shares (including land dividend) and labour compensation. Average income: 12,714 Yüan per cooperative in 1955
Higher-stage APCs	Collective	Households: 160;150 ha (June 1958)	Farm operations, subsidiary occupations and large-scale agrotechnical projects	Mainly compensation for labour, with little or no compensation for land
People's communes	Collective	Households: 5,000; 4,564 ha (1959)	Farming, forestry, fishery, animal husbandry, subsidiary jobs, local industries, etc.	From 20 to 30 per cent of income in free supplies of food, sometimes clothing; the rest in wages (1960)

[1]) Agricultural Producers' Cooperatives
Source: Lichnowsky (1972)

In an eight-point programme the communes were assigned the following tasks:

1. Construction of water storage projects, using manpower reserves not needed for agricultural work;
2. increased and more judicious use of chemical fertilisers;
3. introduction of scientific crop rotation;
4. instruction of the peasants in the techniques of deep ploughing and soil conservation;
5. raising yields by closer planting of crops;
6. protection of crops by plant protection agents;
7. increased input of improved tools and implements;
8. better leadership and improved management of production inputs and products.

The character and meaning of the people's communes has for a long time been a controversial issue, both in the East and in the West. In the socialist camp, the Chinese claimed to have bypassed the collective farms on the path to the final goal of communism, since many more collective decisions were transferred to the people's communes and their field of activities was much wider than was the case in the collective farms of the Soviet Union. This implied a questioning or even a heretical denial of the leading role of the Soviet Union. In the West, reports circulated of the separation of families in the people's communes, with mass dormitories segregated according to sex, etc.

It is difficult to organise work schedules for tens of thousands of people labouring in the fields; and economies of scale cease to accrue above a certain limit. Mass mobilisation of labour cannot serve any useful purpose except for vast building projects for which modern earth-moving and construction plant is not available. Perhaps the people's communes are administrative units operating at a level above that of the agricultural production enterprises and charged with the task of establishing local industries. In some places canteens supplying staple foods have been installed as a substitute for government rationing schemes and as a form of social security for the aged and disabled. Furthermore, all social, cultural and administrative services at the district (hsiang) level are integrated in the commune. Thus, schools, police, local administration, etc. are in fact locally paid and do not burden the central budget.

In describing the organisation and tasks of the people's communes, Biehl (1965) notes the passage in the Central Committee resolution of September 1958 on the establishment of people's communes, which said:

"The people themselves are demanding the opportunity to organise in military fashion for work and to lead a collective life." (P. 41).[66]

He goes on to describe structure and tasks of the people's communes as follows:

> "The people's commune covers not only all the branches of the rural economy; it embraces in addition all walks of life: the peasant, the artisan, the industrial worker, the militia man. It absorbs the lowest unit of the state administration, the district or 'hsiang' as well as the local branches of the state banking and trade organisation and of the health and education services." (p. 41)

During the initial period, the structure of the lower echelons, as taken over with the agricultural producer co-operatives, was to be left intact, changes to be introduced only in cases of proven urgency, in order to avoid any interference with production. In the Party's view, the time had not yet come when it would be appropriate to take the step from group ownership (collective) to ownership by the whole people (nationalisation). Even if that step were to be taken at some time in the future, the people's commune would still be a socialist rather than communist institution, that is to say, it would still be based on the principle of 'from each according to his ability, to each according to his contribution'. Even though the system of distribution (remuneration for work) does not give to each according to his needs, the people's commune is nonetheless the form of organisation best suited to the attainment of socialism and the gradual advance to communism. Such was and is the Communist Party's position, Biehl points out.

Liu Shao-ch'i, who at that time was a leading politician, stated:

> "Many people's communes operate a supply system which ensures free food supplies at an appropriate level for all members. Generally, such free allocations make up 20 to 30 per cent of the members' income. The main purpose of this method is to safeguard the sustenance of the physically disabled and the children. This is an excellent way of establishing a form of social insurance in our rural areas..." (Biehl, 1965, p. 96).

At the beginning of 1959, supplementary guidelines were issued for the reorganisation of the people's communes, which settled the question of the ownership of the means of production. According to these guidelines, the ownership of the assets brought into the commune is vested in the production brigades – the successors to the producer co-operatives out of which the commune was formed – while the property vested in the commune is to be built up gradually from newly created and newly acquired assets such as irrigation plant and stocks of agricultural machinery, which represent the fruit of the members' common effort. In work organisation, too, the production brigade remains the fundamental unit.

The institutions of 'collective life' – canteens, crèches, children's nurseries, old-age homes – served the practical task of enabling the women to devote as nearly as possible their entire working time to the collective. At the same time the directives for housing construction provide for the continued existence of the family, even though its economic functions may radically change.

According to the new guidelines, 'existing old dwelling houses must be replaced step by step', that is to say, not precipitately – 'by new ones... In the construction of new living quarters, care must be taken to ensure that the houses are suitable for the accommodation of man and wife, the aged and the children of each family living together'.

It had been common practice in the past for the village community to entrust the farming of a portion of the village fields for a whole year to a fairly small work team, whose members might not all be drawn from the same lineage. Under the new regulations such annual contracts for the farming of small areas may be concluded even with single families belonging to the village community.

The socio-economic and political tasks and aims of the introduction of the people's communes can be tentatively formulated as follows:
1. Breaking up the enslaving social functions of the old family;
2. end of the economic function of the family as the sole agent of rural capital accumulation;
3. public capital accumulation and collection of the agricultural surplus on a larger, publicly supervised level;[67]
4. local "industrialisation", locally financed, production of all goods not requiring large-scale factories;
5. formation of a basic administration, financially sustained by the population itself.

The establishment of the people's communes has ushered in a radical institutional reform, a change of the production relations. But there are very few new tractors, motor vehicles and agricultural machines, representing the new productive forces. Traditional technology continues to prevail.

Modern equipment is mostly allocated to the new state farms, set up in underpopulated regions, frequently near the state frontiers. The aim is twofold: farmland is to be extended and production increased, and the border regions are to be settled with soldier-peasants producing their own food.[68] Table 4.14 gives data for state farms, but only up to 1964, when they numbered about 2,500, farming more than 5 million ha, of which a large part was newly reclaimed. They employed a workforce of

Table 4.14.: Acreage and equipment of State farms [1]

Year	Number	Total agri-cultural land	Arable land	Work-force	Trac-tors [2]	Har-vesting combines	Re-claimed land	Grain pro-duction
		1,000 ha			1,000		1,000 ha	1,000 to
1949	18	31	31	4	401	13	.	.
1952	404	565	255	390	1,792	283	149	193
1957	710	1,199	1,025	500	10,177	1,537	271	595
1958	1,442	2,655	2,272	990	16,955	1,982	829	.
1960	2,490	5,230	.	.	28,000	.	.	2,500
1964	.	4,130	.	.	.	.	.	2,035

[1] State farms (including stock-breeding farms) under the Ministry for land reclamation. Small experimental farms under regional administration are excluded
[2] In 15 h.p. units

Source: Länderberichte

about one million and were equipped with tractors equivalent to 28,000 units of 15 h.p.

In 1965, there were 2,263 State-owned farm machinery stations. No data are available concerning their equipment and level of performance.

4.2.3. *Farm policies*

For a considerable time to come, agriculture is bound to remain the key sector on which the progress of industrial development must depend. Agriculture supplies raw material and, on the basis of terms of trade loaded against it (price scissors), also supplies capital: low producer prices of foodstuffs contrast with high prices of agricultural production equipment and materials and consumer goods. The main points of current agrarian policy are:

Maintenance of collectivisation combined with toleration of private production on the household plots; gradual expansion of the culti-vated area, in particular by state farms in the interior of the country; fostering of agricultural production by expansion of fertiliser in-dustry, construction of dykes as flood protection, irrigation; supplementing domestic production by imports in case of need; measures designed to force migration from the land are unnecessary as well as impracticable; mechanisation of agriculture to be accomplished gradually rather than through a crash programme.

During an agricultural conference, held in the model commune of Tachai in the autumn of 1975, "mechanisation of farming" was proclaimed as a new objective. It is not entirely clear, however, what the real meaning of the word is in the actual Chinese context. It could imply: improvement of traditional tools and techniques, electrification of villages, mechanisation of regular irrigation operations, or finally introduction of tractors for tillage and transport.[68a]

The problem of collectivisation and mechanisation constituted one of the main issues in the ideological conflict, in which Mao Tsetung and Liu Shao-ch'i were the principal protagonists. Mao wanted to ensure the formation of communes – the transformation of production relations – as a first step, even though it was not yet possible to provide new inputs (means of production). It should be left to the communes partly to make them, partly to pay for their acquisition. In Liu's view, however, mechanisation should have been the first step, involving the supply of pumping engines and tractors, the building up of machine and tractor stations, etc. The creation of new productive forces was to have raised production and to have helped the peasants both materially and psychologically to accomplish the transition to new production relations. This dispute can be traced back to 1958, the year in which the Great Leap Forward was launched, the leap that failed.

Liu thus favoured a sequence of steps of change contrary to Mao's proposals: tractors etc. first, collectivisation second. Such a development path logically implies a different approach also in other fields of the economic, domestic and foreign policy, and thus an alternative mode and trend of political thought.[69]

4.3. *The non-agricultural sectors*

4.3.1. *Industrialisation*
What little industry existed prior to 1949 was concentrated in the large ports and the Manchurian heavy-industry region of Anshan-Harbin. This capacity was further diminished by war damage and dismantling. After 1949 a planned build-up of industry was launched with Soviet assistance. Plant was built for the production of basic materials, heavy machinery, public transport vehicles, lorries and the most important basic consumer goods. Soviet aid was withdrawn at the end of the 1950s. China does not now receive any financial aid from abroad, but she is buying technological industrial processes, chiefly from Japan, West Germany, France and Britain. Thus the starting speed of China's industrial development is slow, but, then, her foreign indebtedness is slight and the burden of interest small. All the capital must be formed on

the internal capital market. Thus China is politically independent, yet at the same time politically and technologically isolated.

The construction of new factories led to the emergence of new industrial zones and growth centres, which promoted decentralisation and, above all, geographical dispersion and regional development. Location of industries at the end of the sixties is presented in Chart 4.2.

Chart 4.2: Location of industries

Region	Local centre and line of production
Southern Manchuria	Anshan – steel; Penki – steel; Shenyang – electrical machinery; Talien – shipyard, cars, refinery; Fushun – chemicals, slate oil, coal; Shuifeng – hydroelectric power.
Central and Northern Manchuria	Changchun – cars and lorries, railway rolling stock; Kirin – chemicals, paper; Harbin – electrical engineering and precision engineering; Chiamussu – paper; Taching – oil.
Inner Mongolia	Paotow – steel; Huhehot – chemicals.
North-East	Peking – steel, cars, electrical engineering; Tientsin – steel, machinery, radio and television; Loyang – tractors; Chengchow and Shih-chia-chuang – textiles; Taiyuan – machinery, steel, chemicals, textiles; Sanmenchia – hydroelectric power; Tatung – locomotives, machinery; Tsinan – cars.
South-East	Shanghai – products of heavy and light industries; Nanking – cars, chemicals; Wuhan – steel; Hangchow – tractors, silk; Canton – synthetic fibres, cameras, paper.
North West	Lanchow – oil refinery, hydroelectric power, chemicals, steel; Yumen – oil wells, refinery; Lenghu, Karamai – oil; Urumchi – uranium, steel.
South West	Chungking – steel, machinery, oil; Chengtu – cement, food; Kunming – motors, food; Kochiu – lead; Kweiyang – bauxite, food.

Source: Länderberichte

4.3.2. *Long-term economic developments*

The results of industrial development till 1970 and development trends up to 1975 are summarised in Table 4.15. Data have been collected by Hidasi (1972) from very different and heterogeneous sources: for 1952 and 1957 from official statistics, 1959 and 1960 partly from corrected semi-official figures, partly from correlation calculations. Later years have been extrapolated by the author and other foreign research workers, mainly on the basis of correlations from earlier years. For the year 1970, the concrete announcements of Chou En-lai could be used. Trend extrapolations had to be utilised for missing back years and for the projection till 1975.

The Table shows a strong upward trend for all basic commodities,

Table 4.15.: Basic trends of economic development

Category	Unit	1952	1957	1959	1960	1962	1965	1970	1975
Industry									
Electricity	1,000 mill. kWh	7.2	19.3	41.5	47.0	30.0	60.0	90.0	130.0
Coal	Mill. to	66.5	130.0	310.0	375.0	225.0	225.0	310.0	380.0
Oil	Mill. to	0.4	1.5	3.7	5.5	6.5	10.0	20.0	35.0
Steel raw	Mill. to	1.4	5.4	12.0	17.0	9.0	13.0	18.0	33.0
Steel rolled	Mill. to	1.3	4.5	9.0	12.0	7.8	11.5	16.0	30.0
Cement	Mill. to	2.9	6.9	12.3	12.5	7.0	11.0	16.0	24.0
Fertilizers	Mill. to	0.2	0.6	2.0	2.5	2.1	6.0	14.0	30.0
Cotton fabric	1,000 mill. m	4.2	5.0	7.0	6.5	3.3	7.0	8.5	11.0
Sugar	Mill. to	0.5	0.9	1.3	1.5	2.1	2.6	3.5	4.8
Vegetable oil	Mill. to	1.0	1.1	1.3	0.9	1.1	1.8	2.4	3.2
Agriculture									
Grain	Mill. to	155	185	192	160	220	220	240	280
Raw cotton	Mill. to	1.3	1.6	1.8	1.4	1.2	1.5	2.1	2.8
Pigs	Mill. animals	90	146	150	120	135	150	180	220
Value of gross production									
Industry	1,000 mill. Yüan[1]	31.0	70.4	152.5	168.0	100.0	156.0	225.0	310.0
Farming	1,000 mill. Yüan	43.0	53.7	57.5	47.0	56.0	64.0	75.0	90.0
Industry + farming	1,000 mill. Yüan	74.0	124.1	210.4	215.4	156.0	220.0	300.0	400.0
Industry + farming	1,000 mill. US $	33.1	55.7	94.3	96.3	70.0	98.7	134.3	179.0
National income									
	1,000 mill. Yüan	62.0	95.0	121.0	125.0	103.0	125.0	178.0	230.0
	1,000 mill. US $	27.8	42.5	58.8	56.0	46.2	56.0	80.0	103.0
National income per head									
	Yüan	110	150	198	186	147	170	227	275
	US $	49	67	89	83	66	76	102	123
Population									
	Mill.	560	635	660	673	700	735	785	835

[1] 1 Yüan = 1 Renminbi = 1,27 DM (August 1973)

Source: Hidasi (1972)

though sharply interrupted by the Great Leap Forward. The break may appear excessively abrupt in the statistics, owing to the inflation of production figures by distorted success reports that were publicly and officially denounced after 1960. – The share of the two main productive sectors in gross production is shifting increasingly in favour of industry, whose contribution to the total national product rose in monetary terms from 42 per cent in 1952 to 75 per cent in 1970 and was due to rise to 77.5 per cent in 1975.

In the course of 18 years up to 1970, total gross production has quadrupled in monetary terms,[70] while agriculture was barely able to double its output. Its growth potential remains limited, at least until industrial inputs can be offered in large quantities. In the meantime the value of industrial production has increased more than sevenfold.

National income, calculated by methods entirely different from those used to compute the gross national product of capitalist economies and therefore not comparable, rose by 187 per cent, i.e. almost trebled, from 1952 to 1970. Since the population during the same period grew by 40

Table 4.16.: Average annual growth rates for selected commodities and indices (in per cent)

Category	First Five-Year Plan 1953-57	Great Leap Forward 1958-60	Second Five-Year Plan 1958-62	Rectifi-cation 1961-65	Third Five-Year Plan 1966-70	Fourth Five-Year Plan 1971-75
Industry						
Electricity	21.6	34.4	9.2	5.1	8.5	7.6
Coal	14.4	42.3	11.6	− 7.4	4.0	4.2
Oil	27.4	54.2	34.1	12.7	14.9	11.8
Raw steel	31.7	46.6	10.7	− 5.3	9.0	10.5
Rolled steel	28.2	38.5	11.6	− 0.8	9.4	10.8
Cement	19.1	34.0	0.2	− 3.9	7.8	8.5
Fertilizers	28.5	51.8	28.5	19.1	18.4	16.4
Cotton fabric	5.7	9.1	− 9.7	1.5	3.9	5.2
Sugar	13.9	18.6	18.4	11.6	6.2	6.5
Vegetable oil	2.3	− 6.4	0.0	14.9	5.9	5.9
Agriculture						
Grain	3.7	−12.5	1.6	6.5	1.8	3.2
Raw cotton	4.7	− 4.2	− 5.6	1.4	8.5	5.9
Pigs	10.1	− 6.5	− 1.4	4.6	3.7	4.1
Production value						
Industry	17.9	33.5	7.3	− 1.4	7.6	6.6
Agriculture	4.6	− 4.2	1.0	6.3	3.2	3.7
Industry + agriculture	10.9	20.0	4.4	0.4	6.3	5.9
National income						
total	8.9	9.7	1.6	0.0	7.3	5.2
per head	6.3	7.4	− 0.4	− 1.8	6.0	4.0
Population	2.5	2.0	2.0	1.8	1.3	1.2

Source: Hidasi (1972)

per cent, per-capita income rose by only 106 per cent. The annual growth rates for several products and indicators are presented in Table 4.16. They indicate considerable disproportions between the two main sectors and between various commodities. Furthermore, they reveal heavy cyclical fluctuations between the development phases. The high growth rates of the first five-year plan are explained partly by the low starting level, partly by foreign development aid extended by the Soviet Union. After the Great Leap Forward, agricultural production in particular suffered setbacks, but the industrial sector was also affected. The third plan again showed sufficient positive growth rates, though mostly considerably below those achieved during the earlier periods.

Population policy seems contradictory during the various phases, and its aims not uniform. As a whole, however, growth rates decrease from 2.5 to 1.2 per cent and approach the rates of modern societies.[71] – Whereas in a stagnant economy per-capita income is depressed by population growth, it showed in China a steady increase, except for periods of crisis. Given the size of population, its predominantly agrarian income and the high degree of payments in kind, the indicated per-capita income is even less meaningful than in highly monetised, market-dependent economies. It appears that the internal social differentials are much smaller than in capitalist countries.

Voss (1971b) established seven phases of economic development since 1949, for which he calculated growth rates of per-capita national product:

Phase	Time period	Growth rate per-capita national product (%)
1. Consolidation	1949-52	no reliable data
2. 1. Five-Year Plan	1952-57	5.8
3. Great Leap Forward	1958-59	3.75
4. Crisis	1960-62	−5.55
5. Recovery	1962-66	3.3
6. Cultural revolution	1966-69	no reliable data as yet
7. After the cultural revolution	1969-	no reliable data as yet

Hidasi (1972) estimates somewhat different values for this indicator; generally the compilations of the research workers differ frequently owing to the absence of official statistics over long periods.

If such figures can be taken at face value, they show a steady growth of national income and private consumption. But public investment and public expenditure have risen more rapidly. This has not led to reduced consumption in absolute terms, but to a relative decline accompanied by a slow increase in absolute terms. This seems to reflect a cautious economic policy.

Voss (1972) summarises the economic development in Table 4.17. and comments as follows:

"Under very unfavourable conditions (apart from the wealth of resources), the Chinese People's Republic has launched a successful economic development, characterised by two features: The modern (industrial) sector was given priority; but simultaneously the traditional sector (agriculture, crafts) was intensively developed – though only after 1962. In that way, progress was made at the same time towards the attainment of several goals: industrialisation, independence, overcoming the scarcity of capital, creation of employment, long-term prospects of higher living standards, adaptation of large groups of the population to modern production methods etc. The planners sought to circumvent the most serious difficulty – the deficient infrastructure – by regionalising development politics." (p. 57)

4.3.3. *External economic relations*
Foreign trade doubled in value from 1952 to 1969 (see Table 4.18.). The direction has radically changed owing to the confrontation with the Soviet Union and its political consequences, so that trade is now conducted chiefly with the capitalist industrial countries. In 1960, 60 per cent of all imported goods, measured in monetary terms, came from socialist countries; by 1968 that proportion had dropped to 22 per cent. During the same period the share of the capitalist industrial nations rose from 22 to 61 per cent, while the share of developing countries rose only slowly. The same development can be traced for China's exports: the socialist countries' share fell from 63 to 25 per cent, while that of the capitalist countries rose from 22 to 61 per cent. China endeavours to increase her exports to developing countries. As a result, the volume of these exports has almost reached the level of Chinese exports to the highly industrialised countries. On some occasions, exchanges with socialist economies have been activated. The most important capitalist partners exporting to China are Japan, West Germany, Canada, Australia, France, while the main importers from China are Hongkong, Japan, West Germany, United Kingdom. The marked repercussions of political troubles, tensions and decisions upon external trade relations emerge very clearly.[72]

Export goods for the capitalist world (not including the USA, with

Table 4.17.: Development of selected economic indices

Year	Population	National income	Private consumption	Net investment	Public expenditure	Production of non-agrarian sectors	Grain	Foreign trade	Academic graduates
	mill.	–	| 1,000 mill. Yüan at prices of 1952			1956 = 100	mill. to	mill. US $	(1,000)
1952	575	65.6	54.6	10.2	16.8	56.1	154.4	1,890	40
1953	588	74.8	54.8	14.2	21.5	70.2	156.9	2,295	47
1954	602	78.7	55.0	16.9	24.6	80.2	160.5	2,350	51
1955	615	83.6	57.0	15.8	26.9	80.7	174.8	3,035	59
1956	628	93.6	62.6	19.8	30.6	100.0	182.5	3,120	59
1957	650	98.2	64.5	18.2	29.0	109.4	185.0	3,025	64
1958	654	111.5	–	23.6	41.0	143.0	250.0	3,735	71
1959	668	108.5	–	20.0	52.8	181.6	220.0	4,270	102
1960	682	111.5	–	17.1	56.0	188.5	185.0	3,975	148
1961	697	93.6	–	15.6	42.0	124.2	178.3	3,005	170
1962	705	97.6	61.8	15.7	37.8	109.6	179.1	2,675	189
1963	715	100.0	63.2	16.7	31.7	120.7	182.7	2,755	200
1964	726	108.3	64.7	18.1	37.0	134.9	179.9	3,230	185
1965	737	112.4	66.2	19.5	40.0	147.6	–	3,695	170
1966	750	118.0	67.9	–	44.0	–	–	4,272	–

Source: Voss (1972)

Table 4.18.: Distribution of foreign trade by groups of countries

Year	1952	1957	1960	1961	1962	1963	1964	1965	1966	1967	1968	1969
Mill. US $												
Chinese exports	1,000	1,673	2,075	1,620	1,597	1,651	1,904	2,187	2,452	1,887	1,858	1,980
imports	1,100	1,382	1,931	1,368	1,082	1,166	1,432	1,813	1,939	1,920	1,762	1,893
Foreign trade balance	− 100	+ 291	+ 144	+ 252	+ 515	+ 485	+ 472	+ 374	+ 513	− 33	+ 96	+ 87
Total foreign trade	2,100	3,055	4,006	2,988	2,679	2,817	3,336	4,000	4,291	3,807	3,620	3,873
Exports Mill. US $	1,000	1,673	2,075	1,620	1,597	1,651	1,904	2,187	2,452	1,887	1,858	1,980
thereof in per cent												
communist countries	60	64.6	63.3	59.3	55.6	47.8	37.3	32.2	26.2	24.5	24.9	–
capitalist-industrial countries		13.4	14.5	15.6	13.6	17.3	23.5	27.7	30.8	33.3	31.7	–
developing countries	40	11.6	11.7	13.4	14.7	18.3	20.3	20.7	22.4	25.8	25.8	–
Hongkong + Macao		10.3	10.5	11.7	14.1	16.6	18.9	19.4	20.6	16.2	17.4	–
Imports Mill. US $	1,100	1,382	1,931	1,368	1,082	1,166	1,432	1,813	1,939	1,920	1,762	1,893
thereof in per cent												
communist countries	73	63.7	65.7	51.1	44.3	35.3	27.0	29.0	28.0	20.2	21.8	–
capitalist-industrial countries		21.8	22.3	35.1	39.4	47.3	48.0	47.7	54.0	61.4	60.7	–
developing countries	27	12.9	10.9	12.5	14.9	16.4	24.1	22.6	17.4	18.0	16.9	–
Hongkong + Macao		2.6	1.1	1.3	1.4	1.0	0.9	0.7	0.6	0.4	0.5	–

Source: Delayne (1972)

which trade relations were illegal and indirect up to 1972) were mainly composed of food items and raw materials (see Table 4.19.).

Table 4.19.: Foreign trade with important capitalist countries by commodity groups

Countries	Food + raw materials		Semi-finished goods		Finished industrial goods	
	1964	1968	1964	1968	1964	1968
1. Chinese exports						
West Germany	79.0	76.1	19.5	13.1	1.5	6.1
France	52.0	52.0	42.2	37.9	5.8	9.2
Italy	80.3	77.7	16.4	17.1	3.3	3.6
Great Britain	65.3	38.2	30.0	33.7	4.5	6.0
Japan	63.0	81.6	35.0	12.1	2.0	6.3
2. Chinese imports						
West Germany	–	2.7	60.0	76.6	39.4	20.6
France	65.4	31.9	27.2	53.1	7.4	19.2
Italy	15.7	7.9	76.7	80.7	7.6	12.1
Great Britain	14.5	6.1	42.1	79.2	43.3	10.1
Japan	12.2	2.2	72.8	87.5	14.9	10.3

Source: OECD; Delayne (1972)

There was virtually no market in those countries for Chinese industrial goods, which on the other hand can frequently be found in several African developing countries. Imports are mostly semi-finished and finished industrial goods. France sometimes exports major quantities of foodstuffs; grain surpluses are sold to China with export subsidies paid by the EEC.

4.4. *Educational system and anti-illiteracy campaign*

There are hardly any recent figures on the development of the educational system, though this seems to be a field of undisputed and quantitatively significant success. Table 4.20, which presents data up to 1963, shows a rapid expansion of schools and educational institutions at all levels. Up to the end of 1959, about 100 million adults were taught to read in evening courses. The percentage of illiterates is likely to have dropped rapidly, even though precise recent figures are not available. Pupils and school leavers of primary schools more than quadrupled in a decade. Secondary and high institutions likewise expanded.

In 1958, according to official statistics, the share of female pupils rose

Table 4.20.: Pupils and graduates by institutions (1,000)

Year / Level	Pupils and students					Graduates			
	Primary	Secondary	Higher	Vocational	Academic	Primary	Secondary+tertiary	Vocational	Academic
before 1949 [1]	23,683	·	} 1,496	383	144	4,633	326	73	25
1949	24,391	832	207	229	117	2,387	280	72	21
1952	51,100	2,230	260	636	191	5,942	221	68	32
1955	53,126	3,320	580	537	288	10,254	969	235	55
1956	63,464	5,165		812	403	12,287	939	174	63
1957	64,279	6,281		778	441	12,307	1,299	146	56
1958	86,400	8,520		1,470	660	16,225	1,313	191	72
1960	100,000	10,520 [2]		2,380 [2]	955	·	·	·	135
1962	·	·		·	820	·	·	·	178
1963	·	·		·	1,500 [3]	·	·	·	200

[1] For each type of institution the highest figure ever reached before the communists took power in 1949 is given
[2] 1959   [3] 1965

Source: Länderberichte

to 38.5 per cent. This appears to show that, at least as far as girls were concerned, full school attendance was not achieved by that year. Apart from material difficulties, social obstacles, too, may well be responsible for the tardy progress in this sphere of education.

So much for the quantitative growth, which is impressive. Moreover, in terms of quality and content Chinese education is breaking away from customary notions and received ideas. Tentatively, the following distinctive points can be named:

1. Higher esteem of manual work, integration of theoretical and practical learning;
2. combination of work experience (in factories and farms) with studies in a number of ways, e.g. at evening colleges or by way of alternating years of work and study;
3. priority for children of peasant or working-class origin in academic institutions.

4.5. *The Chinese development model*

China with her social and economic planning obviously follows the Soviet model to some extent, or at least draws on its historical experience. But as time passes, the dissimilarities grow stronger and finally predominate, making the model entirely distinct from the Soviet attempt at full-scale planning of a whole national economy.

4.5.1. *Economic projections and planning*

The economy is centrally planned, though with a wide measure of encouraged regional and local initiative, so as to utilise the locally available and hardly transferable resources. The documents of the planning institutions are not available to the public. Probably, guidelines, aims, priorities and methods have changed several times since planning started.

Voss (1971b) has developed a model projection of economic development, which, however, he introduces with many reservations. It can be roughly assumed that the parameters of the extrapolations come close to the planning intentions. Voss himself feels that his data for economic growth are the lowest estimate. According to this projection (Table 4.21.), the population will grow from 1970 to 2000 by 484 millions (58 per cent). The manpower employed in all non-agricultural sectors is expected to grow from 38 to 195 million (413 per cent). Even then the agrarian workforce will increase by 61 million persons, i.e. 21 per cent. But, the share of farming in the total workforce will diminish from 88 to 64 per cent. For such a development, total capital in the farming sector will have to grow ninefold, i.e. by 807 percent, while capital formation of

Table 4.21.: Projection of economic development

	1955	1960	1965	1970	1975	1980	1985	2000
Population mill.	611	679	756	841	931	1,022	1,111	1,325
Agricultural manpower mill.	208	227	258	286	297	312	334	347
Manpower other sectors mill.	25	36	34	38	68	94	108	195
Share of farming in manpower %	89.3	86.3	88.4	88.3	81.4	76.8	75.6	64.0
Scientists 1,000	320	696	1,454	2,130	2,794	3,451	4,097	5,914
Farm capital 1,000 mill. Yüan	28	48	72	96	145	231	342	871
Capital other sectors 1,000 mill. Yüan	82	143	216	292	440	704	1,045	2,680
Farm production 1,000 mill. Yüan	49	48	46	47	53	54	50	58
National product 1,000 mill. Yüan	82	102	104	124	183	232	263	492
National product per capita Yüan	134	151	137	148	197	227	237	372
Per capita consumption/Yüan	97	100	86	81	92	95	88	101

Source: Voss (1971)

the remaining sectors will grow at a similar rate, but much more in absolute terms. This implies a daunting measure of frustrated consumption, which is expressed in a very slowly rising per-capita consumption, from 81 to 101 Yüan in 30 years, i.e. by 25 per cent. In its turn, such a demand on the masses, who are to feel satisfied with a very slow rise in living standards, calls for a large measure of equality and the assured provision of a social minimum or norm for everybody.

The value of farm production will increase by roughly 25 per cent during the period 1970-2000, while the total national product will quadruple. The main quantitative contribution to growth will thus come from the secondary and tertiary sectors. – The implementation of the presumed development targets will require a great educational effort, so as to raise enough qualified manpower. Accordingly, the numbers of scientific personnel will increase by about 178 per cent. The "capital-output ratio" would, however, show a marked decline. This index value in Voss's projection naturally suggests further doubts about the attempted extrapolation.

4.5.2. *Characteristics of the model*

The basic traits of the socialist planning models for developing countries were discussed in chapter 3.2. At this point, therefore, only specifically Chinese peculiarities will be mentioned.

The economy is divided into three main sectors:
1. Raw materials and heavy industry,
2. consumer goods industry,
3. agriculture.

During the first phase economic policies laid special emphasis on sector 1, later more evenly on 2 and 3 ("standing on two legs"). Since the agrarian sector vastly predominates, the Soviet model with its long-term neglect of farming is politically dangerous and economically unfeasible. "Farming is the basis of the economy. Industry is the leading sector". Agriculture receives ample supplies of fertilisers, but few machines and tractors. Due to the slow pace of industrial growth and the low demand for manpower, a substitution of human labour by farm machinery is not necessary and not yet possible. Since the agrarian sector is quantitatively overwhelming and capable of bringing a great deal of pressure to bear, it receives a high priority in matters of planning and the allocation of investments. With subtle intuition, the planners restrict their demands on agriculture to a low factor contribution, which corresponds to the low productivity.

China's economic and foreign policies serve her desire for independence. Thus the aims most emphatically proclaimed are self-reliance, building up the country through the people's own efforts, avoidance of foreign debts, self-sufficiency, a positive balance of trade. In reality, the principles are not always observed, and the price of self-reliance during this early phase is a retardation of the economic take-off.

Technology in China aims at labour-intensive methods. It seems, however, that the approach is not uniform. In nuclear energy, aircraft construction and similar fields of strategic interest, the highest level of technology is necessary and accepted. In industries of normal importance, modern manufacturing equipment may go hand in hand with labour-intensive transport facilities. Finally, in construction work on the infrastructure and in agriculture the old techniques of production may still prevail, wasteful as they are of costly human energy.[73]

To overcome bottlenecks, to accelerate the adoption of new techniques and processes, the masses are mobilised politically. Material incentives are offered; but in view of the general poverty, they are small. They are therefore reinforced by moral incentives.

The pace of development is slow or is being slowed down. The fact that the goals of the revolution are approached step by step and over long periods of time has eased the process of social adjustment and understanding on the part of those affected by changes adding up to a radical transformation. The Cultural Revolution will prevent the rigid perpetuation of the post-revolutionary social structures and provide new political impulses.

The Great Leap Forward was launched in 1959 simultaneously with the setting up of the people's communes. It was an attempt to force the pace of industrialisation through the operation of small, decentralised units, village furnaces for steel melting, etc. Deficiencies in quality, uneconomic work and spurious statistics led to a setback. In modern industry, technological factors dictate certain minimum sizes of production units, which cannot be ignored with impunity, e.g. a capacity of about one million tonnes for a steel plant. New techniques may make it possible to lower the economical minimum size. The failure of the village furnaces does not imply, however, that all industrial development in rural areas is impossible. Considering the population density in large parts of China, the construction of medium-size factories, financed by the people's communes, can be envisaged. But such developments presuppose a basis of heavy industry and an efficient infrastructure.

Spurious statistics and false victory claims in the end harm their authors. In 1962, candid action was initiated in order to rectify the mistakes. There were food shortages in the large cities. Large quantities of wheat had to be imported. A systematic drive was launched to send townspeople and Party officials into the countryside.

Can these problems be put down to China's specific natural, geographical and demographic conditions? Or are they typical symptoms of transitory growing pains, or simply the result of temporary policy and planning errors? Can they be attributed to factors of geography and space or of history? If the basic factor is space, things will remain largely unchanged. If it is time, it can be assumed that the difficulties and their theoretical explanations will be transient.

4.5.3. *Factors of development*
China is still in the initial stage of its economic reorganisation on the way to becoming a modern nation. The transition from an agrarian to an industrial society for a nation of about 800 millions has no precedent in human history. A new economic model and new technological forms are called for.

The Communist Party adheres to Marxism as it is understood and interpreted in China today. This basic political orientation, however, gives few clues to actual problems, because China's opponents in world politics profess the same Marxism. If classical Marxism is seen as an instrument for sociological analysis and social criticism rather than as a book of recipes for socialist politics, it gives little advice on topical questions of the domestic, economic or foreign policies conducted by socialist governments. The classical Marxism of Marx himself has produced its impact and proved its fertility precisely because it lent itself to adaptation to various specific needs, so that a plurality of "Marxisms" and models of socialism emerged, all of them equally justified and authentic. Marxist thinking, the class character of a state is only one of the factors contributing to formulations of policy in socialist states. The existing natural, economic, technological, cultural and social conditions, power relations and the balance of strength in world politics are further factors entering into the process of decision-making in national politics in any state, socialist or not.

The Communist Party has adapted Marxist thinking and terminology to the country's conditions (Sinisation of Marxism). It has successfully based its strategy and its ideological interpretation on the overwhelmingly agrarian character of society and the economy. Gradually, its strategy and tactics developed independently, and before long in sometimes veiled, sometimes open contradiction to the attempts of the Soviet government and Party leaders to combine the limited aid extended by them with authoritative advice. The Long March, the first experience in communist government in limited regions, the long period of dual power produced a store of specific experience and knowledge and inspired another model of revolution. It was a seizure of power step by step and a social revolution by stages. The confrontation with the Kuomintang and the victory of 1949 did not fit in with Stalin's concept of world politics and with his limited vision.

After the victory in 1949, China's economic and political interests and aims partly coincided and partly conflicted with those of the Soviet Union. The Chinese desire for a rapid economic take-off implied heavy sacrifices for the Soviet Union and its population, suffering as it was already from the consequences of the second world war. The two Parties, both of them big and victorious, fought for ideological and political leadership (hegemony) in the communist movement and the communist world. By its military victory over the formidable war machine of Hitler's Germany, the Soviet Union had become a recognised world power. On the other hand, the Chinese People's Republic was denied its legitimate place among the nations, above all by the United States. The Soviet Union had achieved its ambitions in the second world war and its aftermath, and sought an understanding with the USA and an end to the cold war. China, on the other hand, was still embroiled in a political confrontation with the USA, which regarded its Asian involvement (in

Korea, Taiwan, Japan, Vietnam, Thailand and the Philippines) as a means to containing or even rolling back the Chinese revolution. It took the US government almost 23 years to understand and recognise the historical events that culminated in the formation of a central Communist Government in Peking on October 1, 1949.

China's demand in the early 1960s for Soviet assistance in the creation of its own nuclear defence potential increased the suspicion of her official ally. Soviet policies were led by the group around Khrushchev, which had launched de-Stalinisation. Thus, the Chinese leadership around Mao decided to make a stand in defence of Stalin and his works. The diverging interests of the two socialist big powers were never openly discussed; instead they were veiled and hidden by ceremonial professions of eternal Soviet-Chinese friendship.

The main currents in the leadership of the Chinese party reacted to these problems with controversial concepts. Liu Shao-ch'i formulated concepts of agrarian and economic policy, which, owing to their implications in terms of world affairs, were anathema to Mao. This resulted in controversies and factional struggles inside the leadership, about which very few hard facts have so far leaked out.

5. COMPARATIVE ANALYSIS AND SYNOPSIS

5.1. *General problems of development*

Many definitions have been offered for the concept of development; those of Behrendt (1965), Zimmermann (1963) and Kuznets (1959) seem to be the most functional ones. According to Behrendt,

> "development can generally be understood as directed dynamic cultural change in a social structure, linked with the growing participation of increasing numbers of its members in promoting and directing that change and in benefiting from its results... Development, thus... implies promotion and use of the dynamics for all and by all, particularly those least favoured in pre-dynamic periods – that is to say, it is a dynamic process democratically fertilised" (p. 94).

Zimmermann views development rather from the aspect of its economic results. For him economic progress is realised only, if the long-term growth rate of the gross national product exceeds the rate of population growth, i.e. if and when per-capita income is on the increase. Kuznets emphasises the importance of long-term trends, ignoring temporary variations:

> "Economic growth of a firm, an industry, a nation, a region means (whatever else it may imply) a sustained increase in the output of goods... The increase must be sustained over a period long enough to reflect more than a cyclical expansion, an unusually large harvest, recovery from some acute disturbance or any other transient rise" (p. 13).

Economic growth, frequently identified with development, was usually measured by the yardstick of the total or per-capita gross national product (GNP). The difference between the GNP in developing and developed nations was taken as measure of underdevelopment. But in using this method, the composition of the GNP, the share of subsistence households and market producers, the stratified distribution of the GNP, the social cost and negative effects of the mode of production were neglected. In the meantime, the old views and ideas have lost much ground in the face of a growing awareness of environmental problems and scepticism vis-à-vis social pressures tantamount to terror in the service of consumption, ostensibly under the banner of technological progress, or even technological revolution.

The other extreme became evident at the UN conference on environmental problems, held in Stockholm in 1972, and in the report to the Club of Rome (Meadows and Meadows, 1972). Some people now want to keep the developing nations entirely free from the negative effects of industrial development by altogether abandoning industrialisation and striving to achieve a stable balance by halting economic growth in the developed countries (zero growth). The representatives of the developing nations, in particular Indira Gandhi as their main spokesman, have vigorously rejected this approach.

5.1.1. *Development objectives*
Regarding objectives of development the following 9 theses can be formulated:

1. Humanity must aim at lessening social differentiation in each country and at reducing the development lag between nations for economic and political reasons.
2. In developing countries development can be achieved only through economic growth and a socially equitable distribution of burdens and resulting benefits.
3. Economic development implies industrialisation, at least in large developing countries, modernisation of all traditional sectors, increased productivity, rising living standards, social and geographical mobilisation and mobility, i.e. a shift of manpower from agriculture, accompanied by migration from the villages, urbanisation.
4. Negative technical and social effects of industrialisation have to be minimised by drawing on the accumulated experience of mankind. Social supervision of economic growth is necessary.
5. A comprehensive development of the educational system and speedy elimination of illiteracy – essential factors in ensuring steady active participation of the masses in the process of change – are vital to development.
6. Development, the attempt to eliminate the development lag, must be accomplished in a shorter period than was required by the currently developed societies in order to reach their present level.
7. Swift optimum development involving a minimum of social injustice and private profiteering calls for planning.
8. There is a connection between production relations and productive forces. Obsolete social structures and systems militate against the

deployment of human and material productive forces, and thus
against rapid take-off.

9. There is no development model hitherto, in which agriculture was
strongly intensified without exodus of manpower, without industrial
inputs that increase yields, without inflow of energy and a technical
equipment substituting labour.

5.1.2. *Strategy of economic mobilisation and social change*

For the modernisation of society in developing countries the desirable
strategy can be outlined in 9 points.

1. Industrialisation must be comprehensive, ranging from raw materials
and their extraction to consumer goods. This includes in the first
place large-scale modern units in key industries. Industrial development is a precondition for rapid increase of agricultural production as
well.

2. Under equal economic conditions the most modern and efficient
technologies are chosen, if adaptable to local conditions.

3. The pattern of industrial production must differ from that of developed
(capitalist) economies for three reasons: (a) a greater volume of
demand, (b) cumulative lag in the supply of consumer goods, (c)
positive and negative experience of past industrialisation. Priorities
have to be set differently, e.g. fertilisers before cosmetics, railways
before motorways, buses before cars, schools and housing before bank
buildings.

4. A modern comprehensive educational system, speedy elimination of
illiteracy, a cultural and a technological infrastructure constitute
essential components of development.

5. Planning helps in implementing modernisation as efficiently and
quickly as possible and in catching up with developed economies in a
comparatively short time.

6. Planning is subject to continuous supervision and adjustment. In a
democratic process the daily needs of the consumers-producers have to
be coordinated with the long-term interests of society as a whole.

7. Mankind's accumulated experience and knowledge has to be utilised –
transfer of technology – in suitable form, calculated to shorten the
phases of development. The acceleration of processes, however,
makes it harder for the people to adjust psychologically to new
technologies and social structures.

8. Private profit is not sufficient as an incentive to induce economic
take-off, nor is it a useful regulator in later phases.

9. A radical change in the traditional social structures and production
relations is necessary to liberate the latent forces from old ties and to

mobilise them for the great tasks ahead. The active participation of the masses in the development processes and achievements is necessary on political and economic grounds.

5.1.3. *The transition from an agrarian to an industrial society*
The change from an agrarian to an industrial society and economy passes through three essential phases.

First phase: The peasants form the vast majority of the population; farming is technically primitive, with low yields, production is self-sufficient, chiefly for subsistence. There are few links with markets outside the village, let alone outside the country, to national or world markets. The natural economy with low monetisation is diversified, and has no division of labour between the primary production units.

Second phase: Contribution of manpower – peasants and farmworkers – to the secondary and tertiary sectors. Yet the means of production capable of replacing manpower are still missing or deficient. All capital funds are needed to develop the non-agricultural sectors. Investment in farming is difficult. The machinery needed for production is subjected to wear and tear instead of being improved and expanded. Farm production is lagging behind, at least in comparison with industrial growth rates and with growing demand. Sometimes, agricultural output even stagnates in absolute terms, which causes bottlenecks in supplies of food and industrial raw materials.

Third phase: Industry has developed to the extent of permitting the delivery of agricultural inputs. The agrarian population becomes a minority. Farm production is intensified and then able to satisfy a growing demand for food. – Retrospectively, the impression is created that population growth, urbanisation, industrial development and farm mechanisation in the now industrialised countries have progressed in an harmonious process, whereas acute friction and tensions did exist and still remain.

5.2. *The agrarian sector and its key function*

5.2.1. *The role of peasantry before, during and after revolution*
In agrarian societies agriculture plays an economically and politically decisive role in the great processes of economic, technological and social transformation. There is no full identity of interests between peasants and

industrial workers. Nevertheless, the peasants, economically and socially unfree, had an interest in the overthrow of the existing order. An anti-feudalistic agrarian programme had to lay bare the latent social conflicts in the village and to appeal to the lowest strata in the village, who were mostly not workers in the industrial sense.

Communist parties have seized power in the aftermath of revolution in developing countries where peasants form a majority of the population. Contrary to Marx's predictions, they have so far failed to achieve success in highly industrialised capitalist countries. To gain mass support, the communist leaders in the agrarian countries had to turn to the oppressed and exploited peasants, to analyse their wants and wishes and to formulate a policy that would mobilise their social forces and energies for the overthrow of the old order. Lenin, Bukharin, Preobrazhensky and Mao Tsetung conscientiously examined Russia's and China's agrarian problems before the revolution.

In the development process of agrarian countries it is agriculture which is called upon to create the basis for the expansion of the other sectors by

a. supplying manpower and capital – its factor contribution;
b. raising market production – its production contribution;
c. taking up goods and services from the other sectors – its market contribution. (See also Chart 5.1)

None of these three contributions could be forthcoming without the other two, and the size of each depends on that of the others: no goods can come from the other sectors, nor can agricultural production be raised until after a measure of capital formation. Conversely it can be said that the higher the factor contribution, the lower the production contribution. The higher the social contribution – keeping unemployed people in the village and feeding them – the lower the production for the urban market.

After the revolution, new tasks gradually emerged. In an agrarian country, rapid modernisation implies the expansion of the cultural and technological infrastructure, industrial development and urban construction. The factor contribution of agriculture is decisive. At the same time the urban masses are expected to put up with shortages, owing to the low agricultural production contribution, while compulsory deliveries are imposed on the rural masses without any quid pro quo and enforced through the transformation of agriculture. As early as 1926 – three years before the first Five-Year Plan – these necessities were clearly stated by Preobrazhensky (1926):

Comparative analysis and synopsis

Chart 5.1.: Interdependence between farm and off-farm development

Category of contribution	Contributions of farming to off-farm development	Contributions of town and industry to farm
Production contributions	Food Coffee, tea, tobacco and similar stimulants, Raw materials, Working animals	Farm inputs, Consumer goods for the farming population, Services
Market contributions	Sale of farm products on internal and external markets, Purchase of off-farm goods, Payment of services	Purchase of farm products, Sale of production inputs, consumer goods, services
Factor contributions	Sale of land, delivery of water for urban settlements, industrial estates, roads, etc., Release of manpower, Capital drain	Compensation for land, etc. Offer of employment, Build-up of industries, infrastructure, services
Social contributions	Care for the unemployed, sick and aged, Cost of education and food for released manpower	Acceleration of cultural and and social change

After Kuznets, S.: Economic growth (1963)

'We can formulate a law, or at any rate that part of a law that relates to the distribution of the material means of production. The more backward economically a country is that has made the transition to a socialist organisation of production, the stronger its petty-bourgeois and peasant elements are and the smaller the socialist accumulation fund of the working class which the social revolution inherits; the greater in relative terms will be the extent to which socialist accumulation has to depend on the alienation of the surplus value of pre-socialist branches of the economy (agriculture) and the smaller will be the relative importance of the formation of capital by the socialist economy's own production base; that is to say, the less will capital formation derive from the surplus value created by the workers in socialist industry. Conversely, the more developed economically and industrially a country is in which social revolution triumphs, and the greater the material assets in the form of a highly developed industry and capitalistically organised agriculture, which the proletariat in such a country inherits by nationalisation when taking over from the bourgeoisie, the smaller will be the significance of precapitalist forms in the country in question. And furthermore, the more the proletariat in such a country is obliged by necessity to curtail the non-equivalent exchange of its products for products of former colonies, the more will the main weight of socialist accumulation shift to the production base of the socialist forms; that is to say, the more will it have to rely on the surplus value of its own industry and its own agriculture." [Preobrazhensky's footnote:] "This law must of course be modified in the event of a transfer of means of production from an advanced to a very backward socialist country." (Quoted from the English version, Preobrazhensky, 1965, p. 124; the English translation has been slightly edited.)

The process of the socialist transformation of agriculture and the agricultural population is generally marked by one decisive turning point, which may occasion profound crises of the communist regime. The peasantry shows enthusiasm in making its political contribution to the overthrow of the old feudal order. It is a contribution that is welcome to the revolutionary leadership and indispensable for the victory of the revolution. The dialectical leap from enthusiasm to aloofness and opposition occurs as soon as the factor contribution is exacted from agriculture. The more quickly the contribution is wanted, and the fewer benefits are granted in return, the more abrupt will be the cooling off between the revolutionary party and the peasantry. Control of the soil as their means of production is not enough for the peasants. they want to control the product as well.

This fundamental change in political-social needs was not analysed or explained during the Stalin era. Western agrarian politicians have overlooked, misunderstood or ignored it, and have fastened on the subsequent tension between the peasants and the socialist planners as evidence of a supposed inherent hostility of communist parties to the peasants. Accordingly, the peasants' enduring support for the (agrarian) revolution in Yugoslavia, China, Cuba and North Vietnam is a constant surprise to them.

Soviet economists and politicians recognised the problem, and warnings against rash economic policies (against all too great a 'leap forward') were uttered especially by Preobrazhensky (1926) and Trotsky.[74] Lenin had estimated that under the most favourable conditions the co-operative transformation of agriculture could be accomplished in a decade or two.[75] Stalin accelerated the radical transformation through harsh administrative measures without offering any economic incentives. The process and the traditional stages were duly compressed and shortened. This also made the difficulties of adjustment more concentrated and more painful. The persons affected by change were scarcely allowed time to adjust to the new set-up.

In the process of collectivisation four phases can be distinguished:
1. Formal decision of the peasants to form a collective farm and to join it.
2. Pooling of land, other production resources, cattle etc.
3. Manufacture and allocation or acquisition of new technical equipment for large-scale field production and construction of new cowsheds.
4. Social and psychological adjustment of individual peasants to joint decision and work.

These four component processes develop at different speeds; their harmonisation and synchronisation is a serious problem of economic policy.

New production relations were created, but without new productive forces. This was one of the main reasons for the slight economic impact of the new agrarian structure and its failure to attract support through the force of example. The formal process of the transformation of almost 25 million individual peasant farms into 30,000 collective farms is completed. The corresponding technological development and provision of equipment as well as the social readjustment of the peasants and the transformation of their consciousness cannot be effected by administrative ukase, cannot even be accelerated to any substantial extent. – It seems that the Chinese communists have learned the lesson of the Russian peasants' resistance.

5.2.2. *The role of the agrarian sector in planning and society*
In the process of development, farming is quantitatively the most important sector; the following tasks are allotted to it:
1. To satisfy the demand for food and raw materials, which is growing in terms of quantity and quality;
2. to earn foreign currency by increased exports of agricultural produce;
3. to release manpower for the expanding secondary and tertiary sectors;
4. to contribute to the capital needed for investment in infrastructure and the secondary sector;
5. to provide impulses for industrial development;
6. to be a waiting room, as it were, for workers, who cannot yet find employment elsewhere.

Some observers of communist farm policies, in particular from West Germany and the United States – notably Schiller (1943, 1960), Adams and Adams (1971), Karcz (1967), Laird (1970) – tend to regard peasant resistance to a hostile communist policy as the main reason for the low production contribution of farming. This one-sided explanation seems too simplistic. In fact, the low production contribution of agriculture may be accounted for by a number of reasons:

a. High factor contribution (systematic disinvestment) forcibly exacted by the state;
b. no deliveries of means of production;
c. agrarian structure: accelerated transformation allows the people affected no time to adjust;
d. low remuneration, hence lack of identification, passive resistance on the part of the producers;
e. other causes of low productivity.

The deficiencies of rapid collectivisation in the Soviet Union led to peasant resistance, burying of grain stores, slaughter of animals, declining or stagnating production. But the greatest mistake of all was the proclamation of the Soviet model's universal validity, so that its imitation became compulsory in the countries conquered by the Red Army, in utter disregard of the great difference of the starting situations. The unmodified transfer of Soviet agrarian policy was largely responsible for the occurrence of political crises, some of which seriously threatened the communist governments. In Yugoslavia and Poland collectivisation was first launched, then reversed, giving the peasants full freedom to leave the producer cooperatives; in other socialist countries the share of the household plot was increased, in order to adapt the Soviet model to specific national circumstances.

The position of agriculture changes under the new economic system. It seems likely, however, that in some countries this system represents a tendency rather than current reality. The economic importance of the agrarian sector is recognised, and this awareness is reflected in the plans, where a higher priority is now accorded to the needs of agriculture. More production inputs come out of the new factories and are offered to the agricultural production enterprises. The production contribution of agriculture rises, the factor contribution drops, the market contribution increases. With central dirigism and central supervision abandoned, active participation on the part of the kolkhoz peasants, whose democratic rights had previously existed on paper only, is now possible and indeed required. None the less, after the adjustment of priorities in favour of farming, the disproportions between the agricultural and industrial sectors remain effective for a considerable period.

Several reasons can be given for that:
a. The extent to which natural conditions of production can be controlled is still inadequate. Increased control and guidance calls for

substantially higher capital investment. Natural fluctuations in harvests and yields cannot be wholly excluded, but only mitigated. Thus, planning must be generous and operate with wide safety margins. Commodity stocks also contribute to minimising the effects of harvest fluctuations.

b. Increases in agricultural production comparable to industrial growth rates require preliminary investments as well as a regular supply of equipment and materials necessary to raise production.

c. The number of producers to be integrated into the planned process of economic development is very large. Owing to the peculiar effect of technology in agriculture – dispersal of individuals, social isolation, absence of a division of labour and of a concentration of masses of workers – new socio-technical instruments must be found for the management of production.

Attentive and critical monitoring of planning progress should give early warning, if and when the need for a major change in economic policy arises.

5.2.3. *The impact of agrarian reform*

The transformation of the agrarian structure and of the rural social structure is decisive for economic, political and social reasons. In an agrarian society, land ownership confers many benefits: a working opportunity in the dominant sector and livelihood for the family, a high social status, economic power over landless labourers as well as political influence and power. Radical changes in land ownership affect the entire power structure at all levels from the village upwards.

Agrarian systems are not equal in their adaptability to changing conditions and new tasks; some are unable to adapt themselves. There is a correlation between performance in production, inputs and institutions. The capacity of institutions and production relations to deploy new motive forces is limited; frequently these institutions are the limiting factors. Their continuous adaptation is an urgent task of farm policies.

Three ways are available for the change of agrarian structure:
– slow improvement by adaptation;
– agrarian reform;
– agrarian revolution.

The three forms are distinguished by five essential features:
– speed of the process and time needed for it;
– radical character of measures. If these are compressed into a short period, the pains of transformation are likewise compressed, and more intensely felt in a shorter span of time;

- initiative and activity of the peasantry. There are situations in which social contradictions in the farming sector and the development expectations of the peasants call for an agrarian revolution;
- incentives for the rural masses;
- compensation for the expropriated landowners.

Whether compensation can be paid depends among other things on the role of farming in the national economy. It implies in any case a redistribution of capital in favour of the wealthy and a diversion of the agricultural surplus from the farming sector. Sometimes, this surplus is used for productive investment in industries, sometimes it is wasted in conspicuous consumption. Social justice apart, it is economic considerations which suggest that compensation ought to be rejected in most of the countries, where an agrarian reform is called for.

Agrarian reform or revolution may be accompanied by a drop in total farm production. This phenomenon is not necessarily the consequence of the change in the agrarian structure, for it may well be caused by simultaneous social processes: migration to the new industries and towards the tertiary sector is an important concomitant of agrarian revolutions. New technologies and new inputs are needed to replace human labour. But these benefits cannot accrue to farming until the relevant factories have been constructed and equipped and have started to operate. Production relations and productive forces have to be renewed simultaneously. The two factors can act only together, not separately. Sometimes, a depression following agrarian reform is due not to a drop in production, but to a drop in market supplies. For such a development two reasons can be suggested:

- The beneficiaries of agrarian reform with their families increase their home consumption and thus create a basis for better physical performance at a later stage.
- They refuse to sell their products, if no industrial goods are offered in exchange.

To some extent, the breakdown of the old social institutions can be held responsible for the low production performance in the early stages of a reform or revolution. Referring to the process as a whole, Bukharin (1922) speaks of the social cost of revolution.

Agrarian reform in *India* is gradualist, intended to proceed cautiously step by step. The zamindars and big landlords, who remain in the village[76] and retain large land holdings (for owner-cultivation), receive compensation for the expropriated land. Thus, unproductive payments continue unchanged, sometimes even at an accelerated pace, and the economic and political power structure in the village remains the same. Accordingly, the economic and psychological stimulus for the mobilisation of fettered

175

energies has so far been very weak. The factor contribution of farming towards food supplies and economic development has remained small and grown slowly, if at all. Yields appear to be virtually stagnant in the long term, without an agrarian revolution, whereas – as has been seen – stagnation or declining production are frequently explained as the consequence of such profound social change. In spite of government support, the cooperatives, too, have remained weak, although they intended to take over the neglected tasks of the deposed landlords.

In *Soviet Russia*, the agrarian revolution of 1917 radically destroyed all remnants of feudalism and liberated the peasantry from all unproductive payments to their former landlords, who were forbidden by law to reside in, or return to, their former villages. The peasants thus had won full economic freedom, which was hardly touched by the communist government during the first decade or more. But collectivisation from 1929 to 1933 was the dialectical negation of the earlier phase. At breath-taking speed it created an entirely new agrarian structure (new production relations) without being able to deliver the new means of production that would have assured the productive success of social change. At the same time, it deprived the peasantry of its right to dispose freely of surplus agricultural production, which had been one of the fruits of the revolution.

In *China*, the agrarian revolution was radical, but it was implemented in several phases: reduction, later abolition of land rent and debt payments, distribution of the landlords' land, leaving only a family unit at their disposal. A village tribunal composed of local peasants was formed to punish or purge the feudal lords. Cooperatives were organised step by step, leading finally to the formation of people's communes. Animal husbandry declined. A certain drop in production appeared as a consequence of the social transformation, though it probably was smaller than in Soviet Russia in the early 1930s. So far, no migration from the village has been possible; on the contrary, urban workers and (recalcitrant) officials were directed to the land as a result of urban food shortages and for the purpose of mutual re-education.

5.2.4. *The peasant as a political personality*

In contrast to normal usage, peasants are functionally defined for the purpose of this book as the ultimate producers, all those who in fact cultivate the land, irrespective of their legal relationship to the land title. The specific situation of the peasants implies certain difficulties in their attempts at social change and political power.

1. Physical weakness and dependence on their ties to home and village for food and maintenance;

2. dispersion over a wide area and lack of communications;
3. lack of nation-wide political and vocational organisation;
4. problem of finding leaders within their own ranks;
5. illiteracy;
6. caste system or similar systems of social stratification, their rein-
forcement by religious institutions, inculcating a sense of inferiority
in the broad masses;
7. domestic competition between cultivators for land and market shares
destroys or impairs the awareness of a common destiny and common
social interests;
8. peasants have rarely succeeded in developing a utopian vision or far-
reaching aims appealing to them and mobilising their social energies.
In actual economic history, the share-croppers and tenants of Southern
Asia, the workers in the large plantations, the *inquilinos* of the Latin
American latifundia are the poorest and most oppressed strata or classes
of their societies. They are subjected to twofold or threefold exploitation
by landlords, moneylenders and middlemen, who very often are members
of the same caste, the same clan or the same family. Local exploitation is
aggravated by the fact that many large holdings are owned by foreign
nationals, who seek to transfer their profits to the metropolis.

Among themselves, peasants compete for the land offered for sale or
tenancy, since the land is their sole or main source of income. Competition
becomes more acute with population growth, particularly if no alternative employment or income is available; it impairs or destroys the
awareness of a common destiny and common social interests.

In Europe, the peasant's status of social inferiority and economic
dependence was changed by the agrarian reforms of the 18th and 19th
centuries. Peasant liberation implied two things: (1) Expulsion of all
"non-viable" holders; thus the efficient farmers and landlords were
furthered; (2) establishment of economically independent peasants (or
farmers), who remained independent at least for a long period.[77]

Social differentiation and polarisation form part of a continuous
process, by which members of the lower rural strata are eliminated from
the farming sector. Thus, it is impossible to speak of agriculture or the
rural community as a uniform social group or stratum. It includes different
strata, some closer to the bourgeoisie, others closer to the working class.
There may, however, be a gap between economic conditions and socio-
political consciousness. Poor peasants in many respects are different and
think and act differently from urban workers.

Ignorance of rural social stratification and social consciousness is a
barrier to the understanding of social movements. The specific conjunction of conditions has to be analysed, if the reasons for peasant unrest

and revolt or inaction and inertia are to be explained, if we want to know, why and how peasants emerge as an organised revolutionary force.

In *India*, the peasantry played an active role during the independence struggle, though its organisation was technically weak. Agrarian reform, therefore, became one of the principal official aims of the Congress Party and the government. But distances, low living standards, and ethnic and language barriers combined to inhibit a strong expression of the demands of the cultivators. Thus, agrarian reform has remained ineffective, and the peasantry still is a latent and barely articulate force.

In *Soviet Russia*, the smallholders had a decisive share in triggering off the revolution of 1917, which satisfied their main demands: land to the tiller and peace, i.e. demobilisation of the Tsarist army. When collectivisation started, the embryonic organisations of the peasantry were dismantled, so as to forestall any organised resistance. Not until the late sixties was the formation of a new organisation representing the peasants' interests discussed again. Up to that time, Stalin's explanation that peasants and workers have identical interests and are linked in an unbreakable alliance was taken at its face value.[78]

In *China*, too, the peasants played an active part in the revolution, more active even than in the Soviet Union.[79] As a main pillar of the revolutionary struggle they had to be considered and it was important not to alienate them. Nothing is known, however, of any specific peasant organisation actually representing their demands.

5.3. *Industrialisation*

The establishment of industries is accepted as necessary for the following main reasons:
a. Increase of farm production to assure food supplies for a growing population;
b. supply of industrial commodities in adequate quantities;
c. providing jobs for the unemployed and underemployed of the agrarian sector;
d. improvement of labour productivity, thus creating the prerequisites for cultural progress on a mass basis;
e. economic independence, diversification of the external trade of developing countries, improvement of the terms of trade.

Engineering and science, inventions and discoveries are equal for all cultures and nations and should be the common property of humanity. Given modern communications facilities, it seems unnecessary and wasteful to re-invent techniques already invented or discovered.

5.3.1. Determinant factors of industrial development
The pattern of industrialisation is dependent on a number of factors, the most important of which seem to be:
1. Size of the country and its population;
2. raw materials and their location, natural conditions;
3. settlement structure;
4. infrastructure, communications, educational system;
5. development lag;
6. external aid;
7. economic and social system (see also Chart 5.2.).

1. The size of the country and its population determines the manpower potential, variety and types of production, size of domestic market. Countries with small populations can develop only industries capable of affecting economies of scale under the given limitations (manpower, raw materials, markets). India, the Soviet Union and China, the three most populous nations, need a diversified industrialisation ranging from extraction and processing of raw materials to the most sophisticated instruments and computers.

2. Quantity, variety and location of raw materials and their proximity to natural (water) or technological transport routes influence industrialisation. Lack of raw materials and natural resources can be covered by imports, if other commodities are available in exchange.

3. Sparse settlement precludes the emergence of industrial centres. A dense population makes the dispersal of factories feasible. There are various industries well suited to decentralised location.

4. Technological and cultural infrastructure, transport system and skilled manpower are prerequisites of industrialisation.

5. Development lag and pent-up demand call for efficient mass production in large countries. But if the country has much leeway to make up and its population is large, then the experience of early capitalism points to the desirability and feasibility of a different pattern and product mix of industrial production. What is wanted, then, is a system of ecologically neutral production and products, in which priority is accorded to the needs of the masses, e.g. to mass transport rather than individual transport.

6. Refusal of external aid slows down development. Aid from a single source leads to dependence and prejudices domestic plans. Multilateral aid, on the other hand, offers room for manœuvre so as to safeguard economic independence.

7. Planning accelerates the economic take-off and ensures priority for the interests and goals of society over individual interests and private

179

Chart 5.2: Determinant factors of industrialisation

Determinants	India	China	Soviet Union
1. Area	3 million sq km, sufficient for diversified industrial development	9.6 million sq km; as India	22 million sq km; as India
2. Population (1975)	604 million; potential for diversified, efficient mass production	about 800 million; as India	253 million; as India
3. Raw materials	partly unexplored; sufficient	sufficient	ample; also exports
4. Location of natural resources	remote	remote	very remote
5. Settlement structure	dense, clustered villages, decentralisation feasible in wide regions	as India; border regions frequently with marginal conditions	sparse; decentralisation difficult and expensive
6. Technical infrastructure	existing, needs improvement	partly missing	existing, but in sparsely populated regions weak
7. Cultural infrastructure	existing, but only part of population integrated; socially biased	created after 1949, open to all social strata	created after 1917, open to all social strata
8. Development lag	very great; acceleration necessary	as India	basically overcome; higher priority for consumer goods industries
9. Foreign aid	from many sources, both East and West; growing indebtedness	low volume, from West only, small debts	foreign aid at present more given than received
10. Economic system	mixed economy (private enterprise-cum-planning; very heavy sacrifice of consumption exacted from mass of people)	planned economy, moderate sacrifice of consumption	rigidly planned economy, heavy sacrifice of consumption
11. Social system	caste society, low mobility	socialist revolutionary change aiming at continual rotation of office-holders	revolutionary change, socialist, new social stratification
12. Pace of growth	slow	modest, accelerating	in the early stages rapid, slowing down

profit. It offers an opportunity for a fairer distribution of both the burdens and the fruits of development.

The three countries analysed here are in need of comprehensive industrial development and have the necessary prerequisites for it. But the relative importance of the seven crucial factors varies from case to case.

India's natural resources are still largely unknown. Internal distances are moderate, but technical and cultural infrastructure do not measure up to the demands of a modern industrial society. The great development lag is only slowly reduced. Production is diversified, but insufficient in quantity. External aid is moderate in absolute terms and can at best contribute to pump-priming. The constitution has abolished the traditional social system, but only on paper. In actual fact the caste system continues as before. The mixed economy with a public and a private sector is not very efficient in its development effort.

The *Soviet Union* has virtually overcome the development lag. It possesses an abundance of natural resources, but the distances are enormous. The country is scarcely in need of foreign aid at this stage and is able to buy external know-how. Its industries can satisfy most of the demand for consumer goods, though quantity and quality are sometimes not entirely satisfactory. The revolution abolished the old classes, created a new social system, which, however, appears to engender a new stratification. Economic planning, an experiment without precedent, accelerated development. Planning needs a continuous reappraisal of methods, aims and content.

China faces a situation comparable to India's in respect of the aforementioned factors 1-5, corresponding to determinants 1-8 in Chart 5.2. During certain phases of her development China has refused foreign aid and called for self-help. Social differences were largely levelled by liquidating big landlords and capitalists. Rotation of functions, change between manual and intellectual work and the Cultural Revolution are intended to inhibit the emergence of a new rigid pattern accompanied by social immobility. The economy is directed and developed according to a central plan, which for political as well as economic reasons takes into account and integrates the dominance of the agrarian sector, the slow accumulation of capital and regional needs. At the current stage in the development of resources and of the infrastructure, priority is given to regional initiative, mobilisation of local resources and the decentralised implementation of the general plan.

5.3.2. *Unemployment and strategies of development*
Two main forms of unemployment have to be distinguished: full and

open unemployment and hidden unemployment or underemployment. The latter is difficult to ascertain and quantify, because its extent depends on the production techniques and the degree to which they are inferior to the improved techniques already available. Traditional working methods and tools are tying down a vast workforce in the farming sector of many developing nations. They are active and fully employed only during the short peak periods of demand for labour, while being out of work for the greater part of the year. A new machine that reduces the peak demand for labour completely dispenses with the services of a proportion of the underemployed, and assures the same production with a lesser work-force. The redundant workers are then available for alternative employment. Unemployment and underemployment are largely endemic in developing countries; they depress labour productivity and put a brake on technical progress and its large-scale introduction at a time when technology is still at a low and traditional level. Unemployment, then, cannot be the consequence of mechanisation, of the input of modern machinery, replacing and releasing manpower. The combination of a low level of technology with a high level of unemployment rather suggests the opposite cause: unemployment is largely due to slow development, which is bound up with traditional technology and equipment.[80]

Unemployment is aggravated by population growth, since no alternative employment in other sectors can be offered, because industrial expansion has been made impossible. A full-scale registration of the unemployed is difficult for several reasons.

a. A clear definition and delimitation of work, employment, unemployment is possible only in a modern society, where salaried work is the social norm for the vast majority;
b. registration does not make economic sense until and unless labour becomes a scarce commodity;
c. the administrative machinery is missing;
d. in so far as neither alternative employment nor unemployment allowance can be offered, there is no incentive for registration. As soon as an opportunity arises, thousands and millions register and clamour for work.[81] People in developing countries are doomed to unemployment not by laziness or higher priority for leisure-time, or a lack of the business mentality, but by the absence of employment opportunities and the lack of physical energy.

One of the main levers of economic development is the mobilisation and use of the available manpower. Here different models have been developed. Difficulties hampering this mobilisation are:

1. Maintenance of the level of farm production;
2. mobilisation of a maximum of unemployed;

3. aggregation and utilisation of the manpower of the vast number of underemployed available for work during part of the year only;
4. organisation of manpower;
5. feeding, housing and supplying the other needs of those not employed in farming;
6. provision of tools and materials;
7. prevention of inflationary effects of new wage payments;
8. selection of the most important projects, which promise the most far-reaching and most rapid effect.

Small local projects avoid the difficulties numbered 1, 3, 5, 7, but increase those numbered 2, 4, 6, 8, It is the other way round with large-scale and centrally organised projects. The short-term employment effect as a social objective is largest if a minimum of scarce resources is allotted to modern equipment. On the other hand, efficiency of production and – as a consequence – the improvement in the living standards of the large masses is the greater, the more modern, labour-saving equipment is installed. Additional sources of mechanical or electric energy multiply the work performance precisely of physically weak, underfed people; they accelerate the implementation of projects, thus also the onset of production, and shorten the passive incubation period. Such an acceleration has psychologically a mobilising effect on the rural masses, existing in a state of lethargy induced by physical and social weakness and lack of success.

In *India*, a middle road has been sought in employment strategy. Large-scale, modern, capital-intensive industrial projects have been built, assisted by foreign aid that had been requested for that purpose. Public funds were at the same time spent on the conservation and protection of traditional crafts. To fight against mass poverty a crash programme of rural emergency works was started in 1972. In it, two thirds of the expenditure goes into the (very low) wages, paid partly in cash, partly in kind. Food as payment is provided in part by the Food and Agriculture Organisation of the UN (FAO) through its world food programme.

The *Soviet Union* gave absolute priority to its large-scale projects. Considering the existing settlement structure and the sparseness of the population, that policy resulted in the migration of millions, accompanied by changes in social status. Except for the school system, few funds were allocated for local infrastructure projects. In this way, rural underemployment was radically diminished. But it was difficult to maintain farm production and assure food supplies for the growing urban population.

China has promoted modern, large-scale projects and the regional and village industries. The people's communes, much larger in size than the single villages, are apt institutions for the accumulation and mobilisation of capital, according to the size of population, and they can organise the replacement of labour when needed for external work. Likewise, they are able to mobilise manpower for local works in land improvement (drainage, irrigation, reclamation, forest clearing, flood protection) and regional infrastructure (roads, schools, drinking water, sewerage).

Unemployment and pressure on the employment opportunities can be alleviated in different ways:
1. Education (compulsory school attendance, prolongation of school age, improved vocational training): it reduces the numbers and improves the skill of job-seekers.
2. Social security (old-age insurance): it reduces the numbers af aged workers by early and statutory retirement.
3. Emigration: it reduces the numbers of economically active persons in the "best age groups" and tends to select the occupationally most qualified.
1 and 2 are thus desirable, whereas 3 is macro-economically doubtful and harmful, though micro-economically it may often be the only solution for unemployment and distress.[82]

5.3.3. *Choice of technology*
Regarding the further development of industries, two economic strategies are offered.

Conservative economists and development theorists advocate measures to assist in the conservation of small-scale cottage industries. The main reasons are:
- Lack of technical know-how concerning modern production methods and equipment.
- Lack of capital and foreign exchange for the purchase and importation of expensive machinery.
- Great leaps forward are economically risky and socially undesirable. The industrial societies of today needed 150 years to reach their present levels.
- The first task in a densely populated agrarian country is the creation of employment. Large-scale, capital-intensive factories increase unemployment.
- The labour-capital ratio in modern, capital-intensive industries is unfavourable for a poor country (i.e. few employment opportunities are created per unit of capital).
- Large factories uproot the village population and may easily become hotbeds of social unrest.

Therefore, various measures are suggested to maintain or revitalise traditional occupations and skills.

A variation of this approach is the proposal for the introduction of an intermediate technology, which would permit only slow progress during the early phases of economic development.

The advocates of modern industries refer to the following points:
- In the long rung, only modern industries can compete with foreign goods on world and home markets.
- Increased productivity leads to improved social standards and rising wages, raises the purchasing power and enlarges the home market, which is the prerequisite for competition on world markets.
- It is true, that some modern factories cannot offer much employment inside their gates. But their growth potential and linkage-effect create new employment in subsidiary services (repair and replacement of machinery, transport of raw materials and finished goods) and in the tertiary sector (administration, commerce, social services, housing).
- Some important industries cannot work on a small scale or with an intermediate, labour-intensive technology (electricity, chemical industries, oil refineries, fertilisers, steel, lorries and cars, etc.).
- Industrialisation in a large nation of many hundred million consumers calls for large-scale, modern production units, to meet the demands of the masses.

The economic size of a factory unit is not a fixed quantity, for it depends also on technological developments, which may lead to the design of smaller units. In steel production, for example, a modern plant in a capitalist or socialist economy has as a rule an output of about one million tonnes or more per year. The Chinese village furnaces with an annual capacity of a few hundred tonnes proved an economic and technical failure. But new technical processes available today enable a steel plant with a capacity of 300,000 to 400,000 tonnes to be run economically.

Before independence, colonial countries had no choice but to accept every offer by metropolitan industrialists or businessmen. Today an independent developing nation can choose freely between various propositions, differing in technology and the degree of sophistication. Most likely the modern technology will be chosen, if suited or adaptable to the specific conditions (climate, skill of mechanics and workers, durability).

In certain very backward regions or in certain trades and occupations the rapid switchover to modern technology can cause great hardship. In such cases additional precautions are necessary to lessen the shock and humanise the transition: measures such as protection of local produce, modernisation of design, social assistance and security for old artisans, retraining of the younger ones. If capital and capital goods are lacking, traditional techniques and tools have to be used for urgent projects. This should be understood, however, as a compromise enforced by a lack of material and financial resources rather than as a desirable way or as an end in itself. Official Indian reports show that subsidies cannot preserve the traditional crafts over a long period.[83] At best they can slow down the process of transformation, but are unable to revitalise the traditional sector of village and cottage "industries".

Two reservations have to be made regarding the input of modern technology.

1. Lack of capital does not permit the introduction of modern techniques in all economic sectors simultaneously. Priorities have therefore to be laid down on economic grounds. Thus the continued use of less productive methods is a necessary phase of the transition, which should be shortened as much as possible.

2. The technology of the industrial nations has been developed mainly in and for moderate climates. It must be adapted to the climatic, technical and other conditions of the countries to which it is to be transferred.

The transfer of technology, apart from other aspects, poses a socio-cultural problem as well. There are various methods of accelerating the transfer (see Chapter 5.7.). The methods differ in respect of the demand they make on foreign exchange, of the mobilisation of domestic resources, of the time needed, and of the socio-cultural difficulties arising.

India has chosen a mix of different technologies, with changes of emphasis in different phases of development. For the new industries (steel, armaments, nuclear energy), a modern technology is preferred. But several institutions have been created by the government and the cooperative movement for the protection of traditional crafts. Schools and academies have been organised to train instructors in these crafts. Quotas are reserved for the cottage industries and their output. When the planners feel the pressure of unemployment, modern technology is relegated to the second rank. Farming is mostly excluded from modernisation and mechanisation.

Soviet Russia has officially opted for the most modern technology available. The planned development effort was initially concentrated on large-scale industrial projects. Naturally, even here priorities had to be set. Thus, farming and housing remained under-equipped for a long period, until heavy industry, arms manufacture, etc. were fully up to world level. This, in fact, was one of the main slogans of planning and mobilisation: to attain the world level, to catch up with and overtake the United States.

China has changed her options at different points in its economic development. In the early phases of planning, modern technology and large-scale units were preferred. In the late fifties, local production units with low and local capital input and low technology were proclaimed as the best way to self-reliance. At present, a factual change seems to have occurred, though not yet officially acknowledged, which has led to a dual approach: modern technology, largely imported, if necessary, is used for the strategically important industries, while farming – still the largest sector – has to carry on with its traditional tools and methods. Even that might change, however, in due course, that is to say, when the country can provide modern equipment from its own factories.

5.4. *Models of population transfer*

In most, though not all, developing countries, full productive employment is impossible in the agrarian sector. It calls for the expansion of the non-agricultural sectors, thus for social, and under certain conditions also geographical, mobility.

Different types and phases of mobility can be distinguished.

Social mobility – change from farming to non-agricultural occupations and employment. – Most developing countries have a high proportion of their manpower engaged, though not fully and productively employed, in "agriculture". In developed economies the proportion is low, eventually decreasing to under 10 per cent. Development of secondary and tertiary sectors is almost synonymous with social mobility, shift away from farming. There seems to be no development without mobility. But the opposite is not always true: there can be mobility without development, as demonstrated by the vast slums and the urban sub-proletariat in many developing countries of Latin America, Africa and Asia.

Geographical mobility, migration. – If no gainful employment is available in the villages and in agriculture, people of working age are driven to look for work elsewhere. This can be in other villages, where the position is likely to be similar; in other regions, where at least seasonal demand may arise; in towns and new industries; or, if none of these opportunities is offered or is sufficient for a growing labour force, in foreign countries ("guest workers" in Western Europe). Migration of farmworkers between villages and between regions tends to even out employment peaks and different man-land ratios.

Social and geographical mobility are interlinked in many instances, but not invariably. Generally, the establishment of new towns and industries with their need for manpower induces people to leave farming and move out of the village. Such social and residential mobility is most effectively induced, where regular employment can be offered and expensive capital equipment demands continuous production. Residential mobility is mostly connected with change of occupation or economic sector, while social mobility can occur without urbanisation. This is particularly true in later stages of industrial development.

Social and geographical mobility are closely related to development. Mobility is both a prerequisite and a consequence of development. With higher development, the number of people mobilised and the intensity and range of mobility are increasing.

The three countries differ both in their socio-economic systems and in the size of manpower mobilised and eventually transferred.

For *India*, basic population figures may be more accurate than for China. The dimensions of the transfer problem are enormous and similar to those of China. Rapid population growth since 1931 has inflated the population dependent on agriculture from 187 to 375 million in 1971 (see Table 5.1.). During the 30 years 1951-81, the total workforce is expected to increase more than twofold, from 139.5 to 298.7 million (see Table 5.2.). Thus, with unchanged sectoral composition, the workforce in farming will grow from 97.3 to 207.6 million people. The non-agricultural workforce is expected to increase from 42.2 to 91.1 millions. With unemployment and underemployment already endemic in both the

Table 5.1.: India: Total and agricultural population

Year	Total	Agriculture millions	p.c.	Decadal growth rate p.c.	Workers all sectors	primary	secondary sector per cent	tertiary
					millions			
1891	235	–	–	–				
1901	236	157	66.5	0.4	111.4	71.8	12.6	15.6
1911	252	182	72.2	5.7	121.4	75.9	10.7	13.4
1921	251	183	73.0	– 0.3	117.9	76.0	10.4	13.6
1931	279	187	67.0	11.0	120.6	74.8	10.2	15.0
1941	319	239	75.0	14.2	–	–	–	–
1951	361	253	70.0	13.3	139.5	72.1	10.6	17.3
1961	439	316	72.0	21.6	188.6	72.3	11.7	16.0
1971	547	375	68.6	24.6	183.6	68.6	31.4	

Source: Statistical abstract (1967), Monthly commentary (1971)

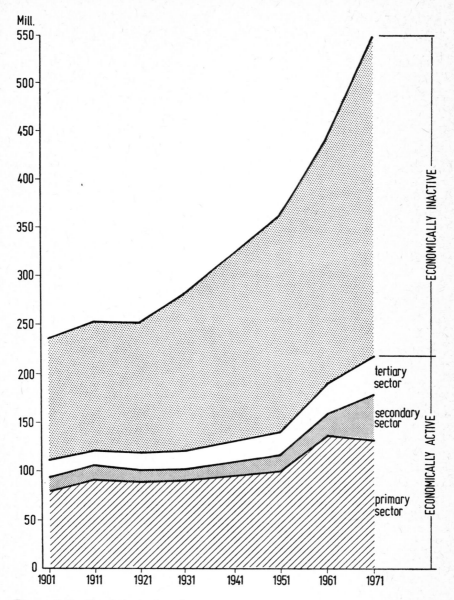

Fig. 5.1. India: Population and employment 1901-1971

Table 5 2.: India: Work force

Year	Agricultural	Non-agricultural workforce millions	Total	Population	Agricultural in p.c. of total workforce
1951	97.3	42.2	139.5	356.9	69.7
1961	131.2	57.6	188.8	439.2	69.5
1971	167.2	73.3	240.5	559.6	69.5
1981	207.6	91.1	298.7	694.9	69.5
Decennial increase					
1951-61	33.9	15.4	49.3	82.3	–
1961-71	36.0	15.7	51.7	120.4	–
1971-81	40.4	17.8	58.2	135.3	–

Source: Dantwala (1968)

urban and rural population, there is little prospect of the self-imposed targets of social and manpower planning being achieved (see also Fig. 5.1).

In the *Soviet Union*, the process was greatly accelerated and compressed within a very short span of time. The agrarian reforms of 1861 and 1905 hardly promoted migration from the land. Neither did the final abolition of feudalism and land distribution in 1917 lead to migration. On the contrary, the destruction of the embryonic industrial machinery in the first world war and the ensuing civil war led to a move back to the land and an urban exodus. Rapid industrialisation began with the first five-year plan in 1929 and called for mass migration to the emerging industrial centres. The collectivisation, launched simultaneously, released (or drove) millions of peasants from the land. The industrial and office workforce grew from about 3 million in 1917 to almost 100 million in 1974. The urban population grew from 18 per cent in 1913 to 60 per cent in 1975. During the same period the total population grew from 159 to 253 millions. The rural population declined more slowly than those employed in, and dependent on, agriculture. The agricultural labour force decreased from 31.3 to 25.8 millions during the period 1940-1974 (see Tables 5.3 and 3.18 and Fig. 5.2). The drastic social transformation and inter-sectoral migration are shown in Table 3.3.

For *China*, precise figures from home sources are hardly available. It seems, however, that Chinese planning adopts a more wary approach to rural-urban migration. There are three main reasons why Chinese planning does not follow the Soviet model: (1) Farming holds an overwhelming position, while the industrial sector is very weak. The capacity

Table 5.3.: Population growth and mobility – Soviet Union

Year	Total	Agricul- tural in millions	Rural	Urban	Agricul- tural	Rural per cent	Urban
1913	159.2	119.4	130.5	28.7	75	82	18
1939	170.6	105.8	116.0	54.6	62	68	32
1956	200.2	86.1	110.1	90.1	43	55	45
1959	208.8	81.4	108.6	100.2	39	52	48
1961	216.1	75.6	108.0	108.1	35	50	50
1963	223.1	73.6	107.1	116.0	33	48	52
1966	231.9	64.9	106.7	125.2	28	46	54
1969	238.9	59.7	105.1	133.8	25	44	56
1972	247.5	?	103.9	143.6	?	42	58
1975	253.3	60.2	101.3	152.0	24 [1])	40	60

[1]) 1974

Sources: Narodnoe chozjajstvo, Information zur politischen Bildung

of farming to produce an agricultural surplus is small. Communications, marketing and distribution are not sufficiently developed and monetised to permit the emergence of a genuine national market and national economy in the modern sense, in which most or all factors are flexible. (2) In view of the size of the population, transfers and migration would involve vast masses, giving rise to economic upheavals and material problems.[84] (3) When agriculture has a very limited capacity for making factor contributions, rapid industrialisation implies either heavy pressure on the agrarian sector or reliance on foreign aid, both politically undesirable. The first alternative could have shaken the domestic political foundations of a power based on the agrarian revolution; the latter would have required foreign policy arrangements with the donor country, thus imposing a limitation on the country's freedom of manœuvre in world affairs.

Social change in the hitherto non-industrialised "Third World" involves much larger numbers of people than all development models of the past. Economists, planners, politicians may well feel overawed in the face of the prospect of mass migration, accompanied by urban slums, social upheavals etc. The pains of change, however, are the price of development. The pains ought to be mitigated by good social planning, extension of the period of transformation,[85] planning of decentralised industries and services.[86]

According to computations by Voss (1971), shown in Table 5.4 and

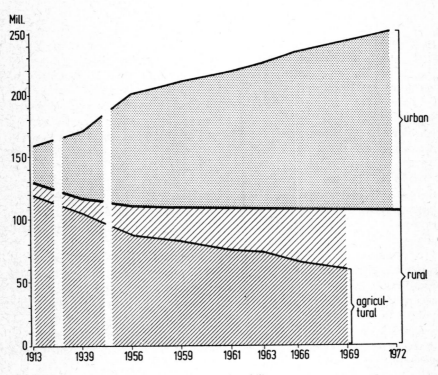

Fig. 5.2. Soviet Union: Population growth and mobility

Table 5.4.: Population growth and employment 1912-2000 [1]) – China

Year	Population				Employment		
	Millions	Growthrate p.a.	Urban rural per cent		Total Agriculture millions		Agriculture percent
1912	430	–	8.5	91.5	–	–	–
1933	500	–	9.3	90.7	–	–	–
1950	547	1.7	10.9	89.1	–	–	–
1952	569	2.0	12.1	87.9	270	238	87.9
1955	611	–	–	–	233	208	89.3
1960	683	1.8	15.5	84.5	263	227	86.3
1965	756	–	–	–	292	258	88.4
1969	799	2.0	14.6	85.4	387	329	85.0
1970	841	–	–	–	324	286	88.3
1975	931	–	–	–	365	297	81.4
1980	1,022	–	–	–	406	312	76.8
1985	1,111	–	–	–	442	334	75.6
2000	1,325	–	–	–	542	347	64.0

[1]) Data are composed from two sources: 1912-52, 1969 Rochlin + Hagemann, the rest and part of the 1960 data from Voss. The authors' estimates differ somewhat. Data from 1970 onwards are estimates by Voss.

Sources: Rochlin + Hagemann (1971); Voss (1971)

Fig. 5.3, China's total population will grow from 841 million in 1970 to 1,235 million in the year 2000. The share of those active in agriculture will slowly decrease from 88 per cent in 1952-1970 to 64 per cent in 2000. That, however, implies a net growth from 238 to 347 million, i.e. by 46 per cent. Those employed in all other sectors will increase sixfold from 32 to 195 million. But even such a rapid growth of non-farming activities implies a further substantial net growth of agricultural manpower.

5.5. *Problems and policies in education*

At the point of economic take-off, the educational system of all developing countries is backward, compared to the "world level" or to domestic needs. One of the principal tasks and at the same time means of development is the deployment of all mental capacities, of the brain capital. Economic, social, cultural and political factors are responsible for this backwardness. Besides compulsory primary schooling and a broad extension of secondary and vocational education, the elimination of illiteracy among adults plays a culturally mobilising role. The handicaps of the lower social classes have to be lessened, and they must be given equality of opportunity. This particular development task needs almost

Comparative analysis and synopsis

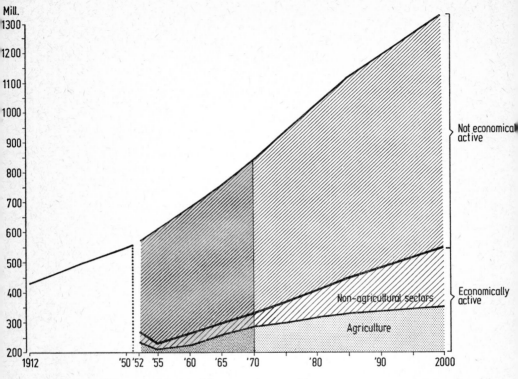

Fig. 5.3. China: Population and its sectoral composition

194

no foreign currency or foreign experts or foreign aid, apart from a few raw materials or scarce material resources. It can and must be implemented mainly with domestic forces and local materials. To offset the earlier discrimination against the working and peasant classes, different methods, operating at different speeds may be adopted: fellowships for specially gifted children of workers, access to higher education for mature working students, broad intake of secondary schools, colleges and universities, priority for children of working or peasant origin.[87]

Problems of education policy are e.g.: how to adapt curricula and courses to the needs of developing countries; how to bar the emergence and establishment of new "elites".

India has probably registered the most modest success in comparison with the two other nations. Primary education was extended, but has not by a long way reached all children of school age. On the other hand, it seems that the universities are educating more academics than the country can employ. In spite of certain protective measures and quotas for the former untouchables, higher education largely remains a privilege of the upper castes, particularly strong in the regions of orthodox Hinduism, much weaker in the south, e.g. in Kerala.

In the *Soviet Union*, general education was quickly extended to the entire population. As a compensation for the historical injustice and in order to mobilise the necessary potential quickly, children of workers and peasants were temporarily privileged by a minimum quota system. Good vocational schools and the stipulation of making university entry conditional on the completion of two years' production experience are to counteract an overvaluation of intellectual as against manual work. In spite of these precautions it appears likely that in actual fact children from families with a university background are again over-represented among university students.

In *China* the efforts to ensure general attendance at primary schools and to reduce illiteracy were probably more successful than in India, though final figures are missing. Chinese characters, however, present more difficulties to general education and literacy than most other scripts. Rotation of office-holders, physical work and other measures are taken to counteract the formation of new elites.[88] – Both in the Soviet Union and China, the Party exercises a measure of control concerning the political reliability of the candidates for university entry.

5.6. *Problems of planning*

5.6.1. *Role and potential of planning*
Societal planning of an entire national economy, and of a backward one at

that, was tried for the first time in human history in the Soviet Union in the twenties of our century. It dethroned profit as guiding motive and motor of economic development. It therefore antagonised its entire – capitalist – environment. The necessity, usefulness, even the feasibility of planning was widely disputed, and planning was considered incompatible with capitalism. At an earlier stage Great Britain and France, at a later stage West Germany abandoned this global rejection of planning. Sectoral and outline planning are accepted as useful, planning is recognised as a scientific discipline. – As for the meaning, objectives, successes and problems of planning, the salient points were mentioned in an earlier section (Chapter 3.2) of this study.

Macro-economic planning implies development of production and services according to the aggregate needs of society and all its members. Initially, it was planning circumscribed by the scarcity of almost all commodities and modern services; thus the most urgent needs, the key projects with the quickest and/or broadest effect on further development were chosen. Choice entails competition for the allocation of scarce resources and the formation of pressure groups trying to influence the decision-making process on behalf of sectional interests. The competing, sometimes antagonistic, interests can involve

sectors   (e.g. armament versus consumer goods industries);
regions   (e.g. underdeveloped versus developed regions, priority for
          growth points versus an evenly spread development strategy)
society   as a whole (e.g. long-term versus short-term goals; social
          versus individual demands, investment versus consumption).[89]
These conflicts of interests are not necessarily antagonistic in the long run, but in the short or medium term they can lead to tensions and even to economic, social or political crises. They can be resolved by economic and political decisions from above (planning commission, government, party central committee), or, after discussion with representatives of the various interests, by changes in the goals and targets of planning. Such a process requires feedback and control mechanisms which limit the power of decision of the planning authorities, confront them continuously with social reality and lead to a democratisation of the planning process. This may slow down the physical implementation of plans, but at the same time it minimises the frictions and losses inherent in a non-democratic procedure leading to lack of identification.

Initially, planning was a clumsy procedure with few data to draw upon, little knowledge of development parameters, few quantitative targets and indices, and a total lack of experience. Today, improved planning techniques are available: a great fund of experience, material achievements of planning and new economic facilities can be put to use. A strongly diversified economy calls for a mode of planning different from the one that served well at the beginning of the economic take-off. In the long run, it ought to be possible to bring the individual demands of consumers into harmony with those of society as a whole.[90]

Planned and profit-oriented economy in their ideal types are contradictions; their mixed forms and their cooperation prove, however, that they form a continuum. Even the socialist countries, without exception, retain sectors of private economy, while capitalist economies introduce planning mechanisms in order to remove apparent abuses and thus to protect the system against crises. All socialist countries look for cooperation with capitalist firms and governments, in production as well as trade (agreements about cooperation, purchase of licences and know-how, turn-key projects, joint ventures etc.).

For all those common traits, distinctions remain between the roles of planning in socialist and capitalist economies, as shown in Chart 5.3.

Chart 5.3.: Comparison of planning in capitalist and socialist societies

Item	Capitalist market economy	Socialist planned economy
Profit as driving force	dominant	subsidiary
Impact of societal needs	moderate	strong
Impact of assured basic social norm	taken into account at a late stage	strong
Equality of opportunity	ignored or rejected	official aim
Income differentials	very large, unlimited	limited, varying from phase to phase of development
Influence of employers' associations and enterprises	strong	limited
Legal status of plan	general directive, not mandatory	law (enforceable by sanctions), plan discipline relaxed in advanced phases of development

The abolition of the private ownership of major means of production gives a new quality to planning and invests the planners with more power for implementing their plans. Earlier institutional reforms create a new basis for the development of the productive forces. As Myrdal (1957) puts it:

"Land reforms have their significance in the national plan not only as a precondition for raising productivity in agriculture, but primarily as a means of shattering the foundations of the old class structure of a stagnating society. Reforms in the field of health and education have also this double purpose of directly raising the productivity of the population and, at the same time, reconditioning individuals and society so that rational motives become of greater consequence." (P. 81f.)

It is a distortion to equate a socialist planned economy with the centrally administered war economy of the Third Reich. Socialist central planning comprises all sectors of society without the participation of capitalist owners of means of production.

5.6.2. *Improvement of the planning process*

From historical experience – though only over a period of less than fifty years – a new vision and understanding of planning emerges. In the Stalin era, the dominant current of opinion held that planning could be successful only by embracing and directing all factors of production. Today we know that planning operating with fewer, but decisive levers can be more successful under certain conditions. Years before the start of the first five-year-plan in Soviet Russia, Bukharin (1922) warned against over-administration as a cause of failure in planning:

"If the proletariat aims at taking too much into its hands, it will need a gigantic administrative machinery. The attempt to replace all small producers by state officials creates so enormous a bureaucratic apparatus, that its cost will exceed the costs entailed by the anarchic conditions of small-scale production. The mode of administration, and the entire economic machinery of the proletarian state will become fetters inhibiting the development of the productive forces. By an act of ineluctable necessity, therefore, these fetters must be broken. If the proletariat will not do that, it will have to be done by other forces."[91]

Oscar Lange, Polish econometrician and Marxist, called for planning improved by econometric methods and cybernetics. Ota Šik, Czechoslovak economist, fought mainly for economic direction and control of planning by a socialist market. In the view of Gunnar Myrdal, the Swedish socialist economist, planning is particularly important for developing countries, though only as a complementary and countervailing force balancing the influence of private enterprise. Other socialist critics of the traditional socialist planning system were Liberman in the Soviet Union and Apelt in the German Democratic Republic.

The market means (for Šik) the ideal meeting place, where a balance is established between social production on the one hand and the aggregate demand of society and all its individual members on the other. Viewed from that angle, the market is no foreign body in a planned socialist economy, but rather an integral and integrating component with regulating and monitoring functions in respect of the plan. During the initial phases of war communism and general scarcity of all commodities, the regulator cannot function. Since socialist planning sets out from aggregate demand (not from the profit motive), planned production and total demand must tally at least in the long term. The market must meet the main needs over a period of reasonable length. If it does not, the plan is poor and inadequate. Failure to meet basic demands leads to economic losses, to a retardation of development, to poor performance on the part of the producers. Such a failure, then, is prejudicial to fulfilment.

The process of planning can be improved chiefly in three ways:
1. Making planning a public process; publication and explanation of social objectives and targets; transparency of the planning process;
2. democratisation of planning, implementation and supervision by the representative bodies of the social groups;
3. creation or improvement of the mechanisms of economic feedback and regulation.

In the initial stages of the take-off, economic growth is slow, while high rates of investment are inevitable. This stage makes high demands on civic understanding, on revolutionary enthusiasm and on voluntary sacrifices of consumption. If the mechanisms of democratic participation and supervision are well developed, it will be very difficult to achieve a high rate of saving with low living standards. Rapid economic take-off and democratic planning seem incompatible, unless reconciled by a high degree of political mobilisation. This is easier to achieve immediately after the revolution, for as time passes, revolutionary enthusiasm tends to fade away.

In *India*, the influence of the Central Planning Commission is weak; planning is only complementary to the initiatives of private enterprise. It is hardly possible to set priorities and to defend and implement them. Economic growth is slow, without being steady, not infrequently interrupted by domestic and external crises.

In the *Soviet Union*, planning had the force of law and was implemented by all available means. Growth rates were high; in the socially and strategically important sectors the development lag was very quickly overcome. The regulating mechanisms, however, did not function satisfactorily. Thus, the sectoral disproportions began to influence and harm total development. Changes in planning came slowly and late.

In *China*, the planning authorities have more weight and influence than in India and are not under pressure from private entrepreneurs. But their freedom of action was limited by the inevitable decentralisation and regionalisation, as a result of which only a part of the national surplus is available for central projects. A political feedback mechanism provided for quick changes after the planning disaster of the Great Leap Forward. The factor contribution of farming remains low; thus growth rates are low also. Political and economic planners are aware and admit that China will remain an underdeveloped society for a long time ahead.

5.6.3. *Man as the decisive factor*
Even the toughest planner will claim that planning in the end must serve man. Thus he exhorts the producers to do their best for plan fulfilment, to forsake individual wishes and needs in favour of the common long-term objectives. In fact, the implementation of the plans is largely dependent on the producers. Their readiness for personal sacrifice depends on numerous factors, such as
- formulation, explanation and acceptability of planning objectives and targets;
- educational level of producers;
- social awareness of producers;
- living standards, social norm and income differentials;
- participation in the successes of planning;
- extent and duration of under-consumption; distribution of burdens;
- participation in planning and supervision.

One of the main socio-psychological effects of a revolution is the mobilisation of mass activity for a quick realisation of great development projects. Revolutionary enthusiasm makes it easier to overcome bottlenecks, to implement difficult tasks with insufficient equipment, to tolerate a low standard of consumption. But, if people are physically overtaxed and denied participation in decision-making, alienation with its negative economic effects is bound to come even under socialism, in spite of the fact that the main means of production are social property. Promises for a better future alone, frequently for coming generations, are no sufficient motivation for sustained effort. If the producers receive no material improvements over long periods, their effort will fade. To mobilise the producers and to give them the feeling of participation, several approaches were tried:
- Workers' participation in, and supervision of, management;
- three-cornered leadership at factory level by Party, trade union and manager (Soviet Union);
- workers' self-management in Yugoslavia (since 1950); in addition producers' councils at all levels;
- workers' participation in management in Poland (after 1956) through bodies composed of Party leadership, trade union leadership and directly elected workers' representatives;
- moral and material incentives in various combinations.

In the *Indian* development model, workers' participation is not included. It would be opposed by old-fashioned capitalists and may be difficult to organise in view of the embryonic state of the industrial proletariat. Moral incentives cannot play an important role, because profit-making is unlimited and income differentials are accordingly very large and conspicuous. No material incentives are needed for employees, as the labour market is a buyer's market.

In all *socialist countries*, the producers are offered material and moral incentives to increase and improve production and productivity. Material incentives are e.g. wages and salaries, bonuses, new housing, additional holidays. Moral incentives are appeals for special performance and voluntary work, public praise, decoration, awards. The mixture of these two elements differs as between the countries and between the various periods. The extent, to which the two types of incentives are applied, depends not so much on ideological purity of the socialist system, as on the development phase. In the early phase, immediately after the victorious revolution, enthusiasm is running high; voluntary work is offered. General poverty prohibits high material incentives. In later phases, enthusiasm is weakening. But increased production enables the government to raise wages and salaries, to offer more bonuses and to combine moral incentives with material gifts. It is only the extent of the income differentials that distinguishes the phases in each country and constitutes the difference between those countries.

5.6.4. *The dual function of trade unions*
As long as a society is stratified, that is to say, divided into social groups, strata, classes with distinct or opposed interests, organised representation of the various interests is necessary. After the abolition of private property of the (principal) means of production, opposing interests survive, even among those who have nurtured the new society and among its followers. Now the demands of the producers, for instance, are confronting the objectives and visions of the planners. The workers' interests are represented by trade unions, even in socialist societies.

Trade unions as socio-economic and socio-technical institutions are called upon to fulfil a double task: they have to represent their members against a centralised general employer with his central departments, all of them dependent on the Ministry of Finance. At the same time, they are institutions of education and socialisation. The many millions of new industrial workers have to be integrated into an utterly different urban society and into industrial life, utterly strange to them also. Here, division of labour, factory discipline, solidarity, understanding of one's own contributory function and of the entire process of production, technical skill, concentration, a high sense of responsibility, regular work performance are demanded. The two functions of trade unions – the socialising task and the fight for the workers' rights – are interdependent; neither can be discharged without the other. If the members ask for higher wages while ignoring the interests of society and the need to discharge efficiently the duties of modern factory workers, the demands cannot be fully met. If, on the other hand, the government compels the unions to deal only with the socialisation of their members without representing their needs and interests in a visible manner, the inevitable result will be the alienation of the workers from their union and of the producers from society. The state no longer appears as a workers' state, but rather as a strange planning bureaucracy without any sense for popular needs. Finally, the trade union loses the ability to influence and educate its members. These begin to act without and against "their" organisation.[92]

To be free to defend their members' interests, trade unions ought to be fully independent – economically, socially, technically – from any influence of their opposite number, be it industrialists, managers or government. These latter, however, are tempted to assist, protect, patronise trade unions in their own field of action. Union officials, on the other hand, may be tempted to make use of such assistance in order to strengthen their hold on the members or to increase their membership, thus raising more money in membership dues. This temptation to accept or invite support from the employer is the stronger, the weaker the working class is in respect of income level, education, class consciousness, all the more so if several unions compete for the same group of workers. Technical assistance in organisational matters may also lead to dependence.

In *India*, trade unions can fulfil the double tasks only to a moderate extent. Due to heavy unemployment, their bargaining position in wage disputes is weak. Because of rapid fluctuations in the workforce they can hardly educate and stabilise their membership. The permanent staffs of the enterprises, on the other hand, may hesitate to join the union either out of a feeling of superiority, or out of fear of the employer's retaliation.

In the *Soviet Union*, trade unions have passed through all postures, from the stubborn defence of their members' interests to total submission of its leadership to Party discipline, and lately again to a more independent position, confronting the economic planners, administrators and managers as their equals. During certain periods they have hardly been more than "transmission belts" passing on Party orders to their membership.

Little is known as yet about the real role of trade unions in *China* today.

Similar points are valid for other socio-technical institutions, as for instance cooperative societies and collective farms. The more harshly they are made to submit to the exalted authority of the plan, the more they are guided, directed, ordered, controlled, the more decisively will they lose the positive features of a genuine cooperative. In a genuine cooperative, control by the state would be unnecessary, since positive action would be in the members' own interest; expensive administration and supervision would be largely replaced by spontaneous action and initiative.

5.6.5. *Social policy and social security*

Economic development and social change deeply affect the social organisation of a society and its institutions. Development, as understood by this author, implies among many other things massive social mobility, vertically, horizontally, geographically.[93] The traditional social-economic units of production and consumption are broken up and replaced partly by smaller social units, partly by larger economic and socio-technical units. If a nation-wide society replaces the self-sufficient family, clan, tribe or village community, the needs of a larger society transcend the potential of the village. The national government is compelled to mobilise the means accumulated hitherto in the small, familial, tribal, local units. The self-sufficient home or family economy is replaced by a national economy, subsistence consumption and barter trade by a monetary economy. The old social units had to offer to every one of their members or clients an indispensable and attainable minimum of social security. The extended family or other social unit offered employment and food, care in illness, food and housing also for those unfit for work owing to disablement or old age. The modern nuclear family is unable to provide these social services, because it is too small, because it has ceased to be a production unit, because most of the man-power is employed outside the family.

The modern economy and society entails more unforeseeable risks, against which the individual cannot protect himself, e.g. unemployment, inflation; it takes an increasing share of the producers' surplus, partly for investment and profit of the employer, partly for social needs. It compels a worker to be mobile through a labour market, over which he has no influence, and which he cannot even fathom or understand.

For all these reasons, modern society needs a social policy and a social security system which is developed at the same pace as the working man leaves the village solidarity and becomes more dependent on the labour market. Thus, social policy acts in part as a substitute for local social solidarity in the dissolving primary social units, in part it repays the production effort and the economic surplus exacted from the workers, and in part it protects the members of society against the vagaries of

economic ups and downs. Social policy is thus an inseparable correlate
of economic policy and one of the means of counteracting the business
cycles.

The construction of a system of social security depends on several
factors: increase in the number of wage and salary earners, reflected in a
decline of the proportion of self-employed manpower in the primary
sector; growth of modern industries and urban agglomerations; income
level. Generally, development of social security leads to broader coverage
of social risks of almost all social groups. If wages are low and work is
not very permanent, as is mostly the case in early phases of economic
take-off, the schemes are restrictive and cover only smaller strata.

In *India*, social security is still largely the responsibility of the primary
social units, extended family, caste and subcaste. Monetisation has not
conquered the whole economy yet. Only permanent employees and
workers in Government enterprises and in private large-scale enterprises
are covered by public old-age insurance. Health and unemployment
insurance do not exist; likewise, there is no general children's allowance.
It will probably take a long while until a large part of the population is
covered by social security.

The social security system of the *Soviet Union* was built up in several
steps, parallel to economic development. There has been a free health
service for every citizen from the 1920s. Old-age insurance was organised
to cover all wage and salary earners and excluded the peasantry until the
mid-sixties. When the peasants were pressed into collective farms, the
latter were obliged to offer a minimum social security to their members at
a lower level than in the scheme for wage and salary earners. The
required funds had to be raised internally with no state subsidy. In the
mid-sixties, a comprehensive, centrally administered scheme of old-age
insurance was introduced with regular contributions, and allowances
close to those of industrial workers.[94] The coverage of all collective
farmers became feasible after their monetary income had increased and
their numbers had markedly declined. – There is no unemployment insurance in the Soviet Union.

Little is known about the *Chinese* system of social security. For the
vast majority, the agrarian population, the people's commune is the
largest institution providing minimum standards of social security. More
cannot be done under present economic conditions. It is probable, that
for workers and employees in the other sectors some basic forms of
social security have been established. In this sphere, China has of
necessity a long way to go before every individual and all social problems
are covered by a comprehensive system.

5.6.6. *The issue of equality*
One current of economic thinking sees growing inequality as a necessary and even desirable effect of economic take-off, as well as a psychological spur to performance. There is another current of thought, represented by those who fear that growing inequality, in particular under conditions of mass poverty, might become an economic disincentive and contribute to politico-social unrest and instability. Once the poor masses feel they can no longer hope to find employment in normal ways, to feed themselves satisfactorily by working and earning, once they realise that the gap between rich and poor is constantly growing, that they do not share in the fruits of development, then their work performance declines and alienation grows.

To look upon inequality as a driving force and on the desire for equality as a cause of stagnation, bound up with a lack of personal effort and incentive, seems unrealistic, if India and China are compared. Indian income differentials are possibly among the widest in the world, and inequality and conspicuous consumption are displayed as an open provocation. The economy is quite close to stagnation. China, on the other hand, professes a belief in equality and resumed her economic development after the setback of the cultural revolution.

Myrdal (1970) is of the same opinion and considers the quest for equality a prerequisite of economic growth in developing countries:

"First, the usual argument that inequality of income is a condition for saving has much less bearing on conditions in underdeveloped countries, where landlords and other rich people are known to squander their incomes for conspicuous consumption and conspicuous investments, and sometimes, particularly (but not only) in Latin America, in capital flight.

Second, since large masses of people in underdeveloped countries suffer from undernutrition, malnutrition and other serious defects in their levels of living, in particular lack of elementary health and education facilities, extremely bad housing conditions and sanitation, and since this impairs their willingness and ability to work and to work intensively, this holds down production. This implies that measures to raise income levels for the masses of people would raise productivity.

Third, social inequality is tied to economic inequality in a mutual relationship, each being both cause and effect of the other. Greater economic equality would undoubtedly tend to lead to greater social equality. As social inequality is quite generally detrimental to development, the conclusion must be that through this mechanism also greater equality would lead to higher productivity.

Fourth, we cannot exclude from consideration that behind the quest for greater equality is the recognition of the fact that it has an independent value in terms of social justice, and that it would have wholesome effects for national integration." (p. 68)

This approach to the problem may be the background to the Indian debate on combating and abolishing poverty. Slogans influencing the electorate like *"garibi hatao"* (abolition of poverty) found their way into official publications. Limited programmes based on socio-political reasoning were planned. But several research workers hold that the army of the poor has in fact further increased. The prospects for a success of this policy of abolition of poverty are not very favourable, given the present economic strategy and plans.

It has been pointed out above (see Chapters 3.6.3. and 5.6.3.) that drastic inequalities of remuneration can have two-edged or outright negative effects. Under Chinese conditions, it can be useful to minimize the gap between high and low incomes in order to maintain a strong motivation for good performance in spite of small remuneration. The same may be valid for India.

5.7. Self-sufficiency and foreign aid

Autarky, self-sufficiency, is feasible in a country with rich natural resources and wide spaces, yet it involves disadvantages and additional costs. It may contribute to political, military and economic independence and it compels the domestic forces to develop the national resources, both material and cultural. But self-sufficiency can also lead to intellectual isolation, thus causing additional costs when ideas and innovations available abroad are re-invented.

Self-sufficiency implies a narrowing of all exchanges with the outside world, be it in commodities or in know-how, a sometimes self-imposed isolation in many fields. Self-reliance, on the other hand, means the full utilisation of domestic resources supplemented by necessary, i.e. beneficial, exchanges with other countries.

The three countries analysed here are probably able to make or keep their national economy self-sufficient on the strength of their natural resources. But they are all deficient in technical know-how and engineering equipment, already developed and tested in other countries. External aid might have speeded up technical modernisation and economic take-off. But for political reasons such aid was for long periods denied to the Soviet Union and communist China. In India, foreign donors tried to give aid with political strings. The optimum solution would be to combine the development of domestic resources and the employment of domestic manpower with external aid taken from many donors, who would neutralise each other's attempts at undesirable interference. If development aid is altogether rejected on principle, development becomes more expensive and is slowed down, and society is excluding itself from discoveries and inventions made elsewhere.

The conditions stipulated by several aid-giving developed nations can be economically harmful: imports of non-essential, luxury commodities, free transfer of capital and profits, sometimes leading to capital flight, emigration or recruitment of skilled personnel to industrialised countries (brain drain).

For the transfer of modern technology several ways can be envisaged:
– Acquisition of blue-prints by industrial espionage;
– employment of experts from highly industrialised countries in the factories;
– training of national experts in industrialised countries;
– foreign experts as instructors for domestic personnel;
– purchase, dismantling, copying of machinery;
– purchase of entire factories or production lines;
– purchase of know-how (patents, licences, production techniques);
– military organisation of technical work;
– adaptation of imported technology.

Development aid frequently leads to soft foreign trade policies, which increase foreign indebtedness. But even without such compulsory or barter imports, payments of interest tend to rise, and since they are deducted from aid disbursements, the net payments decrease and the flexibility of foreign trade policies is more and more circumscribed.

The overwhelming share of development efforts must be fed from domestic forces and sources. The task of development is so enormous, that even if the donor countries were more generous, the impulses have to come from domestic forces, so as to overcome inertia and set an immobile society moving. External aid is desirable, particularly in emergencies, such as harvest failures or food shortages. Such aid can at best speed up, never initiate, an ongoing movement.

Development aid is never an act of charity, whatever country offers it. It is bound up with economic and political ties. For most industrialists from developed countries, aid shall return good, safe and quick profits, i.e. protected against political risks (nationalisation, expropriation, prohibition of profit transfer). Export merchants from donor countries want to tie aid to the purchase of their surplus commodities. (They will, for example, prefer to export fertilisers rather than build a fertiliser factory). Security of investment sometimes implies interference in the receiving country's economic and domestic policies. Import and licensing policies are also influenced: import merchants are keen on large-scale imports and are supported in that aim by their partners in the donor countries.

The political interest of the aid-giving countries is twofold:
1. To assure the safety of investments;
2. to exact political support against the donor country's political enemies.
Governments and planning commissions of large and well administered countries have precise ideas of their domestic needs. Their objectives and methods are clearly defined and mapped out. Occasionally development aid can clash with national planning and economic policies, and then tends to narrow the government's room for manœuvre.

Aid is tied as a rule to the seconding of experts who have, or are supposed to have, specialised technical knowledge. At the same time, they represent the donor country and its economic and political interests. Through its experts, its advice and the conditions of aid a donor country can influence the internal socio-economic development of the receiving country and thus promote social change or social stagnation.

India has readily accepted development aid, but has spread its choice of donors broadly over the world. In spite of its important role in world politics, attempts of donor countries to exert political pressure are not excluded. India has experienced both positive and negative effects of aid. The aim of self-reliance has not yet been attained. At present, a tendency towards national isolation is discernible.

The *Soviet Union* was almost entirely isolated during the greater part of its industrial development, to begin with not of its own volition, but as a result of foreign decisions. The Soviet leadership reacted with a posture of "voluntary" isolation that was maintained for a long time and abandoned step by step only in the fifties.

China has accepted and sought large-scale external aid, mainly from socialist countries, during the initial stages of development. A phase of strong isolation and "self-reliance" followed. Now, a new phase of openings towards capitalist industrial economies seems to have begun.

5.8. *Models of development, of social change, of socialism*

5.8.1. *Models of development*
Various strategies have been tested and elaborated and are today offered

to developing countries. In each of them the agrarian sector is allotted a different role.

(i) *Modern capitalist countries*
Development was and still is a long drawn out process, which took about 150 years or more. Planning was introduced in the late stages. The contributions of the agrarian sector were exacted over an extended period, with long interruptions, by economic and financial instruments, rarely – only in political emergencies or during acute food shortages – by direct administrative or police action. The contributions of the agrarian sector were supplemented by those from the underdeveloped countries. This draining away of the agrarian surplus slowed their own development. Industrialisation was accompanied by a large-scale flight from the land, initiated and promoted in part by the eviction of small-holders, which was legalised by the agrarian reform laws.[95] In the later phases, rural manpower was attracted to industries by economic incentives, by higher income, better social working norms and the atmosphere of freedom in the towns. The early phases of this process were accompanied by hunger, misery, long working hours, child labour in factories and mines, slums of early capitalism, terror against trade unionism.

In the later stages of modern technology, control of environmental pollution, of profit-making, of urban slums and mass unemployment is insufficient. Social checks on the unleashed technical and economic forces are weak or missing. Social and economic planning are in their embryonic stages only.

(ii) *The Japanese model*
Japan needed less time than Europe's capitalist societies, but more than the Soviet Union, for a full transition from an agrarian to an industrial society. Mild agrarian reforms were implemented. European engineering, technology and science, accumulated over generations, were accepted, utilised and improved, not re-invented. That was one of the factors in overtaking other industrialised nations, a characteristic of successful development.

(iii) *The Indian model*
The basic conditions differ from those of all other models. Utter poverty permits only a very small and very slow factor contribution of the rural masses. Compulsory savings and sacrifices of consumption can be exacted on a minor scale only. On the other hand, there is not much time to waste in the face of the impatience, unrest and development expectations of the masses. The agrarian sector cannot be neglected and

deprived of investment. For politico-social and economic reasons it cannot be squeezed too strongly and for too long a period. There are few genuine entrepreneurs, investing according to long-term plans and willing to accept low profits and some risks during the initial period.

Planning is necessary, at least as a complement to the profit-oriented private sector. Industrial development is vital in order to increase farm production and to break the vicious circle of low yields and slow growth. But a cautious balance has to be struck between the three main sectors in order to improve living standards. Basic social reforms are necessary. The technical achievements of the world can be utilised after adaptation to specific local conditions. The economic, social and technical errors of industrialised countries ought to be analysed and avoided. New growth indicators replacing the misleading GNP[96] have to be found.

India is thus in a position, by heeding the lessons of historical experience, to accelerate her own development, to alleviate the pains of social change and to take advantage of the economic resources of many developed countries. That seems to be the essence of economic independence and political neutrality for poor countries in the Third World.

(iv) *The Soviet model*

The basic idea was to compress technological modernisation and economic development into the briefest possible time span. To this end, the social transformation, too, had to be speeded up. Collectivisation, the most radical and comprehensive reorganisation of the social and agrarian structure, itself a vital concomitant of rapid industrialisation, was achieved within four years. The agrarian sector was squeezed to the utmost without regard for the negative side-effects or the sufferings and wishes of the rural masses. Highest priority was allotted to investment in heavy industry, the production of means of production (and armaments). A high rate of compulsory savings, minimum consumption, maximum contributions to economic growth and cultural and technical infrastructure were exacted from all social groups, but most ruthlessly from the peasantry as the largest section of society. The social institutions were formed according to these basic objectives. The development effort was planned and concentrated on the strategic sectors essential for a breakthrough. All remaining sectors were deliberately neglected; their development was postponed to a later phase. No pause or breathing space was permitted. Thus, the peasantry was offered no chance to pause or to receive any exchange values in the course of this process.

(v) *The Chinese model*
It differs from the Soviet model in four main points:
a. The initial emphasis on heavy industry was officially abandoned. After the failure of the Great Leap Forward the efforts were more evenly distributed among the three main sectors: agriculture, consumer goods, heavy industry.
b. External aid was to some extent rejected after 1960. Self-reliance in the spheres of finance and technical know-how was officially proclaimed. The adapted technologies are to be developed through domestic efforts.
c. The pace of development is being slowed down. The long-term plans foresee an extended period of modernisation.
d. Less compulsory savings by the consumers, who ultimately are identical with the producers. The rural masses are not being antagonised, but their desires and needs are taken into account as far as possible.

5.8.2. Social change – from gradualist reform to permanent revolution
In agreement with Behrendt (1965) it is accepted that "efficient development action mostly implies a change of the pre-dynamic structure of social stratification". Without social change, economic growth and technological modernisation remain limited and slow. Conservative development theorists[97] will strongly challenge this proposition. Cautious reformers will try to implement necessary reforms with a minimum of economic, social and psychological upheavals. By advancing little by little at a deliberate pace and combining each step forward with protective social measures, it is hoped to overcome socio-psychological barriers and resistance to change, and to gain the useful cooperation of all those, whose social status will be diminished by those very reforms. Social pressure and revolutionary violence are to be superseded by methods of persuading and convincing, by prayer and temporary social assistance, and shall lead to a voluntary abdication of power by the old ruling classes. Even if successful, such a gradualist reform could entail two disadvantages: (a) By stretching the time factor, reforms are slowed down to such an extent that they will lag behind society's objective needs for reform. There would then be no hope of eliminating the development lag. (b) Any reform proceeding at so deliberate a pace would fail to produce the desired socio-psychological mobilising effect on the masses, who will continue to be oppressed and therefore lethargic. The former big landlords or their representatives remain as lords in their villages, the officials in the ministries, the judges in the courts. Thus, the oppressed cannot believe in a basic change or new departure.

The classics of social revolution (Marx, Engels, Rosa Luxemburg, Lenin and others) regard revolution as a social upheaval, a great historic act reversing and destroying the established power structure and power relations through seizure of power by the proletariat as the new ruling class. According to the model of the Paris Commune (1871), office-holders ought to be elected, and at the same time liable to recall by the electorate. In that way, sabotage of the new order by the servants and representatives of the old order should be avoided. A revolution as a "locomotive of world history" would substantially accelerate the economic, cultural and social processes and would introduce irreversible measures, effectively blocking every possibility of a return to the old system. The new society, however, is not "prefabricated" in form and content or immediately established and completed; rather it is born and fashioned by successive changes, small steps and great leaps, interrupted by pauses affording breathing space. Before the revolutionary act, the revolutionary leader does not reject reforms. On the contrary, he demands and promotes reforms so as to demonstrate the changeability of a society, at the same time showing up its limits and the circumscribed effects of reform.

Thus reform and revolution are not mutually exclusive alternatives. The revolutionary leader understands both as forms of social change, complementary, interacting, with no clear-cut delimitation, points in a continuum.

The great theorists and analysts of revolution were fully aware of the social cost of revolutions. Thus Bukharin (1922) writes:

"The effective cost of the revolution involves an impairment of the reproduction process and a decline of the productive forces. It is compounded of several components, which can be classified under the following headings:

1. Physical destruction of the elements of production;
2. wear and tear of the elements of production;
3. decay of the interrelations between the elements of production;
4. regrouping of productive forces in favour of unproductive consumption." (pp. 118f.).

To get the record straight, however, it must be borne in mind that in countries without successful revolutions, such as West Germany, the historical cost of frustrated, abortive or betrayed revolutions ought to be taken into account.

Social transformations imply basic changes in the class structure, i.e. in the positions and status of the former rulers and the former oppressed. Man needs time to internalise these status changes and to adapt socio-psychologically to the new social environment. The more abrupt and profound the loss or renunciation of status, the more painful will be the adjustment. Gradual change of production relations and of social structures alleviates the adaptation. Here is one difference between collectivisation in the Soviet Union and the formation of people's communes in China.

A comparison of the various processes of agrarian revolution shows that this revolution, too, is not a single, once-and-for-all act, but comprises numerous steps and activities over an extended period of time. The decisive distinction between agrarian revolution and reform, therefore, is not the absence of small steps, but rather the immediate, radical overturning of rural social relations: expropriation of big landlords without compensation, followed by their expulsion from the village; immediate, unbureaucratic land distribution. The radical change dismantles from the outset the established economic, social and political power positions. Thus, all resistance against the subsequent measures becomes unrealistic. This benchmark of irreversibility convinces the former upper class of the uselessness of opposition. And it motivates the activities of the hitherto oppressed. The sequence and speed of the later steps depend inter alia on
- the stage of economic development, i.e. the degree of underdevelopment;
- general economic planning;
- strength of administration and of the revolutionary party;
- cultural and psychological effects of the revolutionary events on the peasantry.

The single steps of transformation are most clearly discernible in China. Both in the pre- and the post-revolutionary periods they led to a gradual development.[98] The different types of collective farms are the formal and psychological steps towards a total integration of the former individual peasants into large-scale cooperative farms.

Newly gained status, however, is liable to establish and harden new social stratifications. Division of labour, specialisation, bureaucratisation, low educational standards, real or imagined foreign threats promote such hardening, which leads to a loss of internal impulses, of motive forces for modernisation, of great initiatives, which could otherwise ease the difficulties of transition.[99] Socialists have offered three answers to this new stratification: permanent revolution, cultural revolution and rotation, democratisation.

Trotsky's theory of the permanent revolution means that a revolution is a decisive historical phenomenon involving irreversible social processes, but it cannot be conceived as a single event occurring once and for all. In his historical perspective, the Russian revolution had to pass from a bourgeois to a proletarian-socialist phase and then would have to see itself only as a harbinger of world revolution, and could prosper only in close alliance with revolutions elsewhere. For Lenin and Trotsky and most of the non-Stalinist leaders of the Russian revolution the hope of revolution in the highly industrialised western countries was the answer to many difficulties resulting from the isolation of the proletarian revolution in a backward country.[100] When the revolutionary risings of West European workers failed and the total isolation of the Soviet Union seemed inevitable, other methods were sought to counteract the threats of bureaucracy and rigidity: the workers' and peasants' inspection was formed in order to control the old-new administration. In the hands of Stalin it became merely another part of the administrative apparatus.

More difficult is the definition of the cultural revolution. The notion of a proletarian cultural revolution was first ventilated in the Soviet Union. During the years 1917-1921 it was a very disputed issue. Different meanings were attached to the term: making culture accessible to the working class, rejection of the "bourgeois culture" and its replacement by a specific proletarian culture (*proletkult*), freedom of experimenting in all cultural fields. Some Left-wing intellectuals opposed these currents and proclaimed the universality of culture: the working class was entitled – so they argued – to enjoy the greatest products of human culture. – There are no theoretical writings of Mao Tse-tung about the cultural revolution, though his group in the CPC initiated and promoted it. It can be explained only by its actions. Its proclaimed objective was to counteract the hardening of the new social structures and thus to avoid the formation of fixed elites with great material privileges and vested interests, even within the Communist Party itself, to preserve or revive the enthusiastic mood of revolution, to remobilise the masses (as during the actual revolution).

This explanation of the cultural revolution can be questioned on the following grounds: Firstly, a revolution develops out of the historical conjunction of a spontaneous movement with organised, organising and politically conscious forces and can succeed when the shifting pattern of social forces reaches a specific configuration. Whether such specific configurations can be repeated at will by initiative from above, must appear questionable to a Marxist analyst. Secondly, a revolution implies an enormous and concentrated physical and intellectual effort. Can people repeat such efforts every few years? And thirdly: only history will tell us whether the Cultural Revolution was not simply the vehicle of a quiet struggle between two groups in the Party leadership contending for power and the realisation of their respective concepts. The leadership seems unable to discuss the controversial issues openly with the Party membership. The protagonists of the two lines of thinking were Mao Tse-tung and Liu Shao-ch'i.

Mao's apologists compare him quite often to Stalin and wish to add his name to the traditional line of "Marxist classics". His adversaries in the official communist movement denigrate him by comparing him to Trotsky. Both views are probably wrong. The Mao leadership after all was and is much less brutal in the factional struggles than was Stalin's. Mao's Stalinist stance was above all a gesture of hostility against Stalin's successors who had openly dethroned him in 1956.[101] Nor is there any similarity with Trotsky's thinking as regards world-political views. In fact, the Chinese revolution has concluded its world-revolutionary phase with the entry into the UN and its Security Council.

Attempts were undertaken inter alia in Yugoslavia and Czechoslovakia to democratise the rule of the Communist Party. In Yugoslavia it goes on, in Czechoslovakia it was abruptly ended by the invasion of five fraternal governments and their socialist armies in August 1968.

5.8.3. *Models of socialism*
The three countries have proclaimed socialism as their goal. Besides these three models, there are several more models propounded by countries, governments, parties, which have formally embraced socialism. Most of these countries are agrarian societies, wishing to effect the change-over to industrial societies. This applies in particular to the nations ruled by communist governments. If they were industrial societies from the outset, socialism was brought to them by the Red Army's military victory, not by genuine revolutions.

Marx and Engels, who wanted to base socialism on scientific thinking and analysis instead of the earlier, utopian socialism of their precursors, defined the features of a socialist society only in very general terms and refused to draft a blueprint of the future. For them, socialism was:

– the dialectical negation of capitalist society;
– abolition of the exploitation of man by man;
– expropriation of the principal means of production;
– end of alienation;
– the proletarian seizure of power;
– gradual transition to a classless society, in which the state as a tool of oppression slowly withers away after removal of the capitalist class;
– full development and deployment of human abilities for the benefit of society;
– provision of goods and services according to need, not according to performance.

As regards the topical tasks facing socialist countries, or governments claiming to be socialist, in domestic, foreign or economic policies, little, if anything can be derived from the classics of Marxism.

The victory of revolution in a backward country,[102] its international isolation, the simplifications of Stalinism led to a generalisation of the Soviet model, the only one that had been successful and had survived the concentrated onslaught of capitalist intervention.[103] The generalised application of a detailed model to many countries in different phases of development completely ignored the time-conditioned natural, socio-cultural and historical characteristics, and its dogmatism caused grave crises within several socialist countries as well as rifts between members of the socialist "community", which was deeply split. In the end, however, the outcome was the emergence and formal recognition of new models of socialist transformation. The first to leave the socialist camp were the Yugoslav communists as early as 1948 (one year before the final victory of the Chinese communists). They sought their own model of transition from an agrarian to an industrial society, from primitive capitalism to socialism. The collectivisation of farming was stopped and reversed by the will of the collectivised peasantry. In factories, banks and administration workers' self-management was introduced. The state was decentralised – a good adaptation to the wishes of a multi-ethnic and multilingual society. The League of Communists endeavoured to influence people and developments by discussion, and persuasion, by setting standards instead of proclaiming its leading position by administrative directives. Thus, a new socialist model of transition to an industrial society emerged – without collectivisation and over an extended period. – De-collectivisation also occurred in Poland in 1956 – this time accepted by the Soviet leadership after dramatic discussions. Cuba after 1959 in turn searched for another type of agrarian transformation: revolutionary, but without collectivisation.

At a conference of communist parties in Moscow in 1956, the Soviet Union explicitly recognised the coexistence of different models with equal rights, which will develop according to the specific conditions of each country.[104] Stalin's monolithism was replaced by Togliatti's polycentrism, though against a rearguard action mounted by bureaucracy. The one and only model of transformation, generally and universally valid, was replaced by a plurality of models, seeking to enrich historical experience by new methods and forms. Marx and Engels had understood socialism as an internationalist, world-wide community of liberated nations on terms of equality. The abuse of internationalism during the Stalin era and afterwards, and the factual inequality of forces within the socialist "community" has provoked the emergence of national communisms, searching for paths of transformation adapted to the national conditions.

Two problems stand out after the deficiencies and difficulties of the first model of accelerated socialist transition to industrialisation:

1. Is socialism good only for developing countries, not for highly industrialised countries?
2. Is the Stalinist distortion an intrinsic feature of socialism, or of Lenin's concept of socialism? Or is it a consequence of the specific difficulties of an underdeveloped economy?

R. Luxemburg, A. Thalheimer, L. Trotsky, N. Bukharin, E. Bloch and several more Marxist theorists have tried to find replies to these questions. It is beyond the scope of this book to discuss all of them at length. But the final judgment and reply will be given by historical development. It has brought about modifications of the Soviet model and in fact new models. Uniformity has been superseded by a variety of paths to socialism competing with each other. None can claim any more to be authentic, all are equally Marxist or not. The future development of socialism will depend on the emergence of further successful models and their mutual tolerance.

5.8.4. *Transitions to socialism*

Political scientists in east and west have begun to discuss the character of those societies that claim to be socialist or to have reached communism. For the emerging doubts about these societies several reasons can be given.

1. Marx and Engels never described their vision of socialist society in detail; for them communism was a contradiction and dialectical negation of the capitalist society, not a final, ideal goal.[105]

2. The realisation of socialism in the Soviet Union was a long march along a poorly lit road, strewn with boulders, and there were many external and internal deviations and distortions. The longer the march towards socialism, the dimmer and more diffuse became the "final" goal. The state and administration, supposed to wither away according to classical Marxism, grew stronger and overwhelmed the personal initiative of the individual, now liberated from capitalist exploitation. Stalin even justified the strengthened bureaucracy by claiming that after the liquidation of capitalism the class struggle, so far from abating, increases in intensity.

3. The question as to how close the various countries had come to the attainment of socialism or communism came to be treated as a scholastic issue, reflecting the position of the member states in the hierarchy of the socialist system. To claim to have advanced faster than the Soviet Union

on the road to socialism – as the Chinese did in 1958 – implied a heresy against the Soviet hegemony in the socialist camp. But as more and more socialist governments came into being, some of them were driven by the logic of facts to modify the Soviet model, which thus lost its monopoly position and became one of several models pointing the way towards a better society.

4. These difficulties were aggravated by two facts. Some countries, such as Czechoslovakia or the (East) German Democratic Republic, were from the outset economically and culturally more advanced than the Soviet Union, even though their socialist transformation started much later. And as political tension rose between China and Russia, each of the two disputed the other's socialist character.

There was a real gap between the western Marxist vision of a socialist society and its first realisation, and this led to prolonged debates as to whether the Soviet Union was a socialist society or merely a special type of State capitalism, where a new class of technocrats had replaced the old capitalists.

Economic historians have found a formal, semantic solution for the problem by calling all these societies transitional societies.[106] It does not seem that the real questions are solved by that formula. But it is made clear, that none of these societies can claim socialism as its sole "property", that all of them are in a process of transition and transformation from capitalism towards something, that is difficult to define once and for all.

This might in due course lead to a better understanding of the problems of socialism as a continuous and infinite process of the progressive improvement of society, a process that does not end with the abrupt transformation ushered in by a radical revolution. Even after such a radical revolution, no ruling party can wipe the slate clean and start from zero point. It has to work under given conditions. Every new society bears the traces and traditions of the old society, which are pervading the social, political and cultural heritage, and the consciousness and behaviour of man, including the revolutionary leaders themselves. Such a new understanding can contribute towards greater equality among these countries, if not in real power, at least in their historical rights, and put an end to all hierarchical thinking.

5.8.5. Involvement and role in world politics
This chapter cannot present a comprehensive review of the three countries' foreign policies and their thinking on world affairs. But certain common features of their role in the world and their three-cornered relationship will be briefly analysed.

The independence of India and the communist revolution in the

Soviet Union and China have profoundly changed the world balance of power. The three nations have become fully independent forces, two of them for long periods isolated from the rest of the world and put into quarantine. By the sheer size of their population they are world powers of the first order, even when unarmed, and much more so when they develop their armies and armaments to the most modern level. Two of them have permanent seats in the UN Security Council with a power of veto on any issue of substance. The emergence of the former colonies and semi-colonies as independent nations and the emergence of socialist states has had and continues to have a lasting influence in the arena of world politics. It implies the decline of the former colonial powers to their natural status (economically and politically) and competition between capitalism and a new economic system opposed to it.

Several factors, some constant, others variable, determine the foreign policies of a state: (a) class character and social revolution, bearing in mind the causal relationship between domestic and foreign policies; (b) geographical circumstances and location, which determine borders, lines of communication, neighbours and enemies; (c) the size of the country and of its population; (d) the international balance of strength.

After independence, *India* favoured a neutral policy of the Third World vis-à-vis the big powers, a concentration on internal development, cooperation of the newly emerging nations, a defensive and pacific foreign policy. A few contentious issues had been inherited from the colonial era: the dispute with Pakistan over Kashmir, the strange configuration of Pakistan, with its two wings "encircling" India from East and West; the undemarcated border with China. The non-aligned bloc[107] declined. When the splits within the "Third World" became obvious, India looked for unprincipled alliances, like other powers. She veered to and fro between the poles of the USA and the USSR. The shifts were conditioned in part by the changing relationships between these two super-powers and India's main opponents, i.e. China and Pakistan. The deepening rift and the military clash with China accelerated the arms race, the alignment with Russia and the confrontation with Pakistan. Growing military strength increased the desire to clear the log-jam and tidy up relations with the smaller neighbours. Thus, India contributed substantially to the break-up of Pakistan and the establishment of independent Bangladesh, and she absorbed the old French and Portuguese colonies[108] and the suzerain state of Sikkim.[109] Twenty nine years after independence the high ideals of a better world policy have faded a as result of external and internal developments. India has virtually become just another big power.

The *Soviet Union* began by rejecting all the rules and usages of capitalist foreign policy. In its first proclamation of 1917 it called for a peace without annexations or compensation, and granted all ethnic minorities the right of self-determination including that of secession. This attitude represented a consistent application of internationalist principles and a reaction to "pan-Russian super-power chauvinism".[110] The isolation imposed upon the new state by almost all powers, by the whole (capitalist) world, strengthened the belief in world revolution as the best way to break out of this ideological and material isolation. The failure of revolutions in the capitalist world, together with domestic consolidation led the changing leadership in the second phase away from old thinking, which gave way to the idea of full self-reliance, withdrawal into the national shell, neglect of the communist world movement or its utilisation as another arm of Soviet diplomacy. International solidarity was offered more and more selectively, according to short-term national interests. In the third phase, the USSR, surrendering its hopes of world revolution and accepting the rules of the game (of world politics), was increasingly accepted by the capitalist world as a power almost like others. This process was furthered by the growing threat of Hitlerite world domination.

The successful defensive and later the victorious offensive against Hitler's armies lifted the Soviet Union in a fourth phase into parity with the other super-power emerging from the second world war. Engaged in a bipolar relationship veering from close collaboration (under Roosevelt) to cold war (under Truman), from a threat of confrontation via mutual understanding to détente and "peaceful" competition, with responsibility for the containment of the ultimate nuclear weaponry, the two super-powers were accepted as such by most nations until the end of the 1960s. During this period of acceptance as a super-power, the impulses of the revolution of 1917, reflected in a new approach to foreign policy, gradually faded away. The constant factors of foreign policies began to dominate: quest for distant naval bases, alliances with capitalist, even reactionary governments, promotion of nationalist feelings where that was considered to serve Soviet interests, military conquest of foreign territory, military confrontation with communist China and attempt at a rapprochement with the stronghold of world capitalism.

China seems to have traversed similar phases, but in a briefer period of time. In the first phase, China's solidarity with the socialist countries, rewarded by external aid and political concessions from the USSR, went together with the hope that her own revolution should produce wider repercussions in Southern and Eastern Asia. Revolutionary governments and movements were supported (Korea, Vietnam, Burma), and progressive alliances were sought with Third World countries. This was a response to the isolation imposed by the main capitalist powers. Internal consolidation and the incipient rift with both India and the Soviet Union radically changed the direction of foreign policy in the second phase. Alliances were sought with various governments irrespective of their political position; military dictatorships and extreme anti-communism were not excluded. China tried to broaden its foreign relations and to seize the leadership in the communist movement and in the Third World. Military confrontations with both India (1962/63) and the Soviet Union (1969) were not avoided. Though they were of a minor scale, involving only a few thousand soldiers, they hardened the rifts and had important internal effects on India, swinging her to the Right.[111] In the third phase, competition with, and hostility against, the Soviet Union seem to be the dominant features of Chinese world politics. This coincides with her final recognition as a major world power (entry into the UN, assuming her seat in the Security Council, resumption of relations with the US). In an old-fashioned power game, alliances are sought with the countries most hostile to the USSR and India. Successes of counter-revolutionary coups are hailed, if they weaken the Soviet position.

There is a certain similarity in the three-cornered relationship between China, India and the USSR to the one between China, USSR and the USA. When India and China were close to each other, the relationship between India and the USSR was cool and vice versa. This can be observed over the whole period since 1947 or 1949.

From this very brief review of foreign policies a few conclusions can be drawn. (1) The internal socialist character of a society has only limited influence on its stand in world politics. (2) The effect of a revolution, however radical, on external relations is gradually fading away and is finally subordinated to the constant long-term national interests. (3) Even relations between socialist governments have so far been determined largely by the balance of strength. No procedure for democratic discussion or the peaceful settlement of contentious problems has been evolved as yet. (4) Socialist great powers behave almost like other great powers.[112] (5) The solidarity of the Third World was a transitory phenomenon in international relations. It was undermined by different, sometimes conflicting, national interests, by changed relations between countries of the Third World, due to social and economic differentiation or even exploitation, and by emerging domestic social conflicts.

5.9. *Comparison of efficiency*

5.9.1. *Notions and indicators*

Efficiency, as defined by Webster (1971), is the generation of the desired result with a minimum of effort, expenditure or loss. According to this definition, then, efficiency can be measured only in terms of specific means and known ends. Seen in this way, socio-economic efficiency cannot be taken for granted by any means, even where purely economic efficiency is undisputed. A distinction must be drawn between micro- and macro-economics. Some forms are micro-economically inefficient, but macro-economically necessary and efficient. Conversely, it may happen that micro-economic efficiency is achieved at the cost of macro-economic inefficiency (for instance state subsidies for a large number of small-scale production units, environmental pollution). Production optimum and financial optimum may be far from coinciding.[113]

Many indicators may be used for purposes of comparison:
a. Productivity per unit area, expressed in yield per hectare. This depends on the climate, input of production equipment and materials, population density (governing demand), and so on. So long as the available area is relatively large and the man-land ratio is high, intensive land use is uneconomic.[114]
b. Productivity of labour. This depends on technological re-equipment, size of production unit, availability of manpower.
c. Per-capita production.
d. Productivity of capital, i.e. production per unit of capital input. Here an input-output analysis might give some partial clues.
e. Monetary income of producers. – However, purchasing power is not reflected in the exchange rates and depends upon price policies, and social and individual priorities, level and composition of consumption etc. Comparisons of the purchasing power of pay per working day mostly show the superior position of the American worker as compared with workers anywhere else in the world, and thus demonstrate the superiority of the economic system of US capitalism. But such figures give no clue to a more profound comparison of living standards in the various social systems.
f. Gross national product (GNP) and economic growth rate. The calculation of these indices varies according to the economic systems and to changes within each system from phase to phase (natural or monetary economy). Therefore their relevance for the comparative evaluation of different systems is small.
g. Distribution of goods and services between the social strata. – This is widely unknown even for countries with good statistical services. But it would be very important for a comparison of GNP figures.
Every one of the above indicators, considered in isolation, is onesided and questionable. Only if all the indicators are considered together and

judiciously weighted can it be at all possible to arrive at an exhaustive and valid measurement. A growing literature deals with this problem, reviewed by Werner (1975) and Beyme (1975). Puhle (1975) proposes to replace indicators and indices by functional equivalents, i.e. to find yardsticks for equivalent functions, which have similar importance in all social systems.

5.9.2. *Problems of comparison*

All the indicators taken together represent only the quantifiable part of the performance, by no means the performance as a whole. So far it has not been possible to express in quantitative terms the following contributions to the national economy and to society:

a. Financial contribution to overall development, capital formation over 150 years for the non-agricultural sectors;
b. discriminatory terms of trade at the expense of agriculture (price scissors);
c. mobilisation of intellectual reserves;
d. cost of food supplies, assuming the entire domestic needs are met through imports under conditions of an ideal international division of labour;
e. economic take-off and elimination of development lag;
f. value of time-saving effect of planning.

In the communist countries, contributions have been exacted for society and the economy which still elude measurement. In the *Soviet Union* collectivisation was the instrument by which domestic capital formation was compressed from 150 into 15 years, a deliberate and planned step taken to eliminate the development lag and prepare for the military conflict with Hitler.[115] In *China*, the peasant masses in their millions were shaken out of their lethargy and mobilised, and their labour potential, until then lying waste, was used for the first time. In all communist countries the people have been made literate and modern systems of education have been set up. In the producer cooperatives, the agricultural producers are able to benefit from the social norms of a modern society, even though material living standards may still be lower than in highly industrialised societies. In *India*, the agonising, though brief convulsions of a radical social upheaval have been avoided at the expense of a long drawn out process of slow growth, accompanied by material misery and the continuance of an archaic social system.

Pure comparisons of production performance thus ignore the aims and achievements of society and the economy as a whole, though admittedly their social cost is no more amenable to quantitative measurement than are the achievements themselves. Cost assessments would have to

compare the cost of agricultural policy in a country with an agrarian structure based on peasant farming (subsidies for a multitude of unprofitable
small production units, advice, price support, storage, other state
measures in aid of peasant farming) with the corresponding cost in a
country with a collectivised agriculture (state support, subsidies for
relatively few unprofitable large-scale production units). New methods
need to be elaborated to measure these benefits and social costs, and
include them in a comprehensive comparison. Communist critics
observing the system from the inside seek to recognise the objectives and
to assess them in their comparisons, while several outside, non-communist
critics ignore the social goals.

For these reasons, Beyme (1975) avoids a comparison between nations
and economies belonging to different social systems. Such attempts will
have to be delayed, until further intensive research finds functional
equivalents and makes them quantifiable. He prefers an intra-systemic
comparison with a new conceptualisation, that yields good insights into
problems and solutions and permits certain cautious judgements about
probable and possible directions of development.

Thus, summing up, the conclusion might be, that inter-systemic
material comparisons are fraught with difficulties, which have not yet
been surmounted. They tend to reflect not so much the real performance
of each society as the ideological and political bias of the research worker.
Intra-systemic comparisons – between societies broadly following the
same pattern of development – may be more fertile, revealing the truly
relevant factors, achievements and failures of growth, modernisation and
change. In such attempts at comparative studies, performance should
not be related to the same actual time, but to corresponding phases of
development.

5.9.3. *Comparisons of the three countries*
In spite of these considerations and the obvious problems involved,
several research workers have been tempted to compare the achievements of some of the three countries.

A long-term comparison of quantitative performance of the agricultural sector of the three countries can be derived from FAO statistics (see
Table 5.5.). *India* shows a long-term growth of total food production in
both periods (1952-62 and 1964-1974), though with marked and repeated interruptions (1966, 1972, 1974). The growth rate of the *Soviet
Union* is definitely higher. *China* is shown to have an intermediate growth
rate, in both periods clearly above India's. Not even the slump of the
Great Leap Forward and its aftermath is visible in the index calculation.
Almost the same picture appears when total agricultural production is

Table 5.5.: Indices of food and agricultural production – India, Soviet Union, China

	1952	1954	1956	1958	1960	1962	1964	1966	1968	1970	1972	1973	1974
			Basis: 1952-56 = 100							Basis: 1961-65 = 100			
Total food production													
India	89	101	106	111	122	122	104	97	111	123	119	127	121
Soviet Union	?	?	?	?	?	?	106	121	128	135	132	153	147
China	88	102	113	127	132	139	104	109	113	122	124	130	133
Percapita food production													
India	93	101	103	103	108	103	102	91	99	105	97	102	96
Soviet Union	?	?	?	?	?	?	105	116	121	123	120	138	132
China	95	102	105	111	111	106	102	103	103	108	106	109	110
Total agricultural production													
India	89	101	107	111	121	123	104	97	110	121	118	127	121
Soviet Union	?	?	?	?	?	?	106	121	127	135	132	152	147
China	88	102	113	127	132	140	104	110	114	123	125	131	135
Percapita agricultural production													
India	92	101	103	103	107	104	102	90	99	104	97	102	95
Soviet Union	?	?	?	?	?	?	105	116	120	125	120	137	131
China	95	102	106	111	107	106	103	104	104	109	107	110	111

Sources: FAO Production yearbook 1966, 1974

compared. In countries with a low share of animal husbandry and, thus, a small loss only in the transformation process, agricultural and food production do not diverge too widely.

In per-capita production indices the influence of population growth on the average availability of food is visible. Here, Indian performance is the lowest of the three, with some years actually showing a net decrease (again 1966, 1972, 1974). China seems to be in a better position, while the per-capita growth rate is highest for the Soviet Union, where population growth has come down to the normal rate of industrialised societies.

No quantitative comparison appears to have been made between the Soviet Union and India. Clearly, the starting conditions are too different.

Rochlin and Hagemann (1971) have presented comparative figures for the quantitative development of structure, inputs and output in the Soviet Union and China over long periods. Yet, they refrained from attempting a comprehensive quantitative comparison. They find similarities in ideology, but the implementation of plans is dissimilar in methods and instruments. The different approach of the two communist parties to the peasantry and the agrarian problems, the cautious farm policy in China, contrasting with the radical procedure in the USSR, is emphasised. The output performance is evaluated as poorer for China.[116]

A few partisan comparisons between China and the Soviet Union have been tried, each dwelling on the other side's failures, seen as a result of its betrayal of the Marxist principles. An exception is the comparative analysis of Schweizer (1972). He sets out from the Marxian theories and discusses their practical application in the Soviet Union and China. Furthermore, he compares work organisation, abolition of the urban-rural differential, capital accumulation in farming and choice of technology in the two countries. – More work has been done to compare the recent performance of India and China. These comparisons will be briefly reviewed.

Some similarities of the two societies are evident, thus attracting the attention of general economists. They are comparable in numbers, they achieved independence at almost the same time (1947 and 1949 respectively). Both had experienced prolonged economic exploitation by colonialism or a semi-colonial status. Both societies were rigid. Natural conditions were similar in part, and so was the settlement structure. Both proclaimed socialism as their objective after independence and set out to promote development by planned effort. They established close contacts and tried to cooperate in world politics for the first part of the 1950s. – Here the similarities seem to end.

Chen and Uppal (1971) in their book do not in fact compare quantitative performance; they offer a collection of papers describing and analysing various aspects of life and policies of the two countries. Biehl (1966) gives a very useful description of conditions at the outset, land tenure and production performance up to 1965, but avoids a real comparison of achievements and results in terms of economic growth. The fact that both Schweizer and Biehl put the main emphasis on social relations indicates their awareness, that quantitative comparisons are difficult and beset with pitfalls.

Bhattacharya (1974) attempts a comparison of the economic achievements of China and India for the period 1950-72. The growth rates for China differ widely in various estimates, and the author accordingly chooses the most conservative estimates. Growth rates of industrial production in China were very high between 1952-59 (18-27 per cent), much higher than for India, while for the sixties figures are very uncertain. For the whole 22-year-period, China's industrial growth is estimated at 8-12 against India's 6.5 per cent. National income grew at 5.3 per cent per annum in China against 3.6 per cent for India. Growth rates in agriculture and foodgrains over the whole period were similar for the two countries. In the author's view they are fairly high, seen in historical perspective. China was more self-reliant, always had a surplus in external trade, while India had a trade deficit all the time. China's overall growth rate of over 5 per cent was well ahead of population growth, which "must lead to significant improvements in the living standards of the Chinese people".[117] For India, Bhattacharya calculates an annual average growth rate of per-capita income of 1.3 per cent and of real national income of 3.6 per cent as against 3.2 per cent and (gross national product) 5.3 per cent for China. The Indian figures

> "may be considered as eminently respectable and represent an improvement upon the economic stagnation that characterised the British colonial period, but they fall short of the objectives of Indian economic development as well as the aspirations and needs of the Indian people". (p. 454.)

The author concludes with the following remarks:

> "Thus, China's economic growth record appears to be substantially better than India's to date, and it has been achieved in spite of the total withdrawal of Russian aid and extreme periods of instability during the Great Leap Forward and the Cultural Revolution. China is one of the very few countries which currently has no debts, either national or external. Moreover, backed by considerable reserves, including gold, China's currency has been free from devaluation or inflation and has remained uniquely stable in a world characterised by the diminishing purchasing power of the currencies of most countries.

Finally, we should not judge the Chinese model in terms of growth alone, because economic growth is a very unsatisfactory index of the rate of economic development, because it ignores the question of distribution of income and wealth, unemployment problems and economic infrastructure. China has gone straight to the roots of the problems that have been plaguing poor countries for many years – the lack of food and low levels of nutrition, gross inequalities of income and consumption, unemployment and a sense of social uselessness, and the blind expansion of the cities. She has been uniquely successful in the development of the people's economic life for the benefit of all instead of for the benefit of the few, and in placing the needs of man before those of machines.

This study indicates better relative performance by China on all fronts. It has eradicated the worst forms of poverty; it has full employment, universal literacy and adequate health facilities. Not only has China been able to solve its unemployment problem, but it has been able to do so without any foreign aid during the last fourteen years. China also stands out as the only developing country without any internal or external debts outstanding and a uniquely stable currency." (pp. 454-457.)

Bardhan (1970) limits his comparison to the performance of the agrarian sector and to a briefer period (1952/53-1964/65). – Yields per hectare were far higher in China. The intensity of cropping also was higher for China. The country's import dependence has decreased. Bardhan sees the correlation between output in agriculture and the relations of land tenure. He points to the quick and thorough success of agrarian reform in China: between 1949 and 1952 almost 40 per cent of the cultivated land was expropriated and 47 million ha distributed among poor and landless peasants. The attempts at agrarian reform in India, on the other hand, were mainly abortive. Share-cropping is widespread and makes it impossible for the cultivators to invest. Bardhan then says:

"... most of the benefits from community development projects in India have accrued to the richer farmers. No wonder that the mass of poor peasants and agricultural labourers do not feel excited by these projects. In irrigation projects also, the distribution of water is very inequitable and is a major reason for the poor maintenance of field channels. Through cooperative management of cultivation, the Chinese have minimized this problem of conflicting self-interest between workers and beneficiaries of a rural capital project.

The emphasis in Indian community development projects has been on coordinated administrative action by the government agencies and not on any programme deliberately planned to effect any change in the rural institutional framework. The village-level workers and extension officers are not merely ill-paid and overworked; they have to operate within a severely constrained institutional set-up. The over-enthusiastic, but technically incompetent Chinese party cadre in his visions of unprecedented socialist transformation attempts too much and quite often fails. The under-enthused Indian village-level worker does and can, under the given constraints, attempt too little." (p. 528.)

But after all, the author remains cautious:
"It is not possible to arrive at clear-cut conclusions about their relative performance." (p. 535).
Richman (1972) restricts his work primarily to a qualitative assessment and will not present a quantitative assessment of economic performance. But he adds:
"In conclusion, it would appear that China has achieved a significant lead thus far over India in overall economic development – in both absolute and per-capita terms. China also seems to have been more effective in creating an overall environment more conducive to substantial and sustained economic growth than has India thus far. Hence, it seems that China's potential for narrowing the development gap between herself and the advanced industrial nations is substantially greater than that of India. And China also seems to be in a position to widen, perhaps considerably, the development gap between herself and India.

In the final analysis, China's economic destiny and fulfilment of her potential depend, in my opinion, chiefly on whether ideological extremism prevails or whether managerial, technical, and economic rationality becomes relatively dominant. If extremism persists and prevails, the chances seem good that India will not only gain on China, but will actually surpass her eventually. However, if relative ideological moderation prevails in China, she is likely to be the undisputed winner in the development race with India, and also to emerge as one of the leading and more advanced world economic powers – at least in absolute terms – by the end of this century." (p. 91.)
Swamy (1973) gives the most thorough quantitative comparative analysis.[118] For the farming sector he finds a definitely better achievement in China. For the industrial sector he starts by comparing the objectives of planning. The Chinese aims are spelt out by Tseng Wen-ching (1959):
"The key link in the development of the national economy during the transition period is the development of heavy industry, because

229

only through the development of heavy industry is it possible to realise the socialist industrialisation of the country, to develop the national economy of the country as a whole, and to provide for the transformation of the economy of the country on the basis of socialist principles."

The Indian Planning Commission (1961) defined its strategic line in the following terms:

"While agriculture and industry must be regarded as closely linked parts of the same process of development, there is no doubt that industry has a leading role in securing rapid economic advance. Industrial development, and especially the development of basic and heavy industries, must be regarded as a part of a comprehensive design of development which ultimately links the industrial and rural economy, the economy of large-scale and of small-scale units, and the economy of the major industrial centres as well as of the smaller towns and villages, bringing them into a close relationship with one another, thus assuming a high degree of mobility and economic integration within the economy as a whole." (pp. 24f.)

An overall calculation of industrial development is presented in Table 5.6. It shows a higher growth rate for China after 1951, though the level at the outset is not clearly discernible. With 1951 as basis, China has multiplied its output 8 times, India only 3 times. But, there were serious breakdowns in China about 1960, while India experienced fewer and smaller interruptions of its upward trend. Swamy sees the reason in the political crises:

"There are, of course, good reasons for these trends. Until 1965 India was making a systematic, though undramatic effort to plan her industrialisation. While many serious errors of judgment and understanding were made, the basic fibre of the Indian system was sound, permitting steady growth and acceleration. In China, the situation was entirely different. The supremacy of politics over economics caused several major dislocations. The Great Leap Forward, rapid commune formation, severe drought and the sudden cut-off of USSR assistance combined to make 1959-62 crisis years, necessitating the abandonment of two successive 5-year plans." (pp. 45f.)

The author finds a picture different from Bhattacharya: The growth rate of the non-agricultural sectors is less for China than for India for the whole period. Therefore the growth rate of the net domestic product is lower (2.2 versus 3.7 per cent). Regarding net domestic investment, the two countries show contradictory trends. In China the growth rate decreased, while India showed a steady increase, finally overtaking

Table 5.6.: Index of industrial production, China and India

Year	China		India	
	1951 = 100	1956 = 100	1951 = 100	1956 = 100
1951	100.0	37.8	100.0	73.5
1952	130.1	48.8	103.1	75.8
1953	169.3	63.5	105.9	77.9
1954	197.1	73.9	113.1	83.2
1955	208.0	78.0	125.0	91.9
1956	266.7	100.0	136.0	100.0
1957	291.1	111.4	141.8	104.3
1958	493.9	185.2	146.5	107.7
1959	687.7	257.9	159.0	116.9
1960	887.5	332.8	117.0	130.1
1961	n.a.	n.a.	188.2	138.4
1962	n.a.	n.a.	204.8	150.6
1963	490.7	184.0	221.5	162.9
1964	564.3	211.6	237.7	174.8
1965	625.6	234.6	250.9	184.5
1966	751.7	281.8	269.7	198.3
1967	n.a.	n.a.	268.0	197.0
1968	689.3	258.5	285.7	209.6
1969	n.a.	n.a.	306.2	225.1
1970	802.2	300.8	320.3	242.0

Source: Swamy (1973)

China also in the actual amount of investment. (See Table 5.7.). In the early 1970s, both countries have come to the same level again, an investment of roughly 9 per cent of the net domestic product. The author then summarises his findings:

"The broad conclusion that we can reach is that (a) the growth rate of the Chinese and Indian economies has been about the same over the period 1952-70, and (b) there has been a significant deceleration in growth rates in China, especially during 1952-65, and a significant acceleration in India." (p. 83.)

Weisskopf (1975) admits the difficulties of qualitative comparison and therefore concentrates on a few economic indicators. Economic growth was stronger in China, both for total and per-capita output with different growth rates for industry and agriculture; as regards industry, the differential was even more favourable to China. Eight indicators of economic equality are then analysed. Income distribution is more egalitarian in China. The urban-rural differential seems to have been smaller and declining in China. Regional disparities may have been reduced more successfully in China. The income differential in the same enterprise,

Table 5.7.: Net domestic product by sectors, China and India (Constant prices; 1,000 million parity Rupees)

Sector	1952	1954	1956	1958	1959	1960	1961	1962	1964	1965	1970
				China (1952 Prices)							
Agriculture	58.46	61.08	66.68	78.40	72.76	59.00	71.20	73.86	86.32	87.24	87.98
Industry	17.18	21.67	29.59	40.19	53.37	54.30	38.21	36.75	42.70	45.96	66.89
Trade, transport, communications, other services	50.34	54.14	58.05	58.40	46.46	32.02	49.15	55.71	66.01	65.39	45.91
All non-agricultural sectors	67.52	75.81	87.64	98.59	99.83	86.32	87.36	92.46	108.71	111.35	112.80
Net domestic product	125.98	136.89	154.32	176.99	172.59	145.32	158.56	166.32	195.03	198.59	200.78
				India (1948-49 Prices)							
Agriculture	44.4	49.8	50.2	50.1	55.6	55.1	59.1	59.1	59.7	65.1	75.7
Industry	15.2	16.5	17.6	18.6	18.8	19.7	21.1	22.1	24.4	25.3	30.2
Trade, transport, communications, other services	31.6	34.0	37.0	40.3	42.3	44.1	47.8	50.1	56.5	60.7	72.5
All non-agricultural sectors combined	46.8	50.5	54.6	58.9	61.1	63.8	68.9	72.2	80.9	86.0	102.7
Net domestic product	91.2	100.3	104.8	109.0	116.7	118.9	128.0	131.3	140.6	151.1	178.4

Source: Swamy (1973)

too, is probably much larger in India. Unemployment seems to be more burdensome for the Indian economy, and basic "insurance" against it better developed in China. Health care is more evenly offered for the Chinese population. Social mobility is much less and women generally more disadvantaged in India, except for the position of Prime Minister. Similarly, as regards economic self-reliance (foreign debt, external aid, technological independence) China has fared much better than India. – Weisskopf summarises his provisional findings with the following remarks:

> "The evidence... leaves no doubt that China's progress in three important dimensions of economic development has been significantly greater than India's in the modern post-war period. With respect to each of eight different indicators of economic equity, China appears to have shown greater improvement than India; in a few cases, the differences in performance do not seem to have been great, but in several cases... the differences have been dramatic. Finally, according to the available evidence on four different indicators, China has achieved a much higher degree of economic self-reliance than India." (p. 185.)

Sinha (1972) tries to find a wider perspective by including Japan and the reform strategy of the Meiji period into his comparison and by extending the period back to the end of the last century. At the same time, he restricts his observations to the farming sector only. His final conclusions are more ambiguous; he is not sure, whether Chinese progress really is so much speedier than India's and sees several similarities between them:

> "To sum up, it seems that in terms of rate of growth of agricultural output or the levels of food consumption, so far the Chinese system has not shown a distinct advantage over the Indian counterpart. In egalitarianism and mobilisation of resources it has a definite edge over the Indian experiment. It is possible to argue that through better mobilisation of resources, a more radical reform of institutions and by consolidation of holdings and enlargement of scale of operations as well as with a stronger industrial base, China is now in a better position than India, in accelerating the rate of growth of its agricultural sector. But on the other hand, if differences of opinion continue to occur in China within the party hierarchy in the future, as has happened in the past, and if this leads to repeated 'purges' and 'vilification' campaigns, chances are that the cadres feel less secure to take initiative and a spirit of cynicism may develop among the masses. Frequent change in institutional set-up on ideological considerations may create further instability and uncertainty as in the past, and thereby prove to be a disincentive to cadres and to the masses." (p. 36.)

NOTES

1 This term no longer fits reality and is therefore put in quotation marks. There are political and economic disparities and differences between the nations calling themselves the developing world, and there are antagonistic social groups in almost all of them.

2 The numbering is doubtful: some newly formed states have a minor status, i.e. a lesser degree of self-administration.

3 For the former untouchables and for backward tribes – two groups experiencing special difficulties in the slowly changing Hindu society – additional protective measures are stipulated in several fields.

4 "O" stands either for "organisation", since this minority group swayed the party administration against Indira Gandhi, or for "opposition". The victorious group under Indira Gandhi is frequently named Congress (R), "R" standing for "ruling".

5 Cf. E. Boserup (1965).

6 About caste see also Chapter 2.5.1.2.

7 The poverty line was put in 1963/64 at a monthly per-capita expenditure of 13 and 18 Rs. respectively for the rural and urban population.

8 This figure is completely unrealistic. But the classification on which employment statistics are based differs markedly from the one usual in industrialised societies with a high proportion of salary earners.

9 Figures about irrigation have to be assessed very cautiously everywhere. They may lump together areas with one irrigation per year, or with full irrigation for one crop, with assured irrigation throughout the year, or with only one additional application after the end of the rain. Water may come from a private well or from a large reservoir providing assured irrigation for thousands of hectares. In certain instances, the potential is not fully used.

10 For further discussion of this problem see Chapter 2.2.6.

11 See also Fig. 2.3.

12 The preliminary figures of the agricultural census are subject to doubt on several points, which cannot be discussed at length (technical and political barriers for data collection). But, the general picture seems to be truly presented. Variation of size and intensity between states and other details have to be neglected in a summary presentation.

13 Madras is now called Tamil Nadu.

14 The total amount of compensation is 6,600 million Rs. The value of the rupee dropped from DM 0.84 at the beginning of 1966 to DM 0.53 in summer 1966 and to DM. 0.33 in February 1973.

15 For legal purposes owner-cultivation is defined as presence of the landowner in the village during harvest season.

16 1 acre = 0.4 hectares. The extremes of ceiling thus vary from 7 to 130 ha.

17 This high figure – one third of all villages in India – probably refers not to revenue villages, the administrative units, but to hamlets and points of settlement, several of which might form one revenue village.

18 Ceiling is the legal upper limit of land permitted to one cultivator with his family.

19 Mann and Kanitkar (1968) in an empirical study have shown that these negative effects

of price rises are felt in the villages, too, leading to further income differentials and social polarisation.

20 For the counterproductive effect of European price policies in developing countries see also Abercrombie (1967).

21 This survey, though never officially published, is quoted extensively by Nayar (1971).

22 Supervised credit: the client does not get cash, which might go into consumption, but inputs in kind to be used for productive purposes only.

23 Central Government regulations are not necessarily applied by the Federal States, which mostly feel free to adapt official rules on entitlement to benefit to the natural and social conditions prevailing in their respective regions.

24 About this drain of resources see also Chapter 2.5.1.3.

25 Vinoba Bhave's defence of village drafts is a case in point.

26 This point involves the development model and its objectives, to be further discussed in Chapter 5.8.1.

27 See also Dandekar and Rath (1971) and Breuer (1967).

28 A survey by a large economic research bureau in Bombay is under way. But as yet no results or data are available.

29 Employment in the private sector may well be underestimated, since some employers, in order to avoid taxes, insurance contributions, etc., and subsequent checks, evade registration. Employment in the public sector was markedly increased by the nationalisation of 14 large banks and of some coalmines.

30 This refutes the statements of some observers from developed countries, who assert that high wages are being paid in modern factories at the expense of the really poor and that the workers, by striking for wage increases, exploit the poor masses.

31 R. F. Behrendt (1965) opposes this widespread view and says:
> "There are substantial differences regarding talent and interest between individuals of all cultures and races. But on the basis of actual knowledge, we may rest assured that the biological differences of the collective types which constitute the races do not determine the degree of ability to set up and man technical and organisational installations... The real problems are not biological and racial, but cultural and social." (pp. 190f.).

32 The writings of Marx about the Asian mode of production have given rise to a spate of publications. Among the more recent ones, reference may be made to Sofri (1969), Barrington Moore (1969), Tökei (1969).

33 Thus, contrary to unequivocally expressed Indian wishes, caste was included in the information required for the census. The state parliaments permitted by the British were composed according to caste representation.

34 Table 2.1 gives the data about these castes and tribes. – Below the protective measures and special laws are briefly mentioned.

35 The Swatantra is now amalgamated with the BLD. See chapter 2.1.3.

36 Cf. the theory of colonial drain put forward by the Indian economists Naoroji and Ganguli (1965).

37 For the largest and very heterogeneous republic, the RSFSR, a further subdivision of data would be useful. Owing to lack of space, this has to be omitted.

38 Cf. Table 3.1. and Fig. 3.1.

39 Not all who had to leave the land have left the villages. Furthermore, changes in the statistical definition of villages and towns may have influenced the apparent trend.

40 No information is available, however, on the procedure by which those are selected and on the relative strength of the various sectors.

41 This quasi-theoretical slogan by Stalin was in fact a response to isolation and its consequences.

Notes

42   The absolute numbers represent annual averages. In the peak season, substantially larger numbers are engaged in tillage work, while in lean seasons the actual figures are lower. Owing to the slow pace of mechanisation, there is still underemployment in the countryside.

43   Sakoff (1972) reports a gradual decline in the share paid in kind.

44   With the exception, up to 1960, of tractor drivers and mechanics employed by the MTS and working in the collective farm.

45   The figures for the workforce are annual averages, ironing out seasonal fluctuations.

46   Alienation is a Hegelian term used by Karl Marx to describe the relationship between a factory worker in a capitalist system and his produce. It seems, however, that alienation also occurs in socialist societies, at least during the early stages of take-off, when high contributions are exacted, while remuneration is low.

47   Swedborg (1975), however, shows that the virgin lands are complementary to arable farming in the rest of the country inasmuch as they have inverse cycles of good and poor crops. When there are good harvests in the RSFSR, they are poor in Kazakhstan and vice versa.

48   Possible reasons for the wide fluctuations will be discussed in Chapter 3.5.3.

49   For this comparison and its problems see Chapter 5.9.2.

50   The agrarian triangle is roughly delimited by the towns of Leningrad, Gorki, Omsk, Novosibirsk and Odessa. It comprises most of the really important and productive regions of the country.

51   It should be noted, incidentally, that the evaluation of official data presented in Fig. 3.4. points to the reliability of present-day Soviet statistics, which give a fair picture of reality, with its abrupt variations. Some problems, however, remain in the interpretation of these statistics. Thus, the figures of grain production usually refer to the biological harvest, i.e. in the field, not in the grain silos. The difference is anybody's guess.

52   It means: If collectivisation is based on the old equipment of the private smallholding, it holds hardly any economic advantage over the old organisation and, therefore, cannot convince the old peasants of its superiority.

53   For the problems of comparison see Chapter 5.9.

54   See Chapter 3.5.1.2.

55   Cf. also Chapter 3.5.4.1.

56   This mobility raises intricate juridical problems about continuity of land ownership, which cannot be elaborated here.

57   The latest published figures are for 1968.

58   About their results see Sakoff (1972). The rest are mainly computations made in other countries.

59   Cf. Chapter 5.6.4.

60   Bhattacharya (1974) gives a colourful picture of this problem:

    "Vice-Premier Li Hsien-nien, in an interview with a Cairo journalist published on November 18, 1971, made some frank remarks on the divergent population estimates by various sectors of the Chinese economy:

      'We have been racing against time to cope with the enormous increase in population. Some people estimate the population at 800 million and some at 750 million. Unfortunately, there are no accurate statistics in this connection. Nevertheless, the officials at the Supply and Grain Department are saying confidently that the number is 800 million. Officials outside the Grain Department say the population is only 750 million, while the Ministry of Commerce affirms that the number is 830 million. However, the Planning Department declares emphatically that the number is less than 750 million. The Ministry of

Commerce insists on the larger number in order to be able to supply goods in large quantities. The Planning Department's men reduce the figures in order to bring the plans of the various government departments into line.' " (p. 442).

61 About the assessment of irrigation data see above, note 9.
62 Figures given by *Länderkurzbericht* (1974) are somewhat lower than those quoted by Rochlin and Hagemann (1971).
63 The reference here is to the later, summarised version, which dispensed with many finer details referred to at length by Alavi (1968/1972).
64 The official figure of 300 million seems improbable unless it is meant to include all the members – or at least all the working members – of the households of beneficiaries of agrarian reform.
65 About the function and socio-economic role of the individual plot see Chapter 3.5.1.2.
66 This and the following quotations about the internal organisation of the people's communes are taken from Biehl (1965).
67 Shillinglaw (1971) shows that, under prevailing conditions of infrastructure and low monetisation of the whole economy, the people's commune is the most suitable unit of capital accumulation.
68 Another purpose may be the settlement of Han people (of Chinese stock) in regions inhabited by ethnic minorities, which are mostly border regions.
68a After the ascendance of Hua Kuo-feng to chairmanship at the end of 1976, a re-interpretation of Mao's thoughts seems to be under way regarding mechanisation of farming. The agrarian sector shall be equipped with all modern technology available or produced in the country.
69 About these problems see also Chapter 3.5.4.2. and an article in *Current Scene*, Hong-kong, VI, 17.
70 Given the different price policies and systems, these figures cannot be compared to those of capitalist economies. They reflect the trend of domestic economic developments.
71 There seems to be some contradiction between the practice of family planning at home and declarations for foreign consumption – e.g. at the world population conference in Bucharest in 1974 – designed to gain popularity among underdeveloped nations and their narrow-minded representatives.
72 Thus, when Cuba on one occasion made a political statement siding with Moscow, China retaliated at once by stopping rice deliveries.
73 The pictorial reportage about the model people's commune of Tachai (1969) shows only one two-wheel tractor and no draft animals. All tillage operations are carried out by human energy. Yet, for the construction of the Tanzam-railway, a large number of heavy earth-moving machines, trucks, cranes etc. were employed, all of Chinese origin.
74 For Trotsky's position see Bukharin et al. (1973) and Deutscher (1963).
75 See Lenin's article 'On Cooperation', *Collected works*, vol. 33, Moscow-London 1966, pp. 467-486.
His thinking in that respect was very close to that of Engels (1884), who had stated repeatedly that socialism, once in power, would use only persuasion and give the peasants a long period to make up their minds and arrive at a voluntary decision whether or not to join the production cooperatives.
76 Better: they are not denied access to their former village. If they are absentees, their representative remains on the spot.
77 Today, vertical integration and new production techniques are keeping farmers subject to a new type of economic dependence on strong external forces.
78 For details see Chapter 3.5.1.

Notes

79 The Chinese peasants' role is described and analysed in several works, e.g. Roy (1930), Wolf (1971).

80 It goes without saying that the level of employment depends also on economic policies and the economic system.

81 Cf. the millions of rural workers who have migrated over thousands of miles to work in Western Europe.

82 For the problem of migration and population transfer see also Chapter 5.4.

83 On this point see e.g. Dandekar and Rath (1971), Patil (1972), Breuer (1967).

84 In some periods of acute food shortage an urban migration to the countryside was organised and forced upon reluctant townsfolk.

85 On the other hand, the extent to which progress can be slowed down is limited by population growth and "development expectations" (cf. Behrendt, 1965).

86 This view is shared by Kuznets (1963), quoted by Dantwala (1968):

> "When modern economic growth does occur, it is the combination of the marked rise in the productivity of labour in the agricultural sector with the secular limits on the demand for its products that results in a sharp and uniform reduction of the agricultural sector in the labour force".

Kuhnen (1972) supports this opinion and advances

> "the thesis, that even with complete utilisation of all employment possibilities in agriculture by necessary agrarian reform measures in some regions, not all the available labour force can be employed. Here, unemployment and underemployment will continue with their adverse effects on progress in agriculture." (P. 47).

Dovring (1959), however, is much more sceptical:

> "In most of the less developed countries of the world today, there is no reason to expect a reduction in the absolute numbers of the agricultural population in the near future. In several of them, continued increase of the agricultural population must be expected for a long time to come. It will take decades before agriculture ceases to employ and support the majority of the world's population." (P. 11).

Khusro (1962) estimates the demand for non-agricultural labour and relates it to the probable supply from within the same sectors. He concludes, as Rao (1960) did before him, that

> "agriculture will continue to give employment not only to all the labour force it is now giving employment to, but also to many more millions of persons for many years or decades to come. From this it follows (i) that policy will have to work towards a speedier reduction of the birth rate and a reduced rate of growth of India's population, if the problem of employment is to become more manageable; and (ii) that agricultural policy has to be employment-oriented and cannot encourage capitalist farming or labour-displacing technology. On the contrary, what emerges is a justification for intensive farming with increasing inputs per acre, accompanied of course by increasing inputs of other factors of agricultural production such as water, fertilisers, pesticides, etc., the need for occupations allied to agriculture, and an economic justification for a ceiling on individual land holdings." (P. 35).

An ILO paper (*Framework*...,1974) summarises three documents on agriculture and employment in the following theses:

> "1. The main burden of employment creation in most developing countries will fall on the agricultural sector.

2. The process of structural transformation that occurred in the Western countries, which led to a speedily declining share of the agricultural workforce in the economically active population, will not be repeated in the same manner in developing countries.

3. The model of agricultural development has to be based on high-density farming which will have to be upgraded technologically within an employment-intensive strategy." (P. 617).

87 It can be laid down, for instance, that at least 50 per cent of all students must be of workers or peasant origin, or that children from families without a background of higher education may be allowed a bonus in final examinations.

88 It remains to be seen, however, whether such measures are efficient and successful in a modern society, which is based on the division of labour and on specialisation.

89 Here it must be noted that the totality of consumers is identical with the totality of producers.

90 It is difficult, however, to define and quantify individual needs and demands. These are changing continuously with qualitative changes in society and a rising standard of living.

91 Quoted after Löwy (1969), pp. 161f.

92 See the events in Poland in 1956, 1970, and again in 1976.

93 The various forms of mobility are briefly discussed in Chapter 5.4.

94 The allowances are about 15 per cent lower than for industrial workers, in recognition of the lower cost of living in the country.

95 See, for example, the agrarian reforms of Sweden, England, Ireland, Prussia and Russia.

96 Gross national product. For a brief criticism see Chapters 5.1. and 5.9.1.

97 Cf., for instance, W. Arthur Lewis (1956).

98 Events in Czechoslovakia followed a similar course.

99 This rigid bureaucracy was probably the leading force opposing all reform proposals after Stalin's death, and contributed strongly to Khrushchev's overthrow.

100 In his book *Radicalism, an infantile disorder of communism*, written in 1920, Lenin commented on the international applicability of the Soviet model abroad:

"... [Certain] fundamental features of our revolution have a significance that is not... Russian alone, but international... It would, of course, be grossly erroneous to exaggerate this truth and to extend it beyond certain fundamental features of our revolution. It would also be erroneous to lose sight of the fact that, soon after the victory of the proletarian revolution in at least one of the advanced countries, a sharp change will probably come about: Russia will cease to be the model and will once again become a backward country (in the 'Soviet' and the socialist sense)."
V. I. Lenin, *Collected works*, vol. 31, Moscow-London 1966, p. 21).

101 Thus, Chinese delegations started after 1959 to lay wreaths at Stalin's memorial bust in the Kremlin.

102 Most Marxists had expected revolution in a highly developed capitalist country.

103 One slogan frequently used was: "To learn from the Soviet Union means to learn victory".

104 After many detours, a resolution on the same lines as that of 1956 was again adopted in 1976 during a conference of communist parties in East Berlin.

105 See Marx-Engels (1845-1846), Deutsche Ideologie.

106 On this question see Hennicke (1973) and Mandel (1973).

107 This self-image of the major new nations and their loose alliance is a contradiction in terms.

108 Pondicherry was taken over by agreement with France, Goa and a few smaller exclaves were occupied by India after the negotiations with Portugal had failed.

Notes

109   Suzerain means a state, which does not enjoy full sovereignty, but is under military and diplomatic dependence of another government. This status of semi-dependence of Sikkim was established during British rule in India and continued after 1947 until 1975.

110   These were the terms used by Lenin and his associates in government.

111   Whatever the legal or other foundation for the Chinese territorial claims may be, the resort to military action seems to have been a major political blunder and failure.

112   The term "imperialism" is deliberately avoided. Since the first world war imperialism has been associated with the capitalist character of a state. While the character of the Soviet Union and China is open to discussion, it is agreed that they are not capitalist states.

113   Thus, it may be very profitable micro-economically to produce, sell and consume a maximum of pesticides or pharmaceutical products. But it may be more recommendable from a social point of view to sell and consume a minimum.

114   It can be proved that the circles of intensity discovered by J. H. von Thünen are valid both for capitalist and socialist systems. The different intensity of land use between socialist countries can be explained by economic reasons. See Bergmann (1976).

115   The speeding up was deliberate. The first five-year plan started in 1929, Hitler came to power in Germany 1933, and the Russo-German war began in 1941. Without independent industrialisation, the Soviet victory might have been more expensive and might have taken even longer.

116   At that time (1971), the Soviet Union had good harvests, while China was compelled to buy millions of tons of grain abroad. While this book is being prepared (end of 1975, early 1976) the position is reversed.

117   P. 452. This statement is not conclusive. It is very possible, even likely, that a very large part of economic growth is allocated for public investment and a small share only for increased individual consumption.

118   Some of his calculations are questionable, e.g. his finding that the Chinese yield per hectare of food grains is about twice that of India (p. 13).

LITERATURE

1. *India*

1. BANERJEE, J. (1961), Co-operative movement in India. Calcutta.
2. BERGMANN, TH. (1967), Funktionen und Wirkungsgrenzen von Produktionsgenossenschaften in Entwicklungsländern. Frankfurt/M.
3. BERGMANN, TH. (1967), Entwicklungshemmende Faktoren und Produktionsreserven in der indischen Landwirtschaft. In: Zeitschrift für ausländische Landwirtschaft, 6, 2, June 1967, pp. 192-212. Frankfurt/M.
4. BERGMANN, TH. (1971), Grüne Revolution und Agrarreform. In: Gewerkschaftliche Monatshefte, 1971, 2, pp. 99-112, Köln.
5. BERGMANN, Th. (1971), Die Genossenschaftsbewegung in Indien. Frankfurt/M.
6. BERGMANN, TH. (1974), The industrial activities of the cooperative movement in India. Paper delivered at the 4th European Conference on Modern South Asian Studies. Brighton, Sussex (mimeo).
7. BHAVE, V. (1958?), Gramdan – Why and how? Tanjore.
8. BOBEK, H. (1961), Zur Problematik eines unterentwickelten Landes alter Kultur: Iran. In: Orient, 2, pp. 64-68, 3, pp. 115-124. Hamburg.
9. BÖTTGER, B. (1975), 700 Millionen ohne Zukunft? Faschismus oder Revolution in Indien und Bangladesh. Reinbek (Hamburg).
10. BREUER, H. (1967), Die Industrialisierung Indiens unter dem Druck der steigenden Auslandsverschuldung. Berlin.
11. CHOUDHURY, UMA DATTA ROY and PRATAP NARAIN (1975). Current national income statistics – what they tell. Economic and Political Weekly, X, 39, Sept. 27, pp. 1540-1553.
12. DANDEKAR, V. M. und N. RATH (1971), Poverty in India. Bombay.
13. DANTWALA, M. L. (1968), Agricultural employment in a developing economy. In: A. M. Khusro (ed.), Readings in agricultural development, pp. 527-546, Bombay.
14. DESAI, A. R. (ed.) (1961), Rural sociology in India. Bombay.
15. DESAI, A. R. (1966), Social background of Indian nationalism. Bombay.
16. EDWARDES, M. (1961), A history of India from the earliest times to the present day, with 127 photogravure illustrations and 21 maps. London.
17. FONSECA, A. J. (1971), Challenge of poverty in India. New Delhi.
18. GANGULI, B. N. (1965), Dadabhai Naoroji and the drain theory. London.
19. HAELLQUIST, K. R. och INGER SONDÉN HAELLQUIST (1973), Indiens, Pakistans och Bangladesh's historia. Studentlitteratur, Malmö.
⨯20. JOSHI, P. C. (1975), Land reforms in India – trends and perspectives. Bombay.
21. KHUSRO, A. M. (1962), Economic development with no population transfers. Bombay.
22. KHUSRO, A. M. (ed.) (1968), Readings in agricultural development. Bombay.
23. KHUSRO, A. M. and A. N. AGARWAL (1961), The problem of co-operative farming in India. Bombay.
24. KIDRON, M. (1965), Foreign investments in India. London.
25. MANDAL, G. C. (1961), Studies in the problems of growth of a rural economy. Calcutta.
26. MANN, H. H. (1968), The social framework of agriculture. London.

Literature

27. MARX, K. (1942), The future results of British rule in India. New York Daily Tribune, 8th August 1853; here quoted from Selected works in two volumes, vol. 2, London.
28. MYRDAL, G. (1968), Asian drama – an inquiry into the poverty of nations. New York.
29. NAIDU, I. J. (1975), All-India report on agricultural census 1970-71. Government of India. New Delhi.
30. NAMBOODIRIPAD, E. M. S. (1966), Economics and politics of India's socialist pattern. New Delhi.
31. NANAVATI, M. B. and J. J. ANJARIA (1960), The Indian rural problem. Bombay.
32. NAYAR, K. (1971), India – the critical years. Delhi.
33. NEHRU, J. (1937), Letters from a father to his daughter. Being a brief account of the early days of the world written for children. 2nd edition, Allahabad.
34. NEHRU, J. (1961), The discovery of India. Bombay.
35. OOMMEN, T. K. (1972), Charisma, stability and change – an analysis of Bhoodan-gramdan movement in India. New Delhi.
36. OSTERGAARD, G. and M. CURRELL (1971), The gentle anarchists – a study of the leaders of the sarvodaya-movement for non-violent revolution in India. Oxford.
37. PATIL, R. K. (1972), Mobilisation of human resources, employment generation and promotion of popular participation through rural institutions. Report on the Asian regional seminar on the contribution of rural institutions to rural development, particularly employment. Geneva, ILO, (stenciled), pp. 59-75.
38. ROTHERMUND, D. (1967), Die historische Analyse des Bodenrechts als eine Grundlage für das Verständnis gegenwärtiger Agrarstructurprobleme, dargestellt am Beispiel Indiens. In: Jahrbuch des Südasiens-Instituts der Universität Heidelberg 1966, pp. 149-166. Wiesbaden.
39. SEGAL, R. M. (1965), The crisis of India, London.
40. SHAH, C. G. (1963), Marxism, Gandhism, Stalinism. Bombay.
41. SOFRI, G. (1969), Über asiatische Produktionsweise. Frankfurt.
42. THORNER, D. und A. (1962), Land and labour in India. Bombay and New Delhi.
43. Annual plan 1974-75 (?). Planning Commission. Delhi.
44. Basic statistics relating to the Indian economy (1974), Vol. I and II. Commerce Research Bureau. Bombay.
45. Brief on Indian agriculture 1977. (1977). New Delhi (stenciled).
46. Census of India 1971 (1971), Provisional population totals, Paper I of 1971. Delhi: Government of India Press.
47. Commerce, Annual number 1972. Bombay.
48. Draft fifth five year plan 1974-79 (1973). Vol. I and II. Planning Commission, Delhi.
49. Eastern economist. Annual number 1972. New Delhi.
50. Economic survey (annually). New Delhi.
51. Fifth plan and previous plans – some key statistics (1974). Commerce Research Bureau. Bombay.
52. Fourth five year plan 1969-74 (1970). New Delhi.
53. India 1971-72 (1971). New Delhi.
54. India pocket-book of economic information 1971 (1971). New Delhi.
55. Indian agriculture in brief (1971), Eleventh edition. Delhi.
56. Indien – Länderkurzberichte 1974. Stuttgart und Mainz.
57. Monthly commentary on Indian economic conditions, Annual number (1971). New Delhi.
58. Report of the All-India rural credit review committee (1969). Bombay.
59. Staatsbürgerliche Informationen. Der indische Subkontinent I+II, (1965, 1966). Bonn.
60. Statistical abstract of the Indian Union 1973. (1973). New Delhi.
61. Statistical outline of India 1976 (1976). Bombay Department of Economics and Statistics, Tata Services.

62. Statistical statements relating to the cooperative movement in India (annually). Bombay.
63. The All-India rural credit survey – General report (1959). Bombay.
64. The anatomy of Indian poverty (1968). New Delhi: Indian Institute of Public Opinion.

2. *Soviet Union*

1. BERGMANN, TH. (1968), Der Kolchosbauer – sozioökonomische Merkmale und Problematik. In: Sociologia Ruralis, VIII, 1, 1968, S. 22-47. Assen.
2. BETTELHEIM, CH. et alii (1969), Zur Kritik der Sowjetökonomie. Berlin.
3. BEYME, K. v. (1975), Ökonomie und Politik im Sozialismus – Ein Vergleich der Entwicklung in den sozialistischen Ländern. München.
4. BOETTCHER, E. (1959). Die sowjetische Wirtschaftspolitik am Scheideweg. Tübingen.
5. BRUNNER, G. and K. WESTEN (1970), Die sowjetische Kolchosordnung, Stuttgart.
6. BOUKHARINE, N. et alii (1973), La question paysanne en URSS (1924-1929), Paris.
7. BUCHARIN, N. (1922), Ökonomik der Transformationsperiode. Hamburg.
8. CONKLIN, D. C. (1970), An evaluation of the Soviet profit reforms. New York.
9. DEUTSCHER, I. (1963), The prophet outcast: Trotsky 1929-1940. Vol. 3 of the biography. Oxford.
10. DEUTSCHER, I. (1967), The unfinished revolution: Russia 1917-1967.
11. DEUTSCHER, I. (1950), Soviet trade unions: their place in Soviet labour policy, Oxford.
12. DUMONT, R. (1964), Sovkhoze, kolkhoze ou le problématique communisme. Paris.
13. ENGELS, F. (1894/1962), The peasant question in France and Germany. (German original: Neue Zeit 1894), Marx-Engels, Selected works, Moscow 1962, vol. 2, pp. 420-440.
14. ERLICH, A. (1971), Die Industrialisierungsdebatte in der Sowjetunion 1924-1928. Frankfurt.
15. FEDORENKO, N. P., P. G. BUNITSCH und S. S. SCHATALIN (1972), Effektivität in der sozialistischen Wirtschaft, Berlin (Ost).
16. FETSCHER, J. (1967), Karl Marx und der Marxismus. München.
17. GUMPEL, W. et alii (1967), Die Sowjetwirtschaft an der Wende zum Fünfjahresplan – Rückblick und Ausblick. München-Wien.
18. HEUER, K. (1965), Zur Entwicklung der genossenschaftlichen Demokratie im neuen ökonomischen System. In: Autorenkollektiv unter Leitung von Gert Egler, Zum neuen ökonomischen System in der Landwirtschaft S. 232-261. Ostberlin: Staatsverlag der DDR.
19. JASNY, N. (1949), The socialized agriculture of the USSR – plans and performance. Stanford
20. JEFIMOW, A. N. (1969), Die Industrie der UdSSR. Berlin (East).
21. KARCZ, J. F. (ed.) (1967), Soviet and East European agriculture. Berkeley, Los Angeles.
22. KARDELJ, E. (1960), Les problèmes de la politique socialiste dans les campagnes. Paris.
23. KARGER, A. (1968), Die Sowjetunion als Wirtschaftsmacht. Second edition, Frankfurt/M.
24. KERBLAY, B. (1967), Du mir aux agrovilles (L'expérience agricole soviétique). Structures agraires, systémes politiques et économiques, Colloque de Venise, 14-18 octobre 1967 (stenciled).
25. KOLESNIKOV, L. (1970), Agriculture of the Soviet Union. XIV International Conference of Agricultural Economists. Moscow.
26. KURJO, A. (1975), Agrarproduktion in den Mitgliedsländern des Rates für Gegenseitige Wirtschaftshilfe (RGW). Berlin.
27. LAIRD, R. D. and B. A. (1970), Soviet communism and agrarian revolution. Harmondsworth.
28. LANE, D. (1971), The end of inequality? Stratification under state socialism. Harmondsworth.

Literature

29. LENIN, V. I. (1960-1970), Collected works. Moscow-London.
30. LÖWY, A. G. (1969), Die Weltgeschichte ist das Weltgericht – Bucharin: Die Vision des Kommunismus. Wien-Frankfurt-Zürich.
31. LONČAREVIC, J. (1969), Die landwirtschaftlichen Betriebsgrößen in der Sowjetunion in Statistik und Theorie. Wiesbaden.
32. MARCUSE, H. (1971), Soviet marxism – a critical analysis. Harmondsworth.
33. MEISSNER, B. (1966), Sowjetgesellschaft im Wandel – Rußlands Weg zur Industriegesellschaft. Stuttgart.
34. MELLOR, R. E. H (1964), Geography of the USSR. London.
35. NOVE, A. (1969). An economic history of the USSR. London.
36. OSIPOV, G. V. (ed.) (1969), Town, country and people Studies in Soviet society 2. London.
37. POKROVSKY, M. (1933), Brief history of Russia (trl. by D. S. Mirsky), London.
38. POKŠIŠEVSKIJ, V. V. (Herausg.) (1967, Russ. Original 1964), Sowjetunion, regionale ökonomische Geographie. 1. Auflage, Gotha/Leipzig.
39. POLLOCK, F. (1971), Die planwirtschaftlichen Versuche in der Sowjetunion. Frankfurt (First edition: Leipzig, 1929).
40. PREOBRAZHENSKY, E. (1965), The new economics. Oxford (Translation of the first Russian edition, Moscow, 1926).
41. PREOBRAZHENSKY, E. (1975), UdSSR 1975 – Ein Rückblick in die Zukunft. (Edited after the 1922 edition by B. Rabehl,) West-Berlin.
42. RAUPACH, H. (1964), Geschichte der Sowjetwirtschaft. Reinbek (Hamburg).
43. RAUPACH, H. (1968), System der Sowjetwirtschaft. Reinbek (Hamburg).
44. RAUTH, M. (1967), Raumgliederung, Raumordnung und Regionalplanung der Sowjetunion aus landwirtschaftlicher Sicht. Wiesbaden.
45. ROCHLIN, R. P. (1960), Agrarpolitik und Agrarverfassung der Sowjetunion. Berlin.
46. SAKOFF, A. (1962), The private sector in soviet agriculture. In: Monthly Bulletin of Agricultural Economics and Statistics. 11, 9, Sept., pp. 1-12. Rom.
47. SAKOFF, A. N. (1972), Rural and urban society in the USSR – comparative structure, income, level of living. In: Monthly Bulletin of Agricultural Economics and Statistics, 21, 10, October, pp. 1-13.
48. SCHILLER, O. (1931), Die Kollektivbewegung in der Sowjetunion. – Ein Beitrag zu den Gegenwartsfragen der russischen Landwirtschaft. Osteuropäische Forschungen, N.F./ Band 8. Berlin und Königsberg.
49. SCHILLER, O. (1943), Ziele und Ergebnisse der Agrarordnung in den besetzten Ostgebieten. Reich Ministry for the Occupied Eastern Territories. Berlin.
50. SCHILLER, O. (1960), Das Agrarsystem der Sowjetunion. Tübingen.
51. SCHINKE, E. (1967), Die Mechanisierung landwirtschaftlicherArbeiten in der Sowjetunion. Wiesbaden.
52. SCHINKE, E. (1970), The organization and planning of Soviet agriculture. World Agricultural Economics and Rural Sociology Abstracts. March, 1970, [pp. 1-18]. Oxford
53. SHANIN, T. (1971), The awkward class, London.
54. STALIN, J. (1954), Concerning questions of Leninism. Works, vol. 8. Moscow.
55. STRAUSS, E. (1969), Soviet agriculture in perspective. A study of its successes and failures. London.
56. ŠUVAR, S. and V. PULJIZ (1971), The role of rural sociology in Jugoslav agrarian policy. In: Sociologia Ruralis, XI, 1, pp 66-74.
57. SWEDBORG, E. (1975), Sovjetunionens försörjningsläge under första delen av 1970-talet. In: Jordbruksekonomiska meddelanden, 1975, 3, pp. 73-80 Stockholm.
58. SWEEZY, P. M. and CH. BETTELHEIM (1971), On the transition to socialism. New York and London.

Literature

59. THORNER, D., B. KERBLAY, R. E. F. SMITH (eds.), (1967), A.V. Chayanov on the theory of peasant economy. Homewood, Ill.
60. TROTZKI, L. (1922), Between Red and White. A study of some fundamental questions of revolution. London.
61. TROTZKI, L. (1928), The real situation in Russia, London.
62. VOLIN, L. (1970). A century of Russian agriculture. From Alexander II to Chrushchev. Cambridge/Mass.
63. WÄDEKIN, K.-E. (1973), The private sector in Soviet agriculture. Berkeley.
64. WÄDEKIN, K. -E. (1974), Sozialistische Agrarpolitik in Osteuropa-I. Von Marx bis zur Vollkollektivisierung. Berlin.
65. WAGENER, H.-J. (1969), Die RSFSR und die nichtrussischen Republiken: ein ökonomischer Vergleich. In: Osteuropa-Wirtschaft, 14, 2, Juni, S. 113-129.
66. WILMANNS, H. (1969), Zur Struktur und Faktoranalyse bei der Wirtschaftsregionalisierung in der Sowjetunion. In: Osteuropa-Wirtschaft, 14, 3, Sept. 1969. Stuttgart.
67. Die Wirtschaft Osteuropas und der UdSSR 1971 bis 1973, Ausblick bis 1975. Monatsberichte 3/1974. Wien: Institut für Wirtschaftsforschung, pp. 181-191.
68. Third All-Union congress of collective farmers. Moscow, 1969.
69. Informationen zur politischen Bildung. Folge 78/79. 12 Karten und Textbeiträge zur Landes- und Wirtschaftskunde der Sowjetunion (Stand: Herbst 1958), Wiesbaden, 1959
70. Informationen zur Politischen Bildung. Folge 139. Die Sowjetunion – Land und Wirtschaft. Wiesbaden 1970.
71. Narodnoe khozyaystvo (Statistical Year-Book of the USSR) 1922-1972. Moscow, 1972.
72. Narodnoe khozyaystvo (Statistical Year-Book of the USSR) (annual). Moscow.
73. Sowjetunion von A bis Z. Berlin, 1958.
74. Sowjetunion 1974/75 (1975). Innenpolitik, Wirtschaft, Außenpolitik – Analyse und Bilanz. München, Wien.
75. SSSR v cifrach 1974. Moscow, 1975.
76. Osteuropa, Stuttgart.
77. Osteuropa-Wirtschaft, Stuttgart.

3. *China*

1. ALAVI, H. (1968/72), Theorie der Bauernrevolution. Stuttgart.
2. AUGUSTINI, G. (1974), Agrarian reform in China: Objectives, approach and achievements. In: Land Reform, Land Settlement and Cooperatives. FAO, No. 1/2, pp. 26-42. Rome.
3. BEAUVOIR, S. DE (1957), La longue marche: essai sur la Chine, Paris.
4. BELDEN, J. (1973), China shakes the world (reprint of 1949 edition with new introduction by Owen Lattimore), Harmondsworth.
5. BETTELHEIM, C., H. MARCHISIO and J. CHARRIÈRE (1965), La construction du socialisme en Chine. Paris.
6. BETTELHEIM, C. u.a. (1972), China 1972 – Ökonomie, Betrieb und Erziehung seit der Kulturrevolution. Berlin.
7. BIANCO, L. (1969), Das moderne Asien. Fischer-Weltgeschichte, Bd. 33. Frankfurt/M.
8. BIEHL, M. (1965), Die chinesische Volkskommune im „Großen Sprung" und danach. Hamburg.
9. BLUMER, G. (1968), Die chinesische Kulturrevolution 1965/67. Frankfurt/M.
10. BRIESSEN, F. VAN (1972), China – Fakten, Daten, Dokumente. Stuttgart.
11. BROADBENT, K. P. (1968), Two decades of social and economic development in Chinese communist agriculture, 1949-1969. World Agricultural Economics and Rural Sociology Abstracts, 11, 4, Dec. 1968, pp. 1-21. Oxford.
12. BURKI, S. J. (1969), A study of Chinese communes, 1965. Cambridge, Mass.

Literature

13. CHAI, WINBERG (ed.), (1969), Essential works of Chinese communism. New York.
14. CHANG, T. T. (1965), Die chinesische Volkswirtschaft, Grundlagen, Organisation, Planung. Köln und Opladen.
15. CHAO KUO-CHÜN (1957), Agrarian policies of mainland China: A documentary study (1949-1956). Cambridge, Mass.
16. CHEN PO-TA (1971), Klassenanalyse und Partei in China. Frankfurt/M.
17. DELAYNE, J. (1972), Die chinesische Wirtschaftsrevolution. Reinbek (Hamburg).
18. DENG ZHONGXIA (1975), Anfänge der chinesischen Arbeiterbewegung 1919-1926 (Herausg. Meissner, W. und G. Schulz). Reinbek (Hamburg).
19. ETIENNE, GILBERT (1974), China's agricultural development – production, inputs, external trade, research. Studies and Documents, I, 3-4. Geneva (stenciled).
20. FITZGERALD, C. P. (1966), The birth of communist China, New York (expanded edition of Revolution in China, London 1952).
21. FUNG, K. K. (1974), Output vs "surplus" maximization: the conflicts between the socialized and the private sector in Chinese collectivized agriculture. Developing Economies 12 (1), pp. 41-55. Tokyo.
22. Großmann, B. (1960), Die wirtschaftliche Entwicklung der Volksrepublik China. Stuttgart.
23. GURLEY, JOHN G. (1975), Die Entwicklung der ökonomischen Strategie Maos zwischen 1927 und 1949. Monthly Review, Deutsche Ausgabe, I, 4, Sept., S. 52-115. Frankfurt/M.
24. HEALEY, D. T. (1972), Chinese real output 1950-1970. In: Bulletin Institute of Development Studies, 4, 2/3, pp. 49-59. Brighton.
25. HENLE, H. V. (1974), Report on China's agriculture. Rome: FAO (stenciled).
26. HIDASI, G. (1972), China's economy in the early 1970's. Acta Oeconomica, 1, pp. 81-94. Budapest.
27. HINTON, W. (1966), Fanshen: a documentary of revolution in a Chinese village, New York.
28. HOFFMANN, R. (1973?), Entmaoisierung in China – Zur Vorgeschichte der Kulturrevolution. München.
29. HSIA, A. (1971), Die chinesische Kulturrevolution. Neuwied.
30. ISHIKAWA, S. (1967), Factors affecting China's agriculture in the coming decade. Tokyo (stenciled).
31. Jacoby, E. H. (1974), Agricultural development in China, Stockholm: EFI (stenciled).
32. JOHNSTON, J. A. and M. WILLIAMS (1971), The new China. Sydney, Melbourne, Wellington, Auckland.
33. KHAN, A. R. (1976), The distribution of income in rural China. Geneva: International Labour Office (stenciled).
34. KOSTA, J. und J. MEYER (1976), Volksrepublik China. Frankfurt/M.
35. LICHNOWSKY, L. (1962), Agricultural policy in mainland China since 1949. Monthly bulletin of agricultural economics and statistics. 11, 10, Oct. pp. 1-8; 11, Nov., pp. 1-7.
36. LIU SHAO-CH'I (1968), Quotations from president Liu. Melbourne.
37. MAGDOFF, H. (1975), China – Unterschiede zur Sowjetunion. Monthly Review, Deutsche Ausgabe, I, 4, Sept., S. 11-51. Frankfurt/M.
38. MALRAUX, A. (1933), La condition humaine, Paris.
39. MAO TSE-TUNG (1961-65), Selected works, 4 vol. Peking.
40. MARCHISIO, H. (1966/1968), Communes populaires chinoises. La contradiction, moteur de développement dans une commune populaire chinoise. Archives Internationales de Sociologie de la Coopération et du Développement. 20, 1966, pp. 76-132; 23, 1968, pp. 173-214. Paris
41. MYRDAL, J. (1965), Report from a Chinese village, London.
42. MYRDAL, J. and G. KESSLE, China: the revolution continued. London.

43. PAYNE, R. (1953 ?), Roter Sturm über Asien. Salzburg-München.
44. ROBINSON, J. (1969), The cultural revolution in China. London, Reading and Fakenham.
45. ROY, M. N. (1930), Revolution und Konterrevolution in China. Berlin.
46. SCHECK, F. R. (Herausg.) (1972), Chinas sozialistischer Weg. Frankfurt.
47. SHILLINGLAW, G. (1971), Traditional rural cooperation and social structure – the communist Chinese collectivization of agriculture. In: P. Worsley (ed.), Two blades of grass, pp. 137-157. Manchester.
48. SIMONIS, U.-E. (1968), Die Entwicklungspolitik der Volksrepublik China 1949-1962, unter besonderer Berücksichtigung der technologischen Grundlagen. Berlin.
49. SKIBBE, B. (1958), Agrarwirtschaftsatlas der Erde in vergleichender Darstellung. Gotha.
50. SNOW, E. (1968), Red star over China (revised and enlarged edition). London.
51. TRETIAK, D. and B. H. KANG (1972), An assessment of changes in the numbers of livestock in China, 1952-1970. WAERSA, 14, 4 Dec., pp. 1-32. Oxford.
52. UNGER, H. (1956), Merkmale und Besonderheiten der chinesischen Ackerbaugebiete. Institut für Agrarraumforschung der Humboldt-Universität Berlin. Bericht Nr. 2/56. Berlin (Ost).
53. VOGEL, U. (1974), Zur Theorie der chinesischen Revolution – Die asiatische Produktionsweise und ihre Zersetzung durch den Imperialismus. Frankfurt/M.
54. VOSS, W. (1971 a), Probleme und Möglichkeiten der Entwicklungsprognose für die Volksrepublik China. Asienforum, 2, 3, Juli, S. 349-360. München.
55. VOSS, W. (1971 b), Die wirtschaftliche Entwicklung der Volksrepublik China – Darstellung und Prognose. Freiburg/Br.
56. VOSS, W. (1972), China auf dem Sprung nach vorn. Bad Honnef.
57. WEGGEL, O. (1973), Die Alternative China – Politik, Gesellschaft, Wirtschaft der Volksrepublik China. Hamburg.
58. WHEELWRIGHT, E. O. and McFARLANE, B. (1970). The Chinese road to socialism. New York, London.
59. YAMAMOTO, H. (1961), Development of agricultural collectivization in China. Tokyo.
60. YAMAMOTO, H. (1971), On the evolution of the Chinese model of agrarian technology. In: Developing Economies, ix, 4, Dec., pp. 449-474. Tokyo.
61. YU, CHEUNG-LIEH (1975), Der Doppelcharakter des Sozialismus – Zur politischen Ökonomie der VR China. I. Die Revolution auf dem Land. Berlin (West).
62. China und die Revolution in der Dritten Welt, (1971), Frankfurt.
63. China I + II (1962), Staatsbürgerliche Informationen. Bonn.
64. Klassen und Klassenbeziehungen in der Volksrepublik China. (1973). (Published in cooperation with the Social Science Institute attached to the SED Central Committee). Dresden.
65. Le soleil rouge eclaire Tatchai dans sa marche en avant (1969). Peking.
66. Some basic facts about China (1974). China Reconstructs. Supplement January (Peking)
67. The developing economies – Special issue on China (1971). IX, 4, Dec. Tokyo.
68. Volksrepublik China – ein wirtschaftlicher Überblick (1959), Hamburg.
69. Volksrepublik China 1969 – Länderberichte (1969). Statistisches Bundesamt Wiesbaden. Stuttgart, Mainz.
70. Volksrepublik China – Länderkurzberichte (1974), Stuttgart, Mainz.
71. Current Scene – developments in mainland China. (1968), VI, 17, October. Hongkong.

4. *Comparative Analysis and Synopsis*

1. ABERCROMBIE, K. (1967), Die Landwirtschaft im Wandel von der Subsistenz- zur Marktwirtschaft. In: Blanckenburg, P. v. und H. -D. Cremer (1967), Handbuch der Landwirtschaft und Ernährung in den Entwicklungsländern. Stuttgart, Bd. I, pp. 230-239

Literature

2. ADAMS, A. E. and J. S. (1971), Men versus systems. New York.
3. BARAN, P. A. (1962), The political economy of growth. New York.
4. BARDHAN, P. K. (1970), Chinese and Indian agriculture: A broad comparison of recent policy and performance. In: Journal of Asian Studies, XXIX, 3, May, pp. 515-537.
5. BEHRENDT, R. F. (1965), Soziale Strategie für Entwicklungsländer. Frankfurt/M.
6. BERGMANN, TH. (1968), Die Agrarfrage bei Marx und Engels – und heute. In: Kritik der politischen Ökonomie heute – 100 Jahre Kapital, pp. 175-194. Frankfurt/M.
7. BERGMANN, TH. (1975), Farm policies in socialist countries. Farnborough, Hants. (England).
8. BERGMANN, TH. (1976), Analyse comparée des politiques agraires dans les pays socialistes. In: Economie Rurale, mars-avril, 1976, 112, pp. 21-28. Paris.
9. BHATTACHARYA, D. (1974), India and China – contrast and comparison 1905-1972. In: Journal on Contemporary Asia, 4 (4), pp. 439-459. Stockholm.
10. BIEHL, M. (1966), Die Landwirtschaft in China und Indien. Frankfurt/M, Berlin, Bonn, München.
11. BOSERUP, M. (1964), Agrarian structure and take-off. In: Rostow, W. W. (ed.). The economics of take-off into sustained growth. London, pp. 201-214.
12. BOSERUP, E. (1965), The conditions of agricultural growth. The economics of agrarian change under population pressure. London.
13. BRESS, L. und K. P. HENSEL (1972), Wirtschaftssystem des Sozialismus in Experiment – Plan oder Markt? Frankfurt/M.
14. BRUS, W. (1972), Wirtschaftsplanung – für ein Konzept der politischen Ökonomie. Frankfurt/M.
15. BRUS, W. (1971), Funktionsprobleme der sozialistischen Wirtschaft. Frankfurt/M.
16. CHEN, K. J. and J.-S. UPPAL (1971), India and China – Studies in comparative development. New York.
17. CLECAK, P. (1969), Moral and material incentives. In: Socialist Register 1969, pp. 101-135. London.
18. DEUTSCHER, J. (1970), Russia, China and the West 1953-1966. Harmondsworth.
19. DOBB, M. (1960), An essay on economic growth and planning. London.
20. DOVRING, F. (1959), The share of agriculture in a growing population. In: Monthly Bulletin of agricultural economics and statistics, VIII, 8/9, pp. 1-11. Rome.
21. ENGELS, F. (1894/1962), The peasant question in France and Germany, (German original Neue Zeit 1894). In: Marx-Engels, Selected works, Moscow 1962, pp. 420-440.
22. FUKUTAKE, T. (1967), Asian rural society – China, India, Japan. Tokyo.
23. HALM, G. N. (1960), Wirtschaftssysteme, eine vergleichende Darstellung. Berlin.
24. HENNICKE, P. (1973), Probleme einer kategorialen Bestimmung der Übergangsgesellschaft. In: ders. (Herausg.), Probleme des Sozialismus und der Übergangsgesellschaften. pp. 70-125. Frankfurt/M.
25. ISHIKAWA, S. (1967), Economic development in Asian perspective. Tokyo.
26. JACKSON, W. A. DOUGLAS (ed.), (1971), Agrarian policies and problems in communist and non-communist countries. Seattle, London.
27. JAHN, G. (1961), Die Wirtschaftssysteme der Staaten Osteuropas und der Volksrepublik China. West-Berlin, S. 96-105 und 135-141.
28. KHALATBARI, P. (1971), Ökonomische Unterentwicklung – Mechanismus, Probleme, Ausweg. Berlin (Ost).
29. KNIRSCH, P. (1969), Strukturen und Formen zentraler Wirtschaftsplanung. Berlin.
30. KOSTA, J., J. MEYER und S. WEBER (1973), Warenproduktion im Sozialismus. Überlegungen zur Theorie von Marx und zur Praxis in Osteuropa. Frankfurt/M.
31. KRAMER, F. (1973), Kollektivwirtschaftliche Ursprünge des Sozialismus in China und Russland. In: Meschkat, K. und O. Negt (Herausg.): Gesellschaftsstrukturen, pp. 188-213. Frankfurt/M.

248

32. KUZNETS, S. (1959), Six lectures on economic growth. London.
33. KUZNETS, S. (1963), Economic growth and the contribution of agriculture. Proceedings of the International Conference of Agricultural Economists. London.
34. LANGE, O. (1963-71), Political economy, I + II. London.
35. LANGE, O. and F. M. TAYLOR (1964), On the economic theory of socialism. New York.
36. LEWIS, W. A. (1955), The theory of economic growth. London.
37. MANDEL, E. (1973), Zehn Thesen zur sozialökonomischen Gesetzmäßigkeit der Übergangsgesellschaft zwischen Kapitalismus und Sozialismus. In: Hennicke, P. (Herausg.), Probleme des Sozialismus und der Übergangsgesellschaften, pp. 15-37: Frankfurt/M.
38. MARX, K. and F. ENGELS (1845-1846/1976), The German ideology. In: Collected Works, vol. 5, Moscow-London 1976.
39. MARX, K. (1969), On colonialism and modernization (Edited by Avineri, Shlomo). Garden City, N.Y.
40. MEADOWS, D. et al. (1972), The limits of growth. A report for the Club of Rome's project on the predicament of mankind. New York-Washington-London.
41. MOORE, BARRINGTON, JR. (1967), Social origins of dictatorship and democracy: lord and peasant in the making of the modern world. Boston.
42. MYRDAL, G. (1957), Economic theory and underdeveloped regions. London.
43. MYRDAL, G. (1970), The challenge of world poverty. Penguin, Harmondsworth.
44. NOHLEN, D. und F. NUSCHELER (Herausg.), (1975-1976), Handbuch der dritten Welt – Unterentwicklung und Entwicklung in Afrika, Amerika und Asien. Bd. 1-4. Hamburg.
45. PUHLE, H.-J. (1975), Politische Agrarbewegungen in kapitalistischen Industriegesellschaften, Deutschland, USA und Frankreich im 20. Jahrhundert. Göttingen.
46. RAJ, K. N. (1966), India, Pakistan and China – economic growth and outlook. New Delhi (stenciled).
47. RICHMAN, B. (1972), Economic development in China and India – some conditioning factors. In: Pacific Affairs, 45, 1, pp. 75-91.
48. ROCHLIN, R. P. und E. HAGEMANN (1971), Die Kollektivierung der Landwirtschaft in der Sowjetunion und der Volksrepublik China – eine vergleichende Studie. Berlin.
49. SHANIN, T. (ed.) (1971), Peasants and peasant societies. Harmondsworth.
50. SIK, O. (1966), Ökonomie-Interessen-Politik. Berlin.
51. SINHA, R. P. (1972), Competing ideology and agricultural strategy: Current agricultural development in India and China compared with Meiji strategy. Paper delivered at the Third European Conference on Modern South Asian Studies. Heidelberg (stenciled)
52. SOFRI, G. (1969), Uber asiatische Produktionsweise. Frankfurt/M.
53. SCHWEIZER, H. (1972), Sozialistische Agrartheorie und Landwirtschaftspolitik in China und der Sowjetunion: ein Modell für Entwicklungsländer? Bern und Frankfurt/M.
54. SHATIL, J. E. (1968-1972), Criteria of the socio-economic efficiency of the kibbutz. In: Archiv für öffentliche und freigemeinnützige Unternmehmen. Bd. 9, pp. 41-59, 118-138 Göttingen.
57. STOJANOVIC, S. (1972), Kritik und Zukunft des Sozialismus. Frankfurt/M.
56. SURÁNYI-UNGER, T. (1967), Wirtschaftsphilosophie des 20. Jahrhunderts. Stuttgart.
57. SWAMY, S. (1973), Economic growth in China and India, 1952-1970 – a comparative appraisal. In: Economic development and cultural change, 21, 4, Part II, July 1973, pp. 1-84.
58. TÖKEI, F. (1969), Zur Frage der asiztischen Produktionsweise. Neuwied-Berlin.
59. TÜMMLER, E., K. MERKEL und G. BLOHM (1969), Die Agrarpolitik in Mitteldeutschland und ihre Auswirkung auf Produktion und Verbrauch landwirtschaftlicher Erzeugnisse. Berlin (West).
60. WEBSTER, N. (1971), New international dictionary of the English language. London.
61. WEISSKOPF, TH. E. (1975), China and India – A comparative survey of performance in

Literature

economic development. Economic and Political Weekly, Annual Number 1975, X, 5-7, pp. 175-194.

62. WERNER, R. (1975), Soziale Indikatoren und politische Planung – Einführung in Anwendungen der Makrosoziologie. Reinbek.
63. WOLF, E. R. (1972), Peasant wars of the twentieth century. London.
64. ZIMMERMANN, L. J. (1963), Arme und reiche Länder. Köln.
65. DTV-Atlas zur Weltgeschichte I+II (1972). München.
66. FAO – Production yearbook. Rome.
67. FAO – Commerce yearbook, Rome.
68. Agricultural projections for 1975 and 1985 (1968) – Europe – North America – Japan – Oceania – Production and consumption of major foodstuffs. OECD, Paris.
69. Study of trends in world supply and demand of major agricultural commodities (1976). OECD, Paris.
70. World Employment Programme (1974). A framework for an ILO programme on rural employment promotion. February. Geneva: ILO (mimeo).

INDEX

PUBLICATIONS OF THE EUROPEAN SOCIETY FOR RURAL
SOCIOLOGY

edited by

Paul Müller, *FB Wirtschaftswissenschaften Universität Konstanz*
M. Cernea, *Institut de Filozofie, Academia Republicii Socialiste România Bucuresti*
A. J. Jansen, *Agricultural University, Department of Rural Sociology, Wageningen*
M. Redclift, *Wye College, University of London*

1. Theodor Bergmann, *The Development Models of India, The Soviet Union and China*. A Comparative Analysis. 1977

THE DEV... ...HE SOVIET
UNION A...